HANDBOOK FOR ENLIGHTENMENT & ASCENSION

HOW TO BREAK FREE FROM BEING TRAPPED IN AN INSANE EGO-DOMINATED WORLD

JONATHAN PARKER

PUBLISHED BY
QUANTUMQUESTS INTERNATIONAL, INC
OJAI, CALIFORNIA
© Copyright 2022 – Jonathan Parker
www.jonathanparker.org

All rights reserved. This book may not be reproduced in whole or in part, stored in a retrieval system, or transmitted in any form or by any means—electric, mechanical, or other without written permission from the author, except by a reviewer, who may quote brief passages in a review. This book is copyright protected. This is only for personal use. You cannot amend, distribute, sell, or use any part or the content within this book without the consent of the author.

The material in this book is intended for education. It is not meant to take the place of diagnosis and/or treatment by a qualified medical practitioner or therapist. No expressed or implied guarantee as to the effects of the use of the recommendations can be given nor liability taken.

Library of Congress in Cataloging Publication Data
Parker, Jonathan
Handbook for Ascension and Enlightenment
ISBN:

First Printing, October 2022

Table of Contents

Introduction 1
Preface   What Is Enlightenment? 2

Part One
What is Enlightenment

Chapter 1   Enlightenment – Your Natural State 10
Chapter 2   Liberation & Self-Realization 12
Chapter 3   Why Does Enlightenment Seem Difficult To Attain? 15
Chapter 4   The Enlightenment Process 19
Chapter 5   An Enlightenment Fable 24

Part Two
Obstacles To Enlightenment

Chapter 6   The Power Of *Your* Myths 29
Chapter 7   The Origin of the Ego 34
Chapter 8   The Challenges of the Ego 40
Chapter 9   Seven Ways the Ego Tricks You 42
Chapter 10 Seven Keys to Understand & Eliminate the Ego 48
Chapter 11 How to Clear Sub-Personalities of the Ego 50
Chapter 12 Shifting From the Fear Universe to the Love Universe ... 58

Part Three
How To Attain Enlightenment

Chapter 13 3 Steps to Clearing Away Struggles 64
Chapter 14 Let Go: Your Spiritual Solution 68
Chapter 15 Surrender is The Golden Path to Enlightenment 76
Chapter 16 Surrender – The Ultimate Spiritual Path 82
Chapter 17 5 Ways To Quiet Your Mind 87
Chapter 18 The Failure of Meditation 93
Chapter 19 Your Spiritual Journey Through Meditation Practices 99

Part Four
How to Deepen Your Enlightenment Realizations

Chapter 20	How Your Perceptions Shape Your Reality	104
Chapter 21	How Your Beliefs Control Your Life	111
Chapter 22	Your Day of Judgment	120
Chapter 23	The Relentless Call of Karma	133
Chapter 24	How To Apply Hope & Trust In Your Life	149
Chapter 25	The Enlightenment Paths Of Faith, Hope, And Trust	155
Chapter 26	Your Source Of Virtue	161

Part Five
Elevating Your Consciousness to Enlightenment

Chapter 27	4 Levels On The Path To Enlightenment	168
Chapter 28	Higher States of Enlightenment	174
Chapter 29	The Soul's Miraculous Light	180
Chapter 30	6-Step Meditation Instructions	188
Chapter 31	Open Your Heart To Your Truth Of Love	194
Chapter 32	Self-Inquiry To Discover Your True Self	198
Chapter 33	How Grace Opens The Door To Enlightenment	206
Chapter 34	Non-Dual Alignment	212
Chapter 35	The Enlightenment Path to Ascension	219
Chapter 36	Epilogue	237

Appendix

100 Questions and Answers on Your Spiritual Journey 239

This book is dedicated to you who have searched for answers and are ready to evolve to enlightenment.

Introduction

Enlightenment and ascension refer to the raising of your consciousness. They are the most natural and interesting topics to pursue because they pertain to how you experience life and how you evolve.

Enlightenment is not a psychological state or a spiritual fantasy, but the actual realization of who and what you are, the nature of realty, and the key to the freedoms you are searching for.

Enlightenment refers to a higher level of awareness that affects all that you think, feel, and believe. Your consciousness is reflected in your every experience because it determines how your lifeforce is directed to create and attract everything and everyone to your life. What you hold in your consciousness influences your health, relationships, career, and happiness.

Enlightenment is not easy to define, but it is possible to describe the effects. For instance, some of the more commonly reported effects are (not in any particular order): deep peacefulness, happiness, mind expansion, oneness, freedom, mindfulness, fulfillment, satisfaction, compassion, and total acceptance. In addition, the mind becomes very still and quiet, and there is a sense of being complete and happy all the time. You will also be in the present moment or "Now" all the time, automatically, and without effort.

Enlightenment also entails spiritually defined realizations such as a sustained awareness of being one with the Source of all. This is referred to as "Unity Consciousness," and some also have the realization of not just being one with the Source of all, but of *being* non-conceptual awareness out of which all creation arises.

All of this can sound far-fetched to the everyday thinking mind that is usually distracted with making a living, struggling with relationships, and facing other challenges. For those who have experienced the enlightenment shift in consciousness, their lives are forever changed. As you read on you will discover why.

-- **Jonathan Parker**

Preface

What Is Enlightenment?

Enlightenment is a word with many different interpretations. Interestingly, there is a period of European history in the 1700's known as the "Age of Enlightenment," but it has little to do with enlightenment in a spiritual context today. That period of history was characterized by the belief in the power of human reason, but spiritual enlightenment transcends the analytical mind.

Actually, enlightenment is a continuum of evolving awareness that reaches far beyond the blissful and mind-expanding experiences that are often described when a person first experiences a spiritual awakening.

There are limitations to the view that enlightenment is the conclusion of one's spiritual quest. For one thing, many people who have enlightening experiences do not maintain the awareness of their enlightenment, but often express a feeling of being unable to sustain it, or they even describe loosing it completely as they revert back to a former state.

It is not unusual for people to feel a great sense of ease, lightness, and grace pervading their lives for days or even weeks after an awakening experience. However, eventually, and often to their great dismay and disappointment, they begin to experience a return to ordinariness and the resurfacing of conditions they thought had been left behind. When this happens, they may believe they are losing their enlightenment.

This is a common experience. One factor affecting them is that they have had beautiful and transcendent experiences, but did not release and clear their underlying beliefs and programming. Your deep beliefs and programming are much more than ideas in your mind. They also have subtle-energy components in your physical body, your aura, your subconscious, your chakras, and other places of which you may be unaware. In addition, you are influenced, if not controlled, by karmic forces that create and attract the experiences in your life. These components exist as thoughtforms.

Thoughtforms are composed of memories, beliefs, and emotions, and you carry many thousands of them around with you and you usually have little idea of how they filter and influence every thought, feeling, and experience you have. As these patterns rise to the surface, they can trigger reactions that can sometimes be quite discouraging if you do not understand what is happening or what to do about them.

As you progress through this book and apply the clearing methods, you'll find your consciousness changing and your life improving. These consciousness shifts are often referred to as Ascension. Your consciousness ascends to higher levels which leads to freedom from struggles and suffering.

Spiritual awakening, ascension, and enlightenment are within reach for everyone and they are, in fact, your destiny. By clearing away the distorted ideas about enlightenment and dedicating yourself to attaining the highest clearing and realizations, you'll soon notice you are not the same person you thought you were. You will discover a freer and happier person emerging.

As we journey together through this book, many misunderstandings will clear up, and many of your questions will be answered, but most of all, you will find techniques that accelerate your path to enlightenment and ascension.

My Beginning of Awakening

My first spiritual awakening happened when I was 31. I was deeply sincere and relentlessly pursuing truth through self-examination and self-discovery while I was a pastor of a Christian church in Kansas, when I experienced a spontaneous shift in consciousness, and like Dorothy in the Wizard of Oz, I knew I wasn't in Kansas anymore.

I can't say I was doing anything to trigger the shift other than earnestly praying to know truth. At that time, I didn't know anything about meditation or other practices commonly associated with enlightenment. What happened to me felt like recalling ancient memories. I realized that everything I thought I knew was a massive tapestry of stories, myths, and perceptions that had been handed to me by others.

Now I could see everything with a new clarity that I had previously been blinded to. The awakenings were like a series of revelations or epiphanies that came every few weeks. This went on for years. At that time, I was not able to find many books or people to explain what was happening, and since much of what I experienced seemed so radical, I had to keep most of it to myself.

Beyond What I Imagined

Some people consider these states of consciousness to be fantasies, delusions, or hallucinations, probably because they have not experienced them for themselves and therefore do not believe they are real. They may have no internal reference for how such a person feels and responds to life. The enlightened state is only known by experiencing it. Until then all one can do is try to imagine what it is like.

For me, every shift in consciousness was always different and beyond anything I imagined it might be. At first, some of these qualities were transitory, but in time, they evolved into a continuous state. They are far more than momentary altered states, fantasies, mind projections, channeled information, inspirations, visions, or meditative insights; they totally transformed me, as they will you.

Enlightenment is an Ongoing Process

Enlightenment is an ongoing process not a destination, and others have echoed this observation. For instance, in the integral approach to human development described by Ken Wilbur levels of consciousness are divided into major tiers along a rising spectrum. In *Power vs Force*, David Hawkins describes consciousness as progressing along a scale from zero to one thousand with enlightenment starting at six hundred. At each level of consciousness the experience of life changes. For example, a person can feel love in many ways and to various depths. Each experience is love, but the way in which it is experienced can be significantly different for each person depending on the person's consciousness level. The same holds true for emotions, beliefs, and reactions as people move from level to level. At each level perceptions and experiences are significantly different.

Some qualities associated with enlightenment are likely to be temporary prior to permanent enlightenment. They may seem to come and go but they eventually deepen and become continuous and sustained. For instance, some people have a quiet mind and feel peaceful when they meditate, but they do not necessarily have their thoughts completely stop or have all negative emotions eliminated all the time; these states may become permanent with future shifts. I have personally worked with thousands of people in workshops, meditation retreats, and one-on-one sessions and have seen people make shifts at all levels, so I know what is possible for everyone.

What follows is an outline of some of the qualities I have experienced and noticed in those who have had awakening realizations. Not everyone who awakens experiences all of these, and I am sure others could create their own lists of what they have experienced that would vary somewhat from this one. This list is not exhaustive, nor is it my intent to elaborate here on each item, but I'll discuss them in more detail later in this book. I merely want to enumerate them here for you as a "road map" of the territory ahead. They are not in any particular order, but points 1, 2, and 3 are what most people think of as enlightenment.

1. You have a sustained awareness of being one with the Source (or God) and all creation. Separation vanishes. This does not mean being spaced out or non-functional, but having an integrated awareness that is always present while having an awareness of being aware. You are self-consciously aware of being an aspect of a much larger whole.

2. A conscious sense that you are an individualized expression of creation similar to the way a wave is an aspect of the ocean and is one with the ocean. The experience is of a vast spaciousness that holds a field of potentiality in which you create and project your experiences.

3. You have an automatic and sustained awareness of always being in the present moment without trying to be in the present moment.

4. You have a still, quiet, and peaceful mind. There are no unintentional or uninvited thoughts.

5. You have a feeling of being deeply in love with life.

6. You have a complete sense of well-being and everything will work out for you. Every day is wonderful. In fact, there is even a feeling of inner playfulness and joy, and sometimes amusement or laughter at the absurdity of situations that some choose to regard as serious.

7. You have the experience of everyone and everything in creation as deeply beautiful. Everyone and everything is perceived as deep beauty.

8. You have the feeling of always being happy.

9. You have the feeling of loving who you truly are and no longer living through ego identities or masks.

10. There is deep compassion and caring for all creation.

11. There is a state of naturally living from the heart and experiencing deep unconditional love for all.

12. There is an experience of more energy and a feeling of being younger and more vital than before the enlightenment shift.

13. Naturally, and without effort, there is a positive flow of words and actions.

14. You have a naturally increased clarity of mind, perception, and intuition.

15. You have an ease and flow through life in "Universal Harmony" and synchronicity.

16. You have a sense of being empowered, whole, and free, with a correlative feeling of being beyond the control of others.

17. You have a natural state free from fear, worry, anger, stress, lack, jealousy, arrogance, hopelessness, intolerance, resentment, despair, discouragement, competitiveness, addictions, suspicions, loneliness, self-pity, and feeling stuck or victimized. There is rarely or even never a feeling of negative emotions, but rather very strong positive feelings, such as love, joy, happiness, ecstasy, and rich beauty.

18. You have a feeling of continuous lightness of being with lingering periods of bliss and euphoria.

19. You no longer experience mood shifts, and the consciousness level you have attained achieves stability.

20. You have an internal state that external conditions do not alter.

21. Negative people and situations do not disturb your internal state.

22. You no longer have judgments or project criticism or blame on yourself or others.

23. You have a feeling of being safe, secure, and never lonely.

24. You have a realization of being positively transformed and all your experiences with others are also transformed.

25. Your higher consciousness and body integrate and achieve healthy balance.

26. You have an automatic sense of protection and safety.

27. You have freedom from dependencies, wants, and "needs."

28. Negative karma is released and dissolved.

29. You have deep peacefulness and calm.

30. You may have awareness of and sometimes a connection with non-physical masters, angels, and enlightened beings.

31. You have inner contentment, fulfillment, and a sense of being complete.
32. You have a natural ability to relate to others at their level of consciousness.

33. Profound enlightened insights and wisdom come, not from experiences, books, or memories, but from deep stillness and consciousness itself.

34. You have no more seeking, striving, or searching. There is completeness, although deeper realizations may continue.
35. You have a sense of being well prepared for the transition to the next life, whenever it may happen and wherever you may find yourself.
36. You have a knowing that you are free from the wheel of rebirth having completed the need for further physical lives; however, rebirth remains an option.

37. You have an ability to transmit enlightened consciousness influences to others, which assists them with their clearing, healing, and spiritual evolution.

38. The strangest one of all is that friends, neighbors, and those around you are likely to have no idea about most of the above list. This is because people don't really know what they have not experienced, so they don't have a reference to what the enlightening experiences are. In fact, they will project their interpretations about you based on their own experiences and their level of consciousness. There may or may not be perceptible external changes in appearances or style of living, but internally there is a vast difference from what most people experience.

39. In addition, some people experience an opening of many paranormal and intuitive gifts which can be directed intentionally and which have traditionally been regarded as Siddha powers. These can include clairvoyance (an ability to see, sense and understand subtle energy patterns in the aura, chakras, and other dimensions); clairaudience (an inner listening ability to receive messages beyond the range of the 5 senses); clairsentience (an ability to have an inner knowing without information from the 5 senses); telepathy (an ability to sense and know the thoughts and feelings of another person); precognition (an ability to see and know future events); remote viewing; spiritual/energy healing; an ability to sense, know and understand a person's consciousness; and an ability to help others become more clear and awake. The awakening of intuitive abilities is most precious and important to assist you in furthering your spiritual journey.

Part One
What is Enlightenment

Chapter 1

ENLIGHTENMENT – YOUR NATURAL STATE

Enlightenment is your natural state of being. Your body was designed for the enlightened state, yet many consider enlightenment a rare occurrence that mysteriously happens only to a few select individuals. By understanding some of what enlightenment is and isn't, you will see that it does not need to be an impossible dream.

Enlightenment is about becoming free of opinions, judgments, concepts, and ideas that affect your experiences. Input is constantly being interpreted, evaluated, colored, and filtered by your conditioning, pain, judgments, beliefs, and choices. In enlightened awareness, the senses can experience reality without the mind interfering. You turn the tables and use the mind rather than letting it use you. You do not lose the mind but rather you become free of the mind's need for drama, for being right, for judging, for valuing, and for being in control. Uninvited thoughts stop and you become free of emotions and decisions based on past realities and experience life in the moment automatically.

Processes to arrive at enlightenment are varied but they generally include meditations that:

(1) Lead to higher states of consciousness in which self-discoveries reveal awareness below the level of everyday conscious thoughts.

(2) Release ego blocks, limitations, karmic patterns, and illusions of the mind to reveal the underlying clarity of being.

(3) Integrate kindness, gratitude, patience, sharing, politeness, loving, and other qualities of goodness into everyday life.

Your spiritual path is like a journey climbing a mountain. As you climb, your inner spiritual connections and realities become more revealed, your clearing abilities increase, your perceptions become clearer, and you become more refined. Each step along the way brings up issues that must be cleared in order to move to the next higher state.

Enlightenment includes many real-world tangible results that enhance one's life. It is a spiritual journey that leads to:

1. A witness state where you do not attach yourself to what is happening but are able to participate.
2. An absence of negative emotional reactions to past and present events, people, and trauma.
3. An awareness that you are more than your physical body or experiences.
4. An awareness of being connected with everything in the universe and feeling at one.
5. Deep peacefulness, contentedness, and quietness of mind.

To follow this path requires a process of meditation, clearing, and commitment to living a pure and respectful life. As you continue reading, I'll address all of these aspects so you can experience them for yourself.

Chapter 2

LIBERATION & SELF-REALIZATION

Many words have been used to explain enlightenment as people grapple to understand what it is. Some of these include: Awakening, Liberation, Self-Realization, God-Realization, and Ascension. These are terms giving further explanation to the various aspects of enlightenment. In truth, however, no word or words can ever convey the experience because there is no way to adequately explain love, bliss, unity consciousness, and deep and profound peace to someone who has never experienced them. For that matter, how would you experience a sunset if you were blind and had never seen one? You would have to rely on the descriptions of others, but it wouldn't be the same as directly experiencing it yourself. Yet even your own direct experiences are filtered. You perceive the world through your senses, thoughts, opinions, memories, prejudices, and perceptions of yourself and others, and you are convinced that this is reality. But the five senses provide no way to *see* the underlying reality of the world. What you perceive is not all of what is. Your senses reveal part of a picture that you attach meaning to, but a greater reality lies beyond all thoughts and sensations.

Self-realization is also called liberation because when you have clarity on who and what you are, you have freedom from suffering and struggle. It is called Self-Realization because you come to realize and know what your true self is.

Enlightenment is a process, not a one-time event, with significant awakenings or realizations along the way. It is an experience of internal peace, love, and completion that totally eclipses what you have been seeking through control, possessions, or recognition.

The Goal of Your Life

The shift in consciousness we call enlightenment is the goal of human life, for the individual and for the entire human race. When people make the shift, they feel like they are waking from a dream. Essentially, enlightenment is an awakening to who and what you, actually, truly are. It is the emergence of higher awareness and realization of your deepest truth.

For one who has not experienced that shift, statements about it may not make much sense because people would say, "What do you mean awaken? I am awake." However, they may think being awake only means seeing the masks they wear or the roles they play, such as office worker, carpenter, mother, etc., but awakening in the sense of enlightenment is something much deeper and simpler. It is who you are below the surface.

Enlightenment is clearly a different state of consciousness that is not easily quantifiable by scientific analysis, and therefore most people do not understand it because there is no reference for what has not been experienced. You see yourself in the mirror each morning and recognize the form you see, but you probably don't give much thought to who is living inside that form.

One Definition of Enlightenment

A definition of enlightenment I like is that enlightenment is awakening to the consciousness underlying all form, and then expressing that realization in every aspect of your existence.

As you look at the universe and all the life in it, you see that everything is in a process of becoming. Nothing is static. Quantum physicists indicate an infinite number of universes are in constant creation and evolution. You learn, grow, and evolve through lifetimes, and by virtue of what you already know and what you can observe, you discover you are on a journey that will continue. In a sense, enlightenment is just a word for the process you are already undergoing. Enlightenment represents the unfolding of your potential in all aspects of body, mind, and spirit. You are now only beginning to scratch the surface of what lies ahead for you.

As your inner powers of observation open, you will find that nothing is separate, even though you experience the illusion that it is. It is all a matter of perception. For instance: The waves of the ocean arise and have a separate birth, crashing on the shore, but then they merge back into the ocean. They appeared to have a separate existence for a little while, but they never really left the ocean. Yet while you perceive them, they appear separate and distinct, as if they have a separate existence. You are a perceiver. Self-realization is seeing the reality that underlies the perception. It is seeing the bigger picture rather than being caught in the single picture before your eyes.

Day-to-day you are normally watching the movies and stories of life and forming perceptions and conclusions about what you see and experience. Everyone's life is composed of stories perceived by the participants as reality. People are wearing costumes and believing the costumes are who they are. All the costumes were created by thoughts and beliefs. Consciousness is the stage where the projections are played out. The stage is a field of potentiality that sustains the projections. Knowing this is the great secret. You can realize the consciousness of the Source, like a massive brain that holds all the thoughts of existence. Moreover, when you make that shift in awareness, you are taken to experience oneness with all there is.

It is easy to get so engrossed in watching the movie of your life that you forget that you are sitting in the movie theater of your own creation. Self-Realization is taking a big step back to be liberated from the movie while watching the movie. The images, the props, and people in costumes are all there. How did they get there? They result from people thinking and believing in their existence.

When you move behind the illusions and see everything is just a projection from behind the screen, you have an enormous power over the nature of the projections. The difference when you wake up is that you can see how people are creating their lives the way they are and you are much more in a position to be conscious of what you create. Your life is the theater of the ego and the soul. Through a sequence of lives, you play different roles on different stages. At birth, you walk on stage. At death, you walk off that stage.

Enlightenment and Self-Realization are the waking awareness that you are watching wonderful movies and enjoying all of it in its wonderfulness. Enlightenment and Self-Realization are experiences in the finiteness of the physical world, enjoying the stories and myths, experiencing the moments in time including the births and death and the stories in-between. Enlightenment is a state of clarity on all of this.

Chapter 3
WHY DOES ENLIGHTENMENT SEEM DIFFICULT TO ATTAIN?

Levels of Enlightenment

The word "enlightenment" is used very loosely today to apply to a lot of different spiritual practices and mental states. As a result, there are many ideas about enlightenment, and even more ideas about the illusions people project on enlightenment.

There are two major aspects to what is generally called enlightenment. First, is enlightenment that comes through the intellect. This includes understanding many explanations and definitions about a broad range of spiritual and enlightenment topics and experiences. In some cases, the crown chakra opens at the top of the head resulting in transcendent awareness of being at one with everything. People who have knowledge of this often consider themselves to be enlightened.

The second aspect to enlightenment is of the heart, a state often talked about in the Buddhic, Vedantic, and Sufi traditions. Enlightenment of the heart is a different focus from that of the mind and intellect, and enlightenment combined through the intellect and heart is what completes the human experience.

Some people who have used psychedelic drugs to have mystical insights tap into higher realms, cling to the importance of those experiences, and believe they are enlightened. However, such adventures are only a narrow range of realizations and may give rise to many ideas about enlightenment that ultimately prove to narrow one's perspective.

Who Are You, Really?

Besides your physical body, you also have a personality, which is composed of an emotional and mental body. What happens through incarnations is that your soul becomes submerged under the personality, which, in turn, is caught in the pain, struggle, and other distractions that are characteristic of the physical dimension. The experiences in the physical plane, which were supposed to be of love, beauty, and fulfillment, have become distorted into experiences of pain, lack, struggle, and suffering.

The Challenge

Every time someone projects his or her emotions at you, it challenges you to see if you can maintain the love within you that is the core essence of your being. If your lover or boss comes in screaming at you, can you hold the love? If the other person's emotions trigger you, you may entangle yourself in your own emotional reactions. This further encases you in the illusions of the lower emotions.

Ask yourself why you fell into this trap. Why did you forget the realization of *being* love? Why did you lose yourself? You can go into your inner space through meditation and clear that place within you that reacted. As a result, you won't be as triggered the next time it happens. I'll outline a variety of methods for doing that later in this book.

To progress on the enlightened path, you must become neutral in the face of the duality of such things as victory or defeat, profit or loss, joy or sorrow, honor or dishonor, good or evil, or any other pairs of opposites. When you are clear of the causes triggering you, you'll be more neutral and experience feelings of love and acceptance. When you reach this state, others can no longer hook you with their emotions or illusions.

If you are not living with that freedom, you are like a cork floating on water in a storm and being pushed around by the projections of everyone around you by letting their illusions rule and create your reality. If you live this way, you are letting the blind lead the blind. You'd be letting another person's illusions create deeper illusions, and you are locked into in a state of limitation and pain.

You can live free. When someone throws a challenge at you, you can recognize it as an ego delusion, and say, "I love you, but I'm not interested in loosing my peaceful consciousness and leaving my heart." Somehow, humanity has lost track of its spiritual essence and became lost in personalities and lives according to the desires of the personalities.

What if you were to orient your efforts to seeking only your deep truth? Moreover, what if you were to commit yourself to it? What if you were willing to clear the veils of illusion that cover the realizations that emanate from your heart and unveil the full experience of your spiritual nature? This is what awakening and enlightenment have to offer.

The World of Illusions

Many are confused by their emotions, so they live in mental worlds of constant thinking, plotting, reasoning, wondering, analyzing, and trying to figure things out and fix things. However, remember the mind creates illusions about whom and what you are, and they run very wide and deep. Each person's illusions are then projected on others. If you live in illusions and not in your spiritual nature, you will be easily distracted by the philosophies and projections of others, which can only manifest lack and struggle.

Your auric energy field contains subtle-energy patterns that are composed of your deepest beliefs, memories, and emotions. Many, if not most, of your beliefs that are affecting you are warehoused below the level of your conscious awareness. These energy patterns create and attract conditions and situations based on the character and quality of those beliefs. Those patterns also coalesce into cellular memories in the physical body itself. Depending on the nature of those beliefs, your life and health will eventually reflect the quality of the beliefs.

The Faster Track to Enlightenment

Since you have free will, you can choose what to think and how to live. You can play your low-consciousness illusions out for years or decades, but they will eventually show up in your life as emotional pain, physical disease, or psychological neuroses. The path of surrender is the fastest and safest path to freedom and enlightenment.

Many seekers take convoluted paths of lateral movement forever seeking the mysterious hidden alchemical keys that will open them to spiritual ascension. Many seek and search the timeless teachings of mystery schools, modern brain machines, new age music, mysticism, Eastern and Western religions, and other sources that promise answers. The seeking is probably fun and maybe exciting, but outer seeking for enlightenment often leaves seekers wondering about their spiritual quests after decades of searching. After a lifetime, many seekers discover that they did not experience a celebrated life of happiness and resolution; rather they never reached what they wanted. Life was not meant to be this way, and it does not have to stay this way.

Why is Enlightenment so Difficult to Attain?

You may have already spent time with several studies. An incredible amount of information is available today, and most seekers are somewhat lost not knowing where to look, but are always searching for the missing key.

Consider all that is available. Some of the areas you may have looked into could have included: Native American traditions, Tarot, Astrology, Buddhism, Cabalah, Yoga, Hinduism, Mysticism, Huna, Mythology, Numerology, Channeled Teachings, Crystals, Ancient Cultures and Religions, Psychic Development, Theosophy, World Literature, Shamanism, and Zen. Of course, it is OK and likely a good idea to study many of these topics, but why not also take the direct non-stop flight to your inner truth. This is your real goal, isn't it? That is the stated underlying goal of nearly all systems, yet they are filled with an obstacle course of mental illusions on the road to enlightenment.

I have previously mentioned that you have a personality, an emotional body, a mental body, and a subtle-energy body, but you also have something else. By accessing your heart center, you'll find the easiest place to access your soul. This is important because within your soul is the deepest enlightened truth.

If you invested the same time and energy into directly seeking through your heart center instead of searching externally, you would likely be much further ahead on your path. Resolve from this moment forward that your biggest commitment will be to surrender and explore your soul and higher self through meditation and clearing practices.

Chapter 4

THE ENLIGHTENMENT PROCESS

All are evolving spiritually whether they are consciously aware of it or not. As you look around you may not recognize this process because there is a full range of consciousness levels from the most base to those who are truly enlightened. When you think about ascension or enlightenment, you need to think of it as an ongoing process of shedding lower consciousness beliefs and reactions, so that higher consciousness realizations of peacefulness and love emerge. Along the journey peaks and valleys occur as the old ways rise to be addressed and released, which sometimes brings with it challenges and dark periods (sometimes referred to as the "Dark Night of the Soul").

The 5 Phases on the Pathway to Enlightenment

1. The Beginning of Awakening.

Awakening is a natural process that happens when one is ready for it. A person can't be forced to wake up, but a conducive environment can help make it easier. The beginning of awakening occurs when you start to realize something is missing in your spiritual knowledge and realization. Your mind begins to open to other possibilities than what you were aware of previously, and you find it interesting enough to search for more.

This is the searching phase. It includes your acceptance of realities beyond your physical experiences or what you have been taught. Many questions arise leading you to seek answers through books, teachers, or organizations. This is a very exciting phase of new discoveries.

2. Moving Beyond Knowledge.

After gathering a treasury of spiritual knowledge and understanding, you settle into some practices that bring you inspiration and a sense of evolving your consciousness to a deeper level than just the accumulation of more knowledge.

You are likely to have found a path that answers many of your questions and needs, and you find your life becoming more peaceful and fulfilled. You become more aware of the illusions that trapped you previously, and you undoubtedly apply practices and tools that move you along your path of spiritual evolution. Your practices would include some forms of meditation and other techniques that lead you to deeper self-discoveries. As a result, you find your beliefs and reactions to the world around you are more peaceful, loving, and acceptant. In this stage, you may have some "aha" realizations and possibly some mystical experiences. This creates further fuel to continue searching and discovering.

3. Discovering "Who Am I?"

The third major shift in consciousness opens you to deeper realizations of who and what you are. You find you have different interests and probably feel like you are losing passion for things that were previously important. The big realization at this level is that your evolution is tied to the degree you let go of your past beliefs that caused the pain and struggle that led to lifetimes of suffering. You become aware of the fear-based ego aspect of your personality, and you apply methods of deconstructing it.

This is the time when you explore healing and clearing modalities and may want to share what you are discovering with those close to you, and perhaps take it further to teach others what you are learning. At this level of your spiritual evolution, you explore deeper realms of consciousness and disengage from the negative aspects of the ego which previously controlled your thinking and emotional reactions. In place of the ego, your soul rises more to the surface of your everyday experiences and brings the refined characteristics of higher levels of love, fulfillment, and happiness. Your life flows with more synchronicity and you have greater peace. You are also likely to recognize you have a higher purpose than just physical pursuits. You feel guided into new connections with people and groups.

4. Shedding the Ego.

As you let go and clear away the lower energies of the ego which includes the suffering from fear, anger, hate, abandonment, anxiety, arrogance, hopelessness, and guilt, you find the deeper nature of your Soul emerging and taking over your personality and everyday experiences. You integrate a deeper realization of the nature of reality and your connection with it. There can be "flash realizations" of oneness, beauty, radiant love, and inspiration. Your intuitive self becomes more apparent, and you may have some psychic abilities naturally emerge.

Virtuous qualities become a natural part of who you are without your having to try or work at it. You become kinder, more patient, and more compassionate. You find yourself automatically being more present in the now. You notice you are experiencing these elevated levels of being longer through the day as the months go by.

5. Higher levels of enlightenment

Eventually, your mind becomes perpetually quiet and deeply peaceful all the time. You are able to operate in your day-to-day life, while sustaining an awareness of the oneness with all and the nature of all that is observed and perceived as being projections on the field of awareness. The negative ego diminishes and eventually disappears, although your individuality sustains your everyday experiences. Your Ascension is the evolution of your consciousness to higher realizations. The clearer you become, the more love and light you naturally radiate.

Something shifts within you and your mind stops its incessant chatter: No more voices in your head, no more rambling thoughts, no more judgments, no more commentary, no more questions, no self-doubt, no involuntary or uninvited thoughts—just quietness, peace, and expanded awareness. A feeling of being connected with everything opens, and a realization that you are one with the source of everything integrates. Truth becomes a direct experience and no longer a matter of how others have defined it to be. There is a connection with all intelligence and love, and an awareness of being one with and part of the entire vastness of being, yet retaining awareness of individuality without separation.

A realization that also comes is that this is so simple. It feels so simple that you realize a child could experience it. Then you feel like you are a child yourself seeing the reality of life for the first time. You feel that now you will experience life in a whole new way—with new eyes, feelings, and awareness. It's like starting life over from a fresh and new awareness of reality. In Biblical terminology, this is like "being born again."

There is a sense of freedom, lightness, and openness sometimes accompanied with euphoria and bliss. What troubled you in the past seems distant and unreal. You may think you have transcended the physical, and in some ways have, yet the needs of the physical must be addressed and cannot be ignored. You may even run to the mirror thinking, "I surely must have changed in some dramatic way, for I feel completely different." Yet the mirror reflects what it always has, but with perhaps a more relaxed expression.

An awareness that nothing in this physical realm is all that important follows, and the feeling inside is such complete contentment that it doesn't seem to matter what your circumstances are—you have found deep peace. You become aware that you have automatic awareness of being present in the moment—in the now. You no longer have to work at being present or acquiring the spiritual qualities you have admired in others and worked so hard for, not that they are yet fully blossomed, but that they are now automatically unfolding without effort. All of this is an outgrowth of the new being you have become because of your awakening realizations. You now know first-hand that the enlightenment event is like a new birth—a new beginning from which far greater evolution is possible than what was understood or imagined before.

What hasn't happened yet however is the release or complete transmutation of the effects of karma. Because the peace and contentment are so full, you may think you have transcended it, only to discover it still bites. Releasing the karmic energy patterns is now far easier, however, for many of the factors of mind are no longer holding on. To continue the spiritual evolutionary process, each karmic issue must be addressed and released until the ego is eliminated and all pulls and attachments are gone. This happens in shifts in awareness that feel like you are "popping" into new realities. All of the false and imagined sub-personalities and identities are released one-by-one until they are all gone, and then you become empowered in whatever ways will appropriately handle what life brings in the moment. There is always a sense of being beyond it all—a neutral observer and unattached participant, yet fully capable of being more present and involved than ever before. At this point, you know you are now, finally, fully free.

How Do You Trigger Enlightenment?

Many spiritual paths exist, but the path to enlightenment is most definitely accelerated by being with someone who has already achieved higher levels of awareness. Some of the effects may be activated by simply being in the presence of people who have experienced the shift themselves. It can be done even more quickly and completely by directly interacting with such a person with the purpose of releasing whatever illusions and limiting beliefs hold you back.

People usually start out trying to find relief from some struggle or pain, but as they raise consciousness, they learn their evolution encompasses much more than this. To accelerate the process, the beliefs and fixations that keep you anchored to lower levels of consciousness must be released and cleared. These include underlying beliefs that cause anger, hate, fear, abandonment, helplessness, guilt, control, and other ego-based reactions. As you clear away the lower levels of beliefs and reactions, more enlightened awareness automatically surfaces and eventually replaces them.

When & How Does this Happen?

Shifting into these enlightened states of awareness described in this chapter can happen in a matter of seconds. Such shifts are called "Flash Realizations," "Epiphanies," or "Aha Revelations." Depending on whether you continue to explore and deepen into these experiences determines whether your realization sustains, extends, or fades.

Chapter 5

AN ENLIGHTENMENT FABLE

The Sage & The King

There once was a king who ruled his country with love and compassion. He had a beautiful and loving queen, elaborate palaces, dedicated servants, loyal friends, happy subjects, and devoted sons and daughters. People were happy with him as their king, and he was pleased with his lifelong accomplishments.

His entire life had been devoted to the discovery of how to find happiness and make others happy as well. Yet with every accomplishment, every building project completed, and every new discovery, he realized that there was still a lack of complete fulfillment. So he continued pushing on with more projects, and searching for new discoveries. Yes, there was peace in his kingdom. He had a loving family and more possessions than he could ever use, yet he felt there was something missing.

One day as he was contemplating his unfulfilled feelings, he called all of his advisors and consultants together and asked them for their help. Each proposed ideas to help their king, yet none could identify what the king felt was lacking. Not knowing where else to turn for answers, the king remembered he had heard of a sage who lived in the mountains surrounding his village, so he decided to make the journey to find this man of mystery he had only heard about.

He traveled all day with his companions to the remote dwelling where this wise man lived and entered the humble hermitage of the sage and told the sage his story. He related how he had accomplished so much in life for himself and so many others. He explained how his health was good and he was content except for one thing. He felt a nagging pull in his heart that something was missing, but he didn't know what it was. So he asked the sage if there were any way possible to find what was missing so that he could feel complete satisfaction and attain understanding of all things.

The sage said, "You are a good man. Your compassion and dedication have brought you the many rewards this life can hold, but to know of what is missing, you must understand something of knowledge you have not yet discovered. There are two types of knowledge. One is the accumulation of many facts and details of many subjects. After lifetimes of study one may become erudite and perhaps wise."

The king replied, "I have learned much from many teachers my whole life, yet I feel there is something missing."

The sage then said, "The knowledge you feel is missing is only an outer reflection of a much deeper kind of knowledge. Let me show you what I mean. Go find a seed from a banyan tree."

The king went out under a large sprawling tree and found the seed the sage had requested. He brought the seed to the sage and the sage told him to open the seed and tell him what was inside. The king said, "Why there is nothing inside."

"Nothing?" the sage replied. "And yet the seed of nothing produces the giant banyan tree which then produces more seeds of nothing which produces more trees. How is this possible? The seed inside, which you say you cannot see, is like the underlying nature of all existence. It is the awareness out of which everything comes. This is the knowledge that by knowing you shall know everything. There will be no more feelings of something missing."

But the King inquired, "How can something come out of nothing."

"Indeed," said the Sage, "something must come from something, and that something is consciousness itself, which is pure Being, awareness, intelligence, and love that pervades all people and things. Just as by knowing a lump of clay, you understand some things about what is made of clay, and by knowing a piece of gold, you understand some things about what is made of gold. By knowing a drop of water, you understand all water, and similarly, when you know God as the all-pervading essence of everything and the Divine intelligence behind all there is, then you will know all.

You will come to know God by inquiring deeper and deeper into the core essence of reality and your mind. As in peeling an onion, going deeper and deeper into the layers of the onion you feel, see, smell, and sense a deeper understanding of the onion. Layer after layer you go beneath the surface appearances and come to understand what makes up the onion. So too, as you go beneath the surface of your mind, you will discover your needs, reactions, attachments, aversions, wants, pains, successes and pleasures. As you continually explore deeper and deeper, you will come to know the fundamental forces composing your being. You will understand what makes you the way you are. You will understand what is real and what has been created out of needs. You continue the process until you come to a place of deep stillness, perfect peace, and unfathomable love. You will discover your consciousness and come in touch with your essential nature. This is your spirit and your soul, and you will come to know that you are one with every other consciousness, and that all are one. Any sense of separateness will vanish!"

The King then said, "I want this knowledge. I realize this is something none of my teachers ever told me, yet I feel that deep inside of me it is what I am seeking? Can you teach it to me?"

The Sage continued, "There are many ways and means to this discovery. Complex systems and practice have been formulated over the millennia to assist those who seek the deep realizations, but they all reduce to each person asking the fundamental questions, 'Who is it that is feeling this, thinking this, judging this? Who am I?' When you ask these questions, you will find the answers will surprise you. You are not who or what you think. Aspects of yourself are yet to be discovered, and no one can answer these questions for you. You must discover the answers yourself, but you are not alone in your quest.

It is not necessary to live a life of austerity, renunciation, or isolation. You do not need to reiterate sounds, prayers, or pleas. You have only to discover the depths of your true nature by exploring the core of your mind and being. Discovery of your Self is all that is necessary."

The King said, "But no one has ever told me how to do this. I don't know where to begin. How do I find what you are telling me?"

The Sage replied, "You need know only a few things. First, be aware you will encounter obstacles in your path of inquiry and self-discovery. Your own mind is beset with distractions, reactions, and worries. You will find yourself groping like a person in the dark for answers that seem to be elusive, when, in fact, they are right before you.

You are like a person whose eyes are closed who complains of darkness, when all that is necessary is to relax and gently open your inner eyes to what has always been with you and right before you...your own truth. It is really very simple, yet, at first, it does not seem easy. Also, you must be patient as this may take some time, how much depends on how strongly you defend your beliefs, judgments, and pain.

What you seek is peace of mind, peace for the body, and peace in the spirit. Within that peace is everything. In the depths of peace you will find all the knowledge you seek, all the answers to your questions, and all the solutions to your suffering.

"As you search within for the answers to the essential questions, many feelings and thoughts will come to mind. No matter what you experience, say, 'Thank you, I am neither this, nor that. I bless you, and release you.' You will find yourself shedding the many attachments and illusions you have held. Your points of view, judgments, perceptions, emotions, and questions will gradually diminish. They are all phantoms of your mind anyway. In time, the mind will become quiet and that is when the true discovery begins.

And here is a wonderful secret. Remember earlier I said you are not alone on your journey?"

The King said, "Yes, but so far I have felt alone. None of my teachers or advisors has been able to help me."

"And all your searching throughout your life has led you to my door, where your real discoveries begin," said the Sage. "For I have traveled the road before you and I know the way. With my help I can take you higher faster than you could alone. When we join in consciousness, I can help you release what you cling to that holds you in darkness and pain. I can help you open to the wonders of life. I have waited long for you to come to me, for I have known we would explore together.

"You do not need to forsake your kingdom, for you will be able to share your discoveries with many, and bring a light to where none has been. Your kingdom shall flourish as never before. Only come and spend some time with me and a universe of wonder will open before you. I am always here for you, and all who seek."

The King expressed his gratitude and promised the Sage he would return for further teachings and realizations.

Part Two

Obstacles to Enlightenment

Chapter 6

THE POWER OF YOUR MYTHS

Myths are something we all live with, yet most are unaware of them. A myth is a story, idea, or concept without a basis of fact which people adhere to as if it were true and real.

Myths are everywhere. There are many types of stories that people believe are true, but often are not. People usually create and live by myths to justify their actions. An example of myth making in politics, it is called "spin" or propaganda and refers to ways policies are presented to make them more acceptable to the public. In business, myths are created around shrewd strategies or deceit. In relationships, myth-making is sometimes called "white" lies. Additionally, you'll find that modern music and movies are full of myths. In fact, that is how they are constructed. These are just some examples of myths. They can be just as powerful as traditional myths such as those usually associated with gods and goddesses of ancient cultures. Those were the major myths of their day that people incorporated into their lives.

In the spiritual realm, a myth is a spiritual insight told in story form. All the spiritual books of the world are filled with them, and although some of them may be describing actual events, they are still myths because they are based on perceptions, conclusions, and ideas expressed as stories. So a myth may be true, or not, but they are filled with perceptions and beliefs that affect your everyday life. This is a more important subject than you may have realized because myths form the backdrop of your life. Recognizing myths for what they are is important because they regulate your decisions and choices.

In the spiritual realm most of the myths people attach their lives to originated from people who had a revelation that they based on an encounter with a legendary figure. This could include an angel, a god or goddess, or perhaps an extra-terrestrial being. From their experience, which may include visions or voices, they construct a perception, a story, and a myth that the vision or voice was external and real.

In most cases, entire belief systems were created like this. And perhaps one of the most amazing results is that entire groups of people and sometimes very large groups take these stories as absolute irrefutable fact and base their lives on them. In some cases, people even give up their life for the myth. This is testament to the power of myths. The myth is so strong that people think they have experienced ultimate truth, but they don't realize that their beliefs are only perceptions masquerading as ultimate truth.

Some may even claim to be enlightened or followers make the claim for the person, so others assume the person is enlightened and, therefore, what they say must be enlightened truth to spread or impose on the group. Some also project the myth that their group is special and their teachings need to be spread to everyone on the planet. The important point to realize is that the power of myth is far reaching on both a personal and global level.

Everyone is Under the Spell of Myths

Of all the topics you want to be clear on such as emotional reactions, limiting beliefs, and self-defeating behaviors, mythologies are the most difficult to eliminate. The reason for this is simple. You are probably more unaware of your myths than anything else you want to clear because they operate in your subconscious. You may or may not be consciously aware of the myths attached to your beliefs and emotional reactions, yet the myths are right there with you all the time, every day in every interaction but you usually don't realize you are operating from a myth.

Myths become beliefs that you believe are true. You then use the myth as the basis for your words and actions. For example, if you are angry, you know you are angry and you usually know why. However, you don't recognize the underlying myths that caused you to be triggered because they operate in your subconscious and work like filters on your thinking.

You'll notice that myths are all around once you know what to look for. They are part of educational systems, religious systems, political systems, and cultures and are as present in non-religious or non-spiritual contexts as they are in religious and spiritual ones. In other words, an atheist might think he or she is free of myths, and most of them do, because they reject the idea of any form of deity or spiritual experience, but they miss the fact that whatever their view of life is, it is also constructed of myths.

Many human interactions and communications between people are attempts at imposing one individual's myths on another. One person is trying to convince people their myth is truth. Alternatively, some people try to comfort others with their myth because they think the other person's myth is somehow defective. People use repetition to impose myths on others.

Stating a myth repeatedly is an effective method of convincing others the myth is true, or at least the best one to believe in. This method is very effective because one of the ways your subconscious mind becomes programmed is by repetition.

What is also amazing is that even the person repeating the lie may come to believe it. This is a type of brainwashing that works on the person saying it as well as those hearing it; this happens because the mind cannot always distinguish reality from illusion, or truth from lies. In this way, myths become internalized in a similar way as self-talk affirmations affect one's thinking.

Once you recognize the power of myths, you will realize how they affect every aspect of your life on an emotional level, belief level, behavioral level, biological level, and even a cellular consciousness level. Myths have almost everyone under their spell, but understanding how they influence thinking and behavior, you can have them under your power. You can live consciously from a platform of neutrality so that you are not at the whim of unconscious myths.

Living with myths is not wrong or bad; in fact, it is probably not likely you could live without them, but the key is being awake, and not being afraid to acknowledge them.

So where does this leave you?

To live as an enlightened being you have to be willing to look at and maybe throw out much of what you've heard, thought, or believed because it probably came from someone caught in myths. Formulating your philosophy of life out of a book, and especially a book written hundreds or thousands of years ago can be problematic. The best you can do is surmise what you think the myths might mean and project your myths on their myths.

Many myths were created to address fears. Consider that the ego is a fear-based identity built out of myths. The myths are composed of stories, ideas, and beliefs that are conclusions projected on perceptions. The ego is a collection of many myths. In fact, it is an entire warehouse of myths built upon other myths, lifetime after lifetime. When you are completely free of myths, you are also free of the ego.

Everything people base their lives on is based on myths because people's lives are a series of stories linked together to form a person's day. The stories are based on the needs and perceptions of the person telling you the story. Being free from the control of myths is an acknowledgement that it's OK to have and experience myths; however, you must consciously recognize them for what they are as stories constructed to give meaning to your day. You can do this consciously or it can happen automatically, unconsciously, once you are mindfully awake.

Deconstructing myths and becoming conscious is the path of self-discovery that results from self-uncovering. Uncovering leads to self-discovery because it is a process of revealing the stories and beliefs upon which your life is constructed. In other words, when you uncover the myths, you find the real you that lives under them.

How to Discover Your Myths

An effective process for discovering your myths is through discrimination and self-inquiry. Self-inquiry involves asking yourself questions that can lead you to the next step in your evolution. Questions help you see through the myths and illusions. This is done by monitoring your thoughts and actions through self-reflection and asking yourself, "What is the myth I am operating out of now? What is the myth behind what I believe?"

I recommend stopping whatever you are doing at least three times a day, or every hour or two if you are able, and take one or two minutes to ask yourself, "What story, myth, or judgment have I been operating under since I checked in the last time?" If you have made any judgments or had any emotional reactions, you were operating from a myth.

You'll get better at deconstructing the myths the more you do it, but finding the myths is tricky because the myths you live by are mostly invisible to you. They operate in the background of your consciousness causing you to assume they are truths, but they are actually your assumptions about life. If you are really serious and committed to self-discovery through self-uncovering, you will make this a priority.

If in a dream you are thirsty and you take a drink, the thirst is satisfied, but when you wake up both the thirst and satisfaction vanish because they were both dreams, and neither was real.

Similarly, when you wake from the illusions and myths of life, you awaken to a liberating naked truth of what you are. You can discover it for yourself through self-discovery which leads you to realizations called enlightenment. While you are living in the myths, they seem to be useful and meaningful ways of living, just as water in a dream is used to quench the dreamed thirst.

You can only arrive at a point free from myths through constant inner reflection or discrimination. To transcend the myths you must awaken from them by examining and inquiring about your perceptions. You must ask the question over and over. "What myth am I operating with in this moment?" As you do that, you will begin to uncover a simple purity that underlies all the stories.

Chapter 7

THE ORIGIN OF THE EGO

Many lifetimes ago, in order to feel more secure, you started investing yourself in acquiring more knowledge, more control, and more attachments. Eventually you oriented your life around your possessions and attachments. These free-will choices created identities and sustained the illusion of separation from your soul. When you are in separation, you are subject to the physics of that reality.

Over time, you began to awaken memories of a universe of light and love, and you set yourself on a path to re-discover more about it. However, the physical realm challenges you with survival and others who believe physicality is all there is. Education and religion keep you in the ego's finite universe. Even though the universe of light is everywhere, it is masked and hidden. It requires diligence to find the exits from the ego universe to enter the universe of light. The full divine presence is everywhere, yet the distractions of life have been so strong that they held your attention to the needs and desires of the ego.

Perhaps you can realize how difficult it would be to pull someone out of ego identifications because of fearing what might happen. The great fear of the ego is the terror of its end or death. This forms the underlying difficulty with people coming to see light and truth. They already have an inherent fear and insecurity of their separate existence, so they cling to anything that seems to offer them support or some measure of security.

The ego is like a drowning person who will tenaciously cling to a board floating in the ocean for dear life. The drowning person is afraid to let go to reach the lifeguard on the boat. The lifeguard cannot pull the person and the board into the boat, so the drowning person must release the board. The board represents the tools of the ego to defend itself against anything it perceives would diminish or destroy it. When you are willing to admit you are living with fear and feeling cut off, and you are willing to surrender these fears, only then can you be freed and helped.

What typically happens with people is they keep running, doing, trying, striving, seeking, building, achieving, learning, accomplishing, controlling, and accumulating, yet something is perceived to be missing and they never achieve completion and satisfaction no matter how much they accumulate.

They have a frenetic feeling that if they keep trying somehow, someday they will attain completion and happiness, but there will never be completion in the universe of the ego and separation.

Like so many people who immerse themselves in business, sports, religion, and hobbies, they don't realize how they have turned their attention away from the truth of their soul that would give them the completion and fulfillment they seek.

How the Ego Can Trap You

No matter how much you acquire or attach yourself to, you will never feel healed, resolved, or complete. Seeking attachment is like having an insatiable hunger. As long as you align with the ego and separation, you will feel something is missing with no way to resolve it. Because the ego is so deeply programmed, you'll keep trying to find completeness through things that can never make you complete. With this emptiness inside, you are likely to form a number of conclusions there something is wrong because even though you have acquired many things, you still are not completely satisfied. You feel something is still missing and therefore you are incomplete and may conclude there must be something wrong with you.

On the occasion when you accomplish something good and nice, an inner voice often says, "Oh that was too easy. Once you get it, you'll lose it." There is fear from perceived threats and circumstances from people trying to take the good away, and sometimes they succeed. Businesses fail, relationships fail, friends pass on, and conditions change.

The conclusions you reach about what you experience become a contract with yourself and the Universe. This contract has several components. One is that when you seek your dreams, you create obstacles and challenges. Another one is that all your dreams and desires have hidden problems. You do this to yourself to create enough struggles to pay the price to compensate for your feeling unworthy of your dream. This can emanate from beliefs and feelings deep inside that you are not worthy or deserving. Your dream requires earning it through pain and struggle. Then once you have suffered enough, you can have your dream.

Because of deep-seated unworthiness, you may be operating with a program that says, "I need people to lie to me in order for me to fulfill my contract." People then oblige you by lying to you or cheating you. Notice how each contract has slightly different versions of the same pattern. You have to lose something or pay a price in order to have something good. Discovering the belief program is important because when you are releasing blocks, you must be as specific as possible in what you are clearing. You only release and clear what you are aware of clearing.

What you want to do with these contract provisions is to neutralize them so you'll stop feeling as if you have to suffer because of guilt for having something you do not feel you deserve. Once you recognize how this works, you can stop having to pay with pain or loss. When you operate in the universe of separation, you operate under the laws of karma, but you can dispel that by moving into the light where you realize it is all an illusion.

To help you neutralize your ego contracts repeat these words to yourself:

- I surrender and release all need for karmic debts and agreements.
- I surrender and release all need to compensate or balance any past thoughts or behaviors.
- I choose to surrender and release now.

Repeat those statements until you feel lighter and freer. In fact, when you have surrendered deeply you will feel like you've been released from prison. You probably do not even realize how much weight and burden you are carrying. You just know something is wrong and life is a struggle.

The ego is where all your problems start, and the soul is where all solutions lie.

A complimentary part of this clearing process after the contracts clear away is to move out of the darkness of separation and into the light of presence. You will eventually realize the soul and light have been with you all the time. You realize it when you stop what you are doing long enough to invite the soul and light back into your awareness. As you do that, you will begin to feel the emptiness and suffering melt.

It is your inherent nature to be complete. The incompleteness you feel is the underlying illusion. Many philosophers and spiritual seekers have been looking in the dark ego realm for the answers that do not exist there. As long as you are groping in the dark, you will keep bumping into obstacles.

By moving in consciousness to the time before you turned away from love, light, and oneness and embraced the illusion of separation is how you recreate your history and neutralize the karmic trail of all your lifetimes. You do this by raising your awareness where realize that it was all composed of illusions. The fact is you never really separated.

To be fully successful with this, you must completely surrender even the minutest part of you that has any curiosity or longing for what separation offers. For if there is even a minuscule part of you with any pull into separation, you will experience separation and not escape the wheel of rebirth. This does not mean you must become an ascetic to break free of the ego. You will have more clarity on this as you learn more about surrender in future chapters.

Once you have gone into separation and then fully come out of it, you will know both sides of existence. At that point, you can make a choice and commitment to always live in the light and not ever go into separation again.

The Longing Ego

Let's look at the part of you that still loves any part of separation and enjoys illusion. This is the ego and its many identities. In the distorted non-logic of the ego attaching to separation makes sense because that is all it knows. It is like having a history of a relationship with somebody, and then leaving that relationship and longing for the relationship. All of the time and energy the ego has invested in lifetimes of separation creates further attachment through familiarity and ego needs.

The ego interprets letting anything go as loss, so it continues to grasp and hold on. It is telling you, "You will never have this again so hang on. If you let it go, you'll not be happy or safe." This is the energy of attachment: the desire to go back to a painful experience. The ego will hold on to suffering and pain because it fears that if it lets go of what is familiar, then something worse may come along. To address this proclivity it is necessary to surrender all desire, all attachment, all pulls, and all energies related to the ego. Surrender all parts that want to attach and all aspects of needing and desiring.

Be aware that besides wanting to accumulate more of everything, the ego also has desires for what it thinks is missing. This includes everything that has been unlived or not experienced. This aspect of the ego wants experiences. This is the part of you that says, "Just one more taste, one more night, one more ride." Of course, there is nothing wrong with one more thing; the problem lies in what motivates the ego for more. It stems from lack and a belief something is missing.

As you formulate the intention to let go, you'll probably experience resistance. You may feel it in your body as a contraction or tightening, and you may wonder why it is not totally going away. The reason is because the ego is more comfortable with what is familiar to it than the fear it has of the unknown future. However, once you experience liberation through surrendering and releasing, you will wonder why you assumed that something of value existed compared to what you experience in the light of the soul presence. I know it seems bizarre that the ego would want to hold on to pain and limitation, yet that is how the ego operates.

As you continue surrendering, the ego defenses gradually melt like an ice cube on a summer's day. As your surrender continues, you may hear inner voices saying things like, "I must hold on. This is what protects me." Those inner voices speak with all the authority of the ego. The ego has instituted a plethora of defense mechanisms that resist letting go.

Surrender is like erasing a computer's hard drive. As more and more ego qualities dissolve through surrender, the voices will become fragmented and make less sense until they are completely gone. Just observe and allow the feelings and voices to float to the surface and dissolve into the light. Moving from an intellectual understanding to the realization of what the ego is and how to release it by surrender is essential.

This is How to Clear the Ego

The ego's deep grip releases as you identify it, address it, and recognize it is a projected illusion. You can identify the ego components by allowing yourself to move into the space where you recall feeling fearful, angry, hopeless, or abandoned.

Once you have identified the ego components, invite the light and presence of the soul to merge into those patterns. You extend that invitation by prayerfully requesting the soul to merge into the feelings. Let those sensations and realizations of the soul, intelligence, and love move into all the places where you were grasping and attaching. Imagine yourself embraced with the light of healing presence. Call to the soul's light and be the light, and face the darkness with the truth of you, and watch the light dissolve the darkness.

Moving fully into this light and awareness takes complete letting go. There cannot be the slightest attachment to the struggle to attain anything.

As you enter willingness to release and shift into the intelligence of the soul, it will do it for you. At this point, you don't do anything to make it happen except be present and receptive. Presence takes over when you surrender and dissolve resistance. Repeat these words:

- I am willing to completely surrender and release all desires.
- I give my full permission to surrender and let go now.
- I invite the light of the soul to fill me.
- I am fully in the peace and comfort of the light presence.
- I surrender myself to this process.

You don't have to try to make the soul presence do anything. Just invite it in and know that its intelligence guides it to precisely where to go and how to clear the ego illusions. If you then scan yourself for your internal reactions of grasping, fearing, and tensing, you will notice that they are diminishing as you do this.

When you fully let go and embrace the soul presence, you'll notice it feels comfortable and familiar, like coming home. You will experience total comfort and familiarity. The light was always there shinning inside of you, and that light is your soul, who you truly are. Give the light permission to integrate into all areas of your life. You want this light to flow into your work, into your relationships, into everything that you say, think, and do.

This process puts you into a state of mindfulness all the time because it dissolves any impediment that keeps you from being mindful, so it is effortless and automatic. Once this process starts, it will continue whether you are paying attention to it or not.

Chapter 8

THE CHALLENGES OF THE EGO

When you commit to exploring the complex patterns and programs that make up the ego, a simultaneous sense of fear and adventure spontaneously occurs. It reminds me a little of skydiving which some want to try, but they feel fear at the prospect. Something is pulling them toward exploring, yet they recoil somewhat at the idea.

As you move forward toward self-discovery, sometimes you will not be certain where you are or where to go next. At those times, you are somewhat like an innocent child who is lost and looks for a reassuring hand to hold, but can't find it. You don't know where to reach. You feel pushed and pulled by the ego storms of suffering as you drift through the universe of separation. This can be a confusing time as you search for answers and direction.

The ego has a strong sense of being empty and lost, and this energy is frozen in time deep inside of you. As soon as you start to surrender and release, you feel fear and recoil back into loneliness, loss, and abandonment. These painful feelings can seem more comfortable than the terror of the unknown that results from letting go. What are those feelings? There is fear of being vulnerable, oppressed, and helpless. A stream of fear may run through you causing you to contract and become stuck. Ultimately, this is actually fear of the unknown. What is unknown to the ego has captured your mind.

These are some of the ego interpretations and feelings that shaped your destiny. They have diminished the space you live in compressing you into a cocoon of illusions.

Finding Your Way out of the Cocoon of Illusions

At first, you probably don't see any light or feel anything comforting. This can be discouraging, but persistence and practice will reveal the truth of the soul's light. Many people don't apply themselves sufficiently to break free. It takes considerable persistence and dedication to overcome the hurdles and reach the levels you long for. You can't bring the light in while operating from the ego itself; you must draw on the truth of your soul that lives fully in light and truth.

Connecting with the soul presence brings sensations such as love, acceptance, comfort, and nurturing. The wounds you have are the dark places where the light has not been. Inviting the soul's presence to merge and integrate fills the darkness with healing light, love, and acceptance. The nurturing soul presence replaces all the pain and wounds.

This loving energy and presence has intelligence and knows where to go and what to do. Just surrender into it more and more. The soul's intelligence knows you and loves you more completely and unconditionally than you have ever experienced. Keep giving yourself permission to unfold and release into it.

The ego has a number of subtle mechanisms that push enlightenment out of reach while tricking you to think you are getting closer. This is why surrender is vitally important to your spiritual path. Surrender and release all trying, impatience, effort, and excitement about attaining enlightenment. Give yourself permission to connect fully with oneness and love. Feel an immersion into the embrace of loving bliss. Open all your channels to accept it and receive it. Relax yourself into light and soul presence and give yourself permission to feel total acceptance.

Chapter 9

SEVEN WAYS THE EGO TRICKS YOU

The ego's greatest fear is that it will cease to exist. Therefore, the ego has assigned itself one mission: Do everything possible for more safety and security. If the ego can assure these conditions, it believes it will then be immortal and happy. This leads to many ways the ego tricks you in its relentless pursuits.

Everything the ego does is rooted in its survival. The ego fears anything and everything that it thinks might threaten its very existence. The irony is that the ego is actually just a projection of conclusions and beliefs that create an identity that it is a real being. Actually, it is more like a program of recordings of many perceptions. In other words, the ego is like a fictional character in a movie. The ego doesn't know it isn't real. It just thinks it must perpetuate its existence as long as it can, so it has a bag of tricks it uses to convince you that you are the ego and that's all that you are. It has a variety creative ways to trick you.

Trick #1: Your Emotions are Proof the Ego is Real

The ego uses the fact that you have emotional reactions as validation to prove that what triggered your emotions is real. But in reality emotions prove the opposite because they derive from beliefs. For instance, believing something is threatening creates fear whether or not there is a real threat. In most cases, what is feared never happens and therefore the threat is not real, but the fear feels real. The good news is that what you feel you can heal.

Your feelings are one of your greatest assets for dismantling the constructs of the ego and clarifying the ways the ego tricks you. Here's how that can work. When you feel an emotional reaction such as fear, ask yourself, "Who is feeling this? Is it my soul, my memory, my brain?" These are the three main possibilities.

1. The reaction could be coming from your soul if the feeling is positive.
2. It could be coming from a memory recording that is part of the ego.
3. It could be a spontaneous emotional reaction from the brain stem also called the primitive ("reptilian") brain. This includes the

category of subconscious negative programs and ego-thoughtform programs.

The point of asking those questions is to determine if what you are experiencing is coming from your soul or somewhere else. Because the soul is incapable of negative feelings, if a feeling is negative, then you have identified an ego thoughtform. Thoughtforms are subtle-energy recordings of past events and reactions. The thoughtforms are composed of memories, emotions, and beliefs. The ego is composed of many thousands of these. They are what cause the reptilian brain to react, and what determines your subconscious programs.

Once you have made the identification, you can assert that the negative reaction is not who you truly are. Your refuting any reality to the reaction as your identity dis-identifies yourself from false beliefs. At this point, if you also apply a subtle-energy clearing procedure, you can completely eliminate negative thoughtforms, which allows more of the soul to emerge and take over.

Trick #2: Reality is What Your Senses Experience

All the ego knows is what you have experienced in this life or another through the senses. These experiences were recorded from sensory input that seems to have occurred without conscious choice. This is sometimes referred to as being asleep in a dream, yet all the while you think you are awake, but you have been tricked.

After many lifetimes, you begin to "wake up" to the fact that ego programs have been running your life and that you can make choices to change. "Waking up" is becoming consciously aware of the soul's qualities which are fundamentally loving, kind, and generous. The soul is actually what is real. You are right now in the process of awakening, and that process continues until all the components of the ego are replaced with the reality of the soul.

Trick #3: If You Accumulate MORE, You Will Be Safer and Exist Forever.

One attribute that defines the ego's motivations, is a perceived need for more. The need for "more" is driven by a variety of fears, and therefore the accumulation of more is seen as a means of increasing security and safety. Therefore, the ego is perpetually on the lookout for more of anything that could possibly mitigate any threat or lack. The ego is in a relentless pursuit of a wide variety of more accumulations. This can include more of practically anything such as more money, more love, more possessions, more control, and more power. The ego thinks it needs lots of money to have security. It thinks it needs love and acceptance of others to feel fulfilled and complete. It thinks it needs to look a certain way to be accepted, liked, and safe. It thinks it needs to be successful and respected in your career to feel you are fulfilling your life mission. One big problem with this agenda is that there is never enough of anything to reach absolute safety and security; hence, the continual pursuit of more.

Trick #4: Fear, Anger, and Guilt Lead to Greater Security.

The idea that negative emotions lead to security may seem counter-intuitive, but since fear motivates the ego it forms irrational and illogical perceptions.

Guilt is a form of fear. It fears punishment for being or feeling guilty. Anger is another form of fear because when you are angry, you fear something. Anger is a reaction to feeling threatened. Feeling threatened derives from fear. Fear is the deepest core of the ego. It is what drives an ego-controlled person to enact shame and guilt on itself and others in a vain attempt to lead to an improved condition. Fear and guilt are the strongest motivations institutions use to manipulate people to conform to the ego needs of those in control.

However, using fear and guilt for motivation creates increased stress, confusion, resistance, resentment, denial, arguments, and conflict. It can also drive you to conform to what those in control want from you. In more extreme cases, it leads to war.

Trick #5: If You Are More Spiritual, You'll Be More Safe and More Happy.

The problem with this one is what the ego thinks being spiritual is. The ego doesn't actually know what spirituality is. How could it? It operates only through the senses, and true spirituality is a matter of consciousness realization beyond the mind or senses. Because of this the only thing the ego can do is speculate about spirituality, and it uses knowledge and the intellect to gather definitions and methods for accumulating more of each of those.

Many spiritual scholars have vast funds of knowledge gathered from ancient texts and the words of spiritual teachers. Some, of course, also have true spiritual realizations, but in many cases, they mistake knowledge for spiritual understanding and realizations. A certain baseline of knowledge is part of the spiritual realization process, but it is not the same thing. What this premise does is motivate and even reward a person for gaining knowledge on spiritual and religious topics. The ego will inspire and assist a person to keep pursuing more knowledge, more understanding, more techniques, and more initiations. As long as a person is doing something that seems spiritual to the ego, it mistakenly believes they are evolving spiritually. The ego believes accumulating knowledge and information results in security and happiness.

When you think of a spiritual person, you probably have some images in your memory based on what you have seen and been taught. This can include certain types of clothing, postures, demeanor, appearance, vocal tone, and practices. Not that there is anything wrong with this list, but it can divert you from understanding what true spirituality is. It is not anything external, but if you pursue something external in a mistaken belief that you are progressing spiritually, you have fallen into this fifth trap of the ways the ego tricks you.

Pursuing anything externally can become a major diversion from what really serves your spiritual evolution. In fact, anything invested in external pursuits actually ends up feeding and strengthening ego needs. Furthermore, all the external pursuits are like trying to grasp "a carrot at the end of a stick." No matter how delicious it looks, you never reach it and end up disillusioned and dissatisfied.

You can find yourself thinking you are close to attaining a spiritual state yet ever pursuing but never quite reaching it. Eventually, all the outer seeking gives way to the realization that what is being sought is already present within you and can be accessed and experienced.

You progress on a true spiritual path by pausing the relentless external pursuits and deeply observing what you are experiencing and asking some simple questions. Here's a short list to get you started:

- How did I arrive at what I am currently experiencing?
- What do I perceive is lacking or missing in my life?
- What beliefs have I concluded from my experiences?
- What have I been resisting?

- What can I release and let go?
- Who is experiencing this?
- What does my soul and spirit tell me about this?

Trick #6: Suffering Leads to Spiritual Rewards.

The ego harbors a mistaken belief that suffering and struggling are important parts of the spiritual path. The ego's perspective is that more suffering offers more evidence that you are spiritual. The ego has concluded that pain, struggle, and suffering are all payment for its sins and defects. It, therefore, concludes that the more pain and loss you suffer, the more you spiritually progress.

Of course, you can learn from struggles, but they are certainly not prerequisites to spiritual evolution. In fact, a true spiritual path leads to relief from pain and suffering. But this doesn't stop the ego-mind from believing that martyrdom for its beliefs is a high spiritual calling. To think that suffering loss is a foundation for a high spiritual realization is an ego trick. You've heard the expression, "Don't cut off your nose to spite your face." This means needlessly suffering in a vain attempt to solve a problem and improve your condition.

Suffering can make you think you are progressing by making you think God is testing you and refining you. Of course, suffering can sometimes help trigger spiritual awakenings, but it is certainly not a requirement, nor is it an evolved approach to your spiritual evolution. This is an ego distortion of spiritual evolution. You do not need to suffer to awaken spiritually.

Trick #7: It is Somebody Else's Fault Causing You to Suffer.

The ego has a dilemma. It doesn't know why it suffers. In some cases, it criticizes and blames itself for being imperfect and bad. In other cases, it projects the blame on others. Obviously, others have a role to play in your life. They may not understand you or accept you, but what you conclude and how you react depends on your own beliefs. If you blame others, it causes the ego-mind to feel exonerated and validated, so the ego feels a little better about itself.

Suffering is primarily due to internal processing, not external circumstances. Breaking through this ego trick requires that you recognize your role in creating, attracting, and sustaining the conditions you experience. This is often not as they say an "easy pill to swallow" because it requires a high degree of honesty with yourself, including admitting your part in the creation of the experience. It also means that you are responsible for your interpretations, conclusions, and beliefs about your life. It also means that the degree of happiness you feel, the spiritual realizations you have, and your responses to life all emanate from within you. The reality is that nothing outside of you can give you what you don't give yourself internally.

It is time to ask yourself in what ways the ego has been tricking you. Each of the ways the ego tricks you enslaves you to ego control. Your mission, should you decide to accept it, is to reject and release the ways the ego tricks you and embrace your deep soul truth by merging with the soul and letting go of everything else.

Chapter 10

SEVEN KEYS TO UNDERSTAND & ELIMINATE THE EGO

On your spiritual journey, knowing how to deal with and eliminate the Ego in order to end struggling and suffering is important. The Ego is the barrier to enlightenment. The Ego is responsible for all the chaos, pain, and destruction in the world today. Luckily, seven keys unlock ways to understand and eliminate the Ego's hold.

Key 1. The Ego is not bad; it simply has virtually no access to permanent solutions.

The ego is searching for safety, security, healing, and love, but it has no clue where to find any of those, so it is continually on the defensive and searching for something it doesn't have access to. If you approach the core of struggle, suffering, and pain with a sincere intention of bringing healing and love to it, the Ego will relax its resistance and you will begin to find release and clarity. This automatically happens as the soul merges more completely into your everyday awareness bringing permanent resolution and healing. This usually needs to be done in a meditative state. If you try to eliminate the Ego with more forceful means such as will power or control, you will only amplify its resistance.

Key 2. The Ego is composed of judgments and distorted beliefs about every experience.

Distorted beliefs formulate identities, which many mistakenly think is who they are. Beneath every false identity is the true self or soul, which has all the Ego is looking for. In fact, the soul ultimately is the healer.

Key 3. The Ego believes that more is better and safer.

The Ego has been accumulating memories, conclusions, beliefs, and control since its inception. The problem is that these are all distortions, yet the Ego doesn't know any other solution to its misery. The Ego believes that more knowledge, more control, more money, and more things will lead to more security and power. The Ego will do whatever is necessary to acquire more, causing the Ego to become a tyrant and enslave you to its needs. But when you approach the Ego's needs with soul solutions, healing takes place and the grip of the Ego diminishes.

Key 4. The Ego is driven by needs.

Nothing is able to satisfy the Ego for more than a short time. The Ego thinks, "I don't have enough," "I want it," and/or "I need it." When it acquires what it thinks it wants, it feels satisfied for a short time, but soon continues to feel something else is missing. This causes the ego to drive you to keep acquiring more to fill the perception something is missing or lacking. When you address the needs with surrender, the sense of being incomplete and unsatisfied eventually disappears. This in turn creates an attractor field within you that brings completion, happiness, and fulfillment.

Key 5. The Ego strives for immortality.

The Ego is always in survival mode and defends its beliefs so it regards others as rivals or even as enemies. In order to survive, the Ego strives to defend, protect, sustain, and expand itself. It fears its finiteness and thinks that by accumulating control and possessions, it can continue forever.

Key 6. The Ego projects that everyone is a potential threat.

The Ego has a very difficult time with trust. It suspects that anyone or anything may possibly threaten it; therefore, it often exaggerates potential threats. You've heard the saying, "Don't make a mountain out of a mole hill." This speaks to the Ego's proclivity to catastrophize. The soul, on the other hand, lives in trust. Trust derives from surrendering fears. Surrender means letting go of all forms of resistance including judgments, blame, fear, and anger.

Key 7. The Ego keeps people hypnotized and asleep.

The persuasiveness of the Ego is so powerful that people are unaware that their life is governed by a programmed mind. If you are able to observe and address the functions of the Ego, you will be able to clear it and transcend its effects. You must reach beyond your Ego-dominated mind programs because if you don't succeed with doing that, you'll continue to create more struggle and suffering.

Chapter 11

HOW TO CLEAR SUB-PERSONALITIES OF THE EGO

While trying to clear issues and problems from a person's life, many people circle in spirals of recurring problems because they do not go to the source of where all the problems originate, which is the ego itself.

You may have heard the story about the man who one night was crawling around on the street looking for a lost key. A friend stopped to ask him what he was doing and then volunteered to help him look for his lost key. After searching for quite a while, the friend says, "Are you sure you lost the key around here?" To which the man said, "No, I lost it somewhere else" The friend then asked the obvious question, "Then why are you looking here?" The man answered, "Because the light is better here." What this ridiculous story is designed to point out is that people in general go about looking for answers symbolized by the key in all the wrong places. They look to what appears to be the easiest and most accessible places.

The problems we seek answers for are like leaves on many branches of a large tree that you do not want. You can pull the leaves off and even cut off some branches, but the tree will continually grow more. The solution lies in completely chopping the tree down. The tree is like your ego. You can continue chipping away at it and find ways of coping with it, but as long as it exists, it will continue sprouting new ways to express itself.

People usually think they know who they are. They can give you their names, their career, their relationships, their identifying numbers, their degrees and certificates, and the groups they belong to, but these are not who they are.

Part of the problem is that people become wrapped up in their activities and other distractions of the day. They mistakenly think they are an accumulation of their beliefs and emotions. In fact, to suggest otherwise seems like a delusion to most people. This is why the story at the beginning of this chapter about the person looking for the key in the wrong place is what almost everyone is doing: Looking to what seems to make sense to the logical, rational, analytical mind is looking in the wrong places for spiritual answers.

On one hand people believe they are a collection of beliefs, emotions, reactions, and biology, and on the other hand are those who believe they are something more and deeper. When it comes to discovering the latter, we find a convoluted and polluted path. Doctors, psychologists, and sociologists tell you how you are the product of your biology, your environment, your culture, your childhood, and your life experiences. Religions say humans cannot know God directly but must follow rules, regulations, and procedures written down mostly by men who supposedly did have contact with God. All of this is looking in the wrong place. This diverts the search into the realm of the ego and prevents discovering the truth.

The ego is the accumulation of all the disturbances, reactions, beliefs, feelings, perceptions, identities, and personality traits people think they are. The ego permeates the conscious and subconscious realms. It embeds itself in the subtle layers of the aura and chakra system, and its effects are often felt in the physical body. Relentless searching is driven by the deep fear and loneliness the ego experiences because its consciousness is focused in the outer realms through the senses.

The core of the ego experiences separation, abandonment, and aloneness because that is its nature. It was born out of the consciousness of separation. With this as the core driving every human, you can see why there is a relentless pursuit of pleasure, safety, and accumulation of possessions, control, love, and relationships. The ego seeks anything that will potentially alleviate its suffering even if it is short-lived.

The problem with this premise is that no way exists to perpetuate anything. Happiness, fulfillment, love, and peace cannot be found in a permanent and sustained way through people or things, but they can only be found through the discovery of your true inner nature: your soul which exists beyond birth and death and transcends the mind and body. Furthermore, this is the birthright of everyone. In some ways, it seems amazing that not everyone knows this since it's only a matter of discovering your own inner truth. But clearing the distortions created and sustained by the ego are not so easy because everyone has accumulated a great deal of ego programming.

The ego is what is responsible for all your habits, beliefs, identifications, attitudes, and negative emotional patterns. These are all contained in subtle-energy thoughtforms that must be discovered, dis-identified from, deconstructed, and dissolved. This process takes diligent focus and attention sustained over months and years as incremental progress leads to greater degrees of awakening and self-discovery.

A generally accepted perception is that we are striving to become something. This would include creating and building desirable traits, characteristics, and qualities, such as becoming more kind, loving, noble, healing, caring, insightful, generous, supportive, compassionate, wise, and all the other traits we admire in the saints and spiritual leaders of history. Those who possess these traits did not develop them. You heard that correctly. They did not develop them but rather they discovered them and revealed them because they are all the natural traits of your soul. Therefore, as you discover who you are, you will also reveal the very traits you most aspire to attain.

As you delve into the depths of where you house the ego traits and release them, you'll find that the mind becomes more peaceful and quiet, and the heart center opens and expands to radiate its gifts. Your life changes and the path that once challenged you becomes much smoother and easier to travel.

Clearing Sub-Personalities & Identities

The spiritual path is through the purification of the heart and mind to reveal your true self or soul. Something that interferes with this process and keeps you entrapped with the ego are the numerous sub-personalities or identities you mistakenly think are you. It is very easy to think you are the identities and the identities are you, for these are what you experience every day. So you unwittingly find yourself attached to them. The identities or sub-personalities represent a segment or fragment of your personality. They are not a complete personality but an aspect of your personality that has a single objective or characteristic such as depression, pride, anger, or fear. An identity is like a costume you wear that portrays a role you play, such as being possessive, and/or feeling betrayed, fearful, undeserving, hurt, stuck, or confused. Every time you experience any of these, you slip into those roles and live your life for a time through those identities.

A fascinating aspect of sub-personalities or identities is that you can interact with them. For instance, you can address the part of you in fear and ask it why it is generating the fear and what it wants. Remarkably, you can receive insights and answers. Each sub-personality has a limited consciousness of beliefs you can communicate with, but it always answers you from the perspective of what it believes to be true, which is a rather narrow view because it only sees options through the lens of its nature. For instance, fear views situations and responds to events from the perspective of protecting you from something believed to be threatening.

As you communicate with your sub-personalities, you will find that they believe they are you, and they will insist on it. After all, you can feel what they feel, so it's logical to assume they are you. They may or may not have a logical point of view. More often than not, their point of view is completely absurd, but this is the belief from which they operate.

What to Do About Ego Identities

Step 1: Identifying the Identities

Think of the sub-personalities or identities like costumes you wear. This perspective helps you to contextualize them as overlays or recordings, which are easier to recognize as not being who you are. You probably have a collection of several of these costumes in your wardrobe closet, but wouldn't it be better to throw them out and get a new wardrobe, one that reflects who you really are?

There are a number of ways of going about eliminating and replacing dysfunctional sub-personalities and identities. In order to release an identity, you must identify the components of it. This is the most time consuming part of the releasing process as ego identities have considerable history and multiple components. For these reasons, you want to gather as much information about the sub-personality or identity as you can.

The key to accessing the sub-personalities and addressing them is your willingness to be open and honest with yourself. You have to be willing to face questions, confusion, and what is upsetting you. If you find you do not want to look at something, ask yourself why not? Unless you are a fully enlightened and ascended being, I'll guarantee sub-personalities are ego aspects of your identity. Your evolution proceeds from your willingness to discover what they are and then the degree you succeed in letting them go.

The Four Categories of Each Sub-Personality

Four major patterns comprise each sub-personality: the emotional components, the mental components (conclusions and beliefs), the memories, and the physical components.

(1) Identify the Emotions. Start with how the sub-personality presents itself emotionally. This is the way you were triggered and reacted. Describe the emotions and feelings you are experiencing. Feel the emotions such as, sadness, discouragement, anger, resentment, hatred, helplessness, futility, loneliness, anxiety, worry, guilt, revenge, etc.

(2) Identify the Beliefs. Once you feel the emotions then the voices will start to show themselves.

Beliefs produce emotional states. For example, the belief, "I'm not good enough" can lead to sadness, discouragement, or guilt.

A belief sets up the emotion, which you then feel in your body. Sometimes it is subtle, but if it sits there long enough, it can lead to physical symptoms or even disease. For instance, you may have felt sensations like "butterflies" in your stomach when anxiety arose.

Tuning in to the voices or self-talk of the sub-personality is important. What does it believe is true? What does it want? Why is it there? What do you conclude about it? What is the primary voice? The answers are the voices you can address. Be willing to face what you find.

If you were taught as a child that showing anger is wrong, you will likely feel helpless and as a result, suppress your feelings. If you hide the anger and pretend it isn't there, the pattern will find ways to express itself as time goes on. For instance, you may become cynical, blaming, depressed, or passive aggressive. Suppression or denial eventually leads to the pattern asserting itself later.

(3) Identify the Memories. Memories can be like pictures or movies in your mind. Painful memories are what cause you to hold on to the sub-personalities. To the ego-controlled mind, your memories provide the justification for holding on to the sub-personality.

(4) Identify the Physical Effects. What physical sensation do you associate with this sub-personality? Where do you feel or sense it in or around your body?

If something is not going the way you want, sit with your body. Feel how it shows up in your body. Ask yourself, "What do I notice in my body right now?" Maybe it's a tight shoulder, a pain somewhere, or a headache. Let the physical aspect show itself to you. Where in your body would you locate your issue? You can do this by picking some condition, discomfort, or something that draws your attention in your body. Describe what is going on with your body.

(1) If it is pain or tightness, does it seem like it is due to feeling mad, angry, or resentful?

(2) Or, is the pain or tightness connected to fear, concern, or worry?

(3) Or, is the pain or tightness like a feeling of stress? Tune in to what you notice and describe to yourself what the nature of the physical sensations are in the discomfort.

Step 2. Preparing to Let Go

Now that you have gathered some insights and understanding about the sub-personality, you can ask yourself some additional questions that will give the ego mind some good reasons to let it go. The ego mind likes to have rational reasons to let go of something it has been holding on to in some cases for many decades.

When an emotion comes up and you are struggling with something, you can't intellectualize that you are enlightened. You can't effectively tell yourself, "I am one with the universe and I am love," when you are feeling attacked, or are caught with self-hatred or self-judgment, or are blaming yourself or someone else. Your body doesn't respond with love and peace to such intellectualizations. For instance, your stomach doesn't seem to know you are love and are one with God just because you say it is. Therefore, to reach the realization of what you know intellectually, you must first stay with the identity and explore it in order to more completely release it.

Identification with the identities is the first and probably most important part of the clearing and releasing process, for you usually only release what you acknowledge and put your attention on, and much of what needs to be released, either you tend to ignore or you don't know what to do with it.

Ask yourself, "What do I think will happen if I allow this to continue?" For instance, you might answer, "I'll embarrass myself, I'll feel vulnerable, I'll feel afraid, I'll feel stupid, people will reject me, I'll make a fool of myself, I'm afraid I'll fail, or I can't trust people." Answering these questions helps to flesh out the beliefs and sort out what seems to be truth from what really is true.

Step 3. Disidentify Yourself from the Sub-Personality

One of the reasons sub-personalities and identities are held on to so strongly is because they are survival mechanisms. In this step, it is important to:

(a) Acknowledge the identity and describe it in a sentence.
(b) Express gratitude for the identity helping you survive for lifetimes.
(c) Be thankful for the identity revealing itself to you.
(d) Verbally express to yourself that you are ready to heal and willing, and able to release all of the sub-personality.
(e) Verbally state, "I am not this sub-personality. I do not own it, and I do not allow it to own me."
(f) "I am willing to surrender, release, and let go of the need for this."

Add the specific descriptions you discovered about the sub-personality in the previous steps. When you say these releasing statements to yourself, make sure you move your lips even if you do not speak the words aloud. That makes them much more effective.

Gratitude actually begins the releasing process, and, of course, releasing them is the objective. The fact that they have lead to pain, struggle, and suffering is why you want to replace them with something that is more effective. They do not and cannot take you to enlightenment, and they certainly do not make you happy.

Step 4. Apply a Subtle-Energy Clearing Technique.

Every belief, emotion, and memory has a subtle energy component. These can be in your aura, chakras, or your physical body. Generally, if you only verbalize your intention to release the sub-personality, subtle-energy components will remain unless a clearing method is applied. A simple one I recommend is to use your releasing words and intentions while you imagine a vacuum hose six inches in diameter removing all energy in the thoughtforms associated with the sub-personality. You don't need to see this visually in your mind's eye because your intention is enough for it to be effective. This can seem like merely a visualization, but it is also the activation of your intention to release, let go, and be free from the sub-personality. I can assure you this method works as I have helped free thousands of people by using this method. In the realm of subtle energy your intentions are what rules. Intentions are what can free you.

Step 5. Call to Your Soul to Merge into Everywhere the Sub-Personality Was.

As you release the sub-personalities say these words to yourself, "I ask the highest enlightened awareness of the soul to merge into and replace the sub-personality." Name it specifically for the greatest effect. Put the name of the identity in the merging statement.

What Happens Next

Next, pictures or memories will often surface. You are like a warehouse of memories stored from lifetimes. As you call to the light of the soul, you shine light on stored memories of the past, which include your conclusions and beliefs. For instance, you might get a flash back to your childhood of an older brother or sister or relative doing something to you. On the other hand, some people barely react and go on to something else, while others cry and conclude that life is horrible and they can't fix it. Beliefs are attached to the pictures in your memories and they contain energetic components of the events and your conclusions about the events.

Conclusions and beliefs form bridges to more memories and pictures. Calling in the soul and dissolving those pictures will clear the beliefs, which in turn clear the emotions. This potentially clears the physical effects or, in some cases even diseases if you have one. It is necessary to continue clearing the pictures as they come up. Surrender them, release them, and call to your soul. You should repeat the process until you completely return to your soul essence and oneness.

After doing this for a while, soul qualities emerge with gifts to take you further into self-discovery of your true self. Qualities such as joy, deep peace, happiness, blissfulness, compassion, fun, euphoria, overwhelming love, and beauty are all possible.

Chapter 12

SHIFTING FROM THE FEAR UNIVERSE TO THE LOVE UNIVERSE

At least at times, your life probably seems like one emotional storm after another. How do you remain peaceful when facing turmoil and stress? How can you be in the middle of a storm and yet remain calm?

As you keep clearing the patterns that cause turmoil, you will become so purified that you no longer attract or create the storms. The reason storms are still in your life is because the elements are within you attracting the situations and people who trigger you. In other words, your outer world is the projection screen of your inner world.

Nothing can happen to you or exist in your life if a program within you is not projecting it. I know that sometimes this is a little difficult to accept. The reason it is difficult to believe is because you think you should have only what you consciously desire. What gets in your way are the negative energy patterns in your subconscious that you have accumulated over lifetimes. Because most of the patterns that make up who you think you are inhabit places that are unconscious. The challenge is finding the unconscious beliefs embedded in your emotional and mental bodies. Even though they are unconscious they affect your day-to-day life just as surely as a computer program determines what a computer will do.

Every thought, memory, feeling, and emotion is composed of energy thoughtforms. These thoughtforms occupy a place in your aura or energy field and sometimes even embed themselves in your physical body causing pain, disease, accidents, or bad luck. These thoughtforms have size, shape, color, and other characteristics that enable you to discover and remove them. For instance, if you have had past lifetimes as a warrior you will have a carry-over of thought habits from your lifetimes as a warrior. This could include such things as anger, hatred, and fear. You could also tend to approach problem solving as a battle to fight.

Gradually, over many lifetimes these thoughtforms loose their energy naturally; however, you can also accelerate the process by directly removing and dissolving them. As you work on removing these negative thoughtforms, you will eventually reach a state of equanimity and peace.

The biggest challenge is finding what needs releasing. You can remove these programs by working on your own, but it generally takes longer than having someone help you. You will find it is quicker and easier for someone trained in clearing energy to spot these patterns and help you remove them quickly and permanently.

A Simple System for Removal

If you have a troubling pattern such as getting triggered with an emotion, or struggling with your finances, or coping with your relationships, bring your attention to it and describe to yourself what this energy feels like in one or two sentences.

Next, say these words, "I give myself full permission to release and let go of all need for this program."

After making this statement a few times, close your eyes, relax, and observe a healing and transformational presence emerge bringing a comforting feeling.

Then say these words, "I give my permission for this healing presence to dissolve all causes of the reaction now."

At this point, there is nothing to do but allow the healing energy presence to move through you. The intelligent presence knows both what needs to be done and how to do it. As this energy comes in, it will clear the blocked energy wherever it is. This is the energy of purification and transformation. It can sometimes feel like a soothing warm liquid bringing deep peace. As it gradually moves through you, it dissolves the negative thoughtforms.

As the process unfolds, repeat the following words:

"I allow this purification process to release all stuck patterns."
"I give healing energy permission to transform me as I surrender to the purification."

You will notice that the energy is rejuvenating. There is a youthful energy and a lightness that has a revitalizing quality to it.

As you experience this, say these words:

"I give permission for this energy to completely fill every place in my body and aura."
"I allow it to fill me totally from head to toe."
"I ask for the perfect healthy soul blueprint to integrate into me."

The Power of Fear

Prior to clearing the programs, your ego and subconscious have been on different missions. The operating directive has been survival. At certain levels of consciousness, fear is a necessary underlying motivation for survival, and it is where the vast majority of people operate. Fear is good for survival and therefore it has served you, which is precisely why it lives on. But needing fear for survival is an illusion. Fear has been such a core trait that the ego often defines itself in terms of fear. Fear has a single-minded purpose. It is so diligent that it cannot see other options. It is as if it is on a mission. In fact, it is the underlying force of nature. Survival is the goal. Fear believes itself to be on a noble and diligent path leading to your survival and evolution. Fear says, "You have no idea how much I have helped you get you to where you are now. Do not tell me what works and what doesn't work. I know fear works."

Fear and love exist as a duality of opposites. Since this is true, the subconscious fear programming is at odds with the Higher Self or Soul because the Soul is light and love, while the subconscious programming is fear motivated. This means the conscious mind is caught in the middle. Without intervention, the subconscious will win.

When you meditate free of the subconscious and body, you have some clarity free from fear, but as soon as you open your eyes, you enter a world whose underlying fabric is composed of fear. Of course, there are temporary experiences of love, peace, and joy, but unless released, fear remains in the background.

Fear is certainly evident throughout nature and creation. Even great spiritual leaders have admitted they have fear. However, there is a higher level of evolution. Eventually fear must let go because at some point the individual will evolve and transcend any need for fear. At that point, fear will have done its job. Fear will have taken the individual to the place where that person is now ready to enter into the universe of love.

How do you make the transition away from fear?

The most accessible way to move away from fear is to merge with your soul, which is love. In fact, the highest evolution is not possible any other way. Love is a creative energy, and following the path of love is the most logical course to follow because fear will ultimately have to surrender itself to love.

You will affect the transition from fear to love by shifting your focus to merging your full consciousness with the purity of unconditional love. Then love will fill all the places where fear was in all of your cellular consciousness. You must let fear go and fully embrace love as your new prime directive.

Your Body is a Good Place to Start

Many people have an adversarial relationship with their body. You might not think much about your body when you are healthy and feeling good, but what is your relationship with your body when it is not operating the way you'd like?

Your body is a gift. You could not be doing what you are now doing without it. Problems are not your body's fault either. You have projected energy on your body. Your body is processing the energy that you projected on it. If the body needs rest, vacations, or pampering, this is what you need to do. If you have illness, injury or an antagonistic relationship between your spirit and the body, you must address these issues. If you think you have a lot of work to do and do not have time to take care of your body, you need to rethink your approach and take care of your body. This will help you feel better and perhaps live longer giving you more time to accomplish your goals.

By analogy, this is like a man sawing a tree and making slow progress. Another who was observing him said, "Why don't you sharpen your saw?" The man answered, "I can't take the time, and I've got to saw this wood." It sounds a bit silly when you think of it this way, but you must honor the physical laws that promote good health and as a result you will be able to pursue your goals and advance your evolution.

An important first step is to tell your body you love it and accept it:

"I now bless my body with love and healing energy."

"I now clear all energy meridians throughout my body."
"I restore the free flow of lifeforce energy through all my systems."

You can take that method one-step further by talking to each part of your body and all your internal organs and systems and tell them how much you love and appreciate them. Then send healing love to them. This is a good practice to do before you go to sleep at night.

As you do this practice you will be anchoring a new paradigm of Surrender, Love, Trust, Joy, and Peace. This is paramount because it allows energy associated with these qualities to integrate all through you. Allow that energy in all through you until it becomes you and is the only energy that exists in you. As it infuses itself through you, it will erase and dissolve all the old programming.

The Universe is like a Scientific Laboratory

The Universe operates according to energy laws. As such your life becomes a process of learning what the laws are and how to use them. It doesn't matter how long or how hard you've been applying yourself to your evolution. People sometimes tell me they have been working long and hard for decades on their spiritual path and don't understand why they have not progressed further. I then explain it is not the quantity of time, but the quality of what you are doing.

Many people insist they can figure everything out and resolve everything themselves. They wouldn't likely think of learning a musical instrument themselves, or learning a trade or skill on their own, but when it comes to their spiritual growth they choose to struggle on their own. I assure you that your spiritual journey will be quicker and smoother if you avail yourself of the guidance of someone who has mastered what you are trying to master. You will serve yourself well to determine what areas you could benefit from being supported, and then find someone who is an expert at that and seek that person's help.

Part Three

How to Attain Enlightenment

Chapter 13

3 STEPS TO CLEARING AWAY STRUGGLES

Everyone has struggled with something. Struggles come from striving to overcome obstacles or attempts to fix a condition. The question is why does your life have struggles? Is there some cosmic force making it happen? Moreover, most importantly, how can you clear the cause of struggles?

You might say, "I only want to be healthy, wealthy, and wise. Why do I struggle with achieving these ideals?" The problem lies with the causes being unconscious. They developed when you concluded such things as:

- My life is difficult.
- There is something wrong with me.
- I'm not able to succeed.
- I'm just not good at relationships.
- I feel unworthy of life being easy.
- People are dangerous.
- I have the "family curse."
- I must not be a very good person.
- I feel like I have a scar for life.
- I keep running into a "brick wall."
- If I get it I'll just lose it.

These deep unconscious beliefs not only repel happiness, fulfillment, love, and a blessed life, but they also keep you from being aware of why.

Why Does Your Life Have Struggles?

What I refer to as a "core issue" is the subtle-energy pattern that causes all of the struggles. They have been with you for so long that you've come to accept them as just part of who you are like an unrequested destiny forcing struggles on you. In some cases, your nationality or family has certain characteristics that work like filters distorting perceptions and entangling you in ego needs. There are entire cultures that have strong guilt woven into the fabric of their citizens. In some cases, basic beliefs about how to behave, treat others, raise children, and who to be afraid of or hate are part of the cultural inheritance. Some cultures impose heavy burdens of responsibility. These patterns can be deeply ingrained and operate in the background nearly unnoticed like wallpaper.

Your deepest-seated beliefs resulted from conclusions about your past when you were hurt or wounded or witnessed others being hurt. This resulted in a lot of your inner beliefs forming out of pain from your childhood and adolescence. In addition, many of your unconscious conclusions were formed in past lives for which you have absolutely no clue what they are or where they came from, yet they affect you every day.

Since you were a child, you've been forming conclusions about yourself and the world around you. Your parents no doubt disapproved of some of the things you did, perhaps they punished you and in some cases did so severely. You may have had other harsh experiences that shaped the image you formed about yourself. Anything that happened to you that ignited your emotions made the deepest impressions on your subconscious mind and then became part of a blueprint for your life.

That blueprint is your self-image. Your self-image is a manufactured identity you believe to be you. It is composed of all the beliefs you have about yourself, other people, and the world. To cope with life you adopted certain defense mechanisms as part of your self-image such as anger, withdrawal, shyness, depression, anxiety, hopelessness, and more. Those reactions sometimes seemed to protect you, but they also trapped you. The walls you erect for protection also keep out much of what you want. For instance, everyone has experienced struggles, disappointment, and pain from relationships. To protect themselves people put up defensive barriers and, in some cases, don't (or can't) let anyone get close to them again. Yet they want intimacy and love. This creates frustration, struggles, disappointments, and relationship stress.

Here are some common symptoms of core programming causing struggles:

- You want a relationship to make you feel worthy of love and to complete you. This stems from the feeling that something is missing and lacking.

- You have thoughts such as, "I'm not enough," "I am unlovable," "I'm a mistake," "I'm powerless," or "I'm a bad boy or girl."

- You feel loneliness and abandoned, as if no one really understands you or supports you.

- You have a need to excel, accomplish, and perform extremely well. This makes you feel valued and worthy, and you can, therefore, feel good about yourself much of the time as long as you succeed.

- You suffer from not feeling very good about yourself. You see yourself as often failing at your goals. This leads to low self-esteem.

- You feel like you don't know who you really are, where you belong, why you are here, and what you are supposed to be doing in life.

- You are your own worst critic. You judge yourself for so many things.

Healing Your Core of Struggles

Most of your struggles come from deep subconscious programming of being a limited being. People struggle to climb out of limitations. Most are trapped by these forces and struggle with them their entire life. There is a way out, however. The amazing truth about them is they are all made up by your mind or imposed on you by others.

Thinking of them like programs on a computer will help you disown them. They are *not* intrinsic, universal truths. They certainly are not part of your soul or true self. They are made-up thought constructs, and therefore are able to be dismantled and released. Eliminating these destructive patterns is not about learning to compensate for your shortcomings and limitations, but about eliminating those beliefs! Whether you made them up or someone in your ancestry made them up, or some group you belonged to made them up, they are all fabrications. This is important to recognize.

Of course, people and groups can be very convincing that the core beliefs are absolute truth, yet they are just perceptions, conclusions, and programs someone created. Nevertheless, many become convinced they are true, base their life on them, and, in many cases, take them to the grave. Think of people who have been martyred for their beliefs. Often convictions people have died for have elements of truth, but most of them were just ideas formulated by others.

Three Steps to Clearing Away Struggles

First, you must identify the struggles. Define each in one or two sentences. You must be brutally honest with yourself and list all the ways you have struggles and the ways you undermine yourself and sabotage yourself.

Secondly, acknowledge that conclusions and beliefs are nothing more than self-judgments and concepts you formed yourself, inherited, or accepted from someone who convinced you to believe them. The only reality they have is your acceptance of them and your believing them. They are not who you really are and you must affirm that you will no longer identify yourself with the false beliefs. I like to think of these like recordings in your mind including your subconscious mind. They get programmed and play repeatedly until they are accepted as factual, yet they are just recordings that can be deleted.

Thirdly, forgive yourself for accepting the limiting beliefs and declare yourself released. Then assert the positive opposite.

You can apply this process to any of your core programs.

Chapter 14

LET GO: YOUR SPIRITUAL SOLUTION

Many have searched the world seeking the secrets of life and often they stumble over them but don't recognize them. Why is that? One reason is because they are so simple. Some would say the answer is too simple. Regardless of the methods and approaches, they eventually distill down to two words: Let Go. Although this sounds simple, it is not easy to do since it takes serious dedication to discover what to let go and how to do it. Letting go is the process enabling you to make changes in your life.

If you want something to be different, you must let go of what hasn't worked. You might say you must take action in a different direction from what you've been doing. In other words, stop doing what you are doing that creates what you don't want. That makes good sense doesn't it? But, the big question is how to do it.

Some, who want to change, try to change by moving to a different location, change their name, or get a new job. Often they end up recreating what they had before. Why? The simple answer is because they are holding on to what they don't want, and they are afraid to let go of what is not getting them what they do want.

The key to turning the tide and creating lasting change is to ask what needs to be released while letting go of all resistance to what you want. This leads to some very subtle subconscious and non-physical holding patterns that affect you physically, emotionally, and spiritually. Years ago there was a popular song titled, "Let's Hang On." The words went like this, "Let's hang on to what we've got. Don't let go girl we've got a lot." These words reflect a fear of losing something. Letting go can sometimes be a scary process because you get comfortable with where you are and the future is uncertain. So even in the face of something uncomfortable or threatening, many people will resist change and hold on to what is familiar.

Lester Levenson, the author of the *Sedona Method*, discovered an interesting, simple, and effective way of letting go. You may already be familiar with it, but I'm going to guide you through a short variation so you can learn to use it yourself when it would be helpful.

Pick something that you would like to be different in your life and get in touch with the way you hold it. This could be anything you want to release or let go. Then ask yourself these questions:

"Could I let this go, if I had to?
"Could I let this go, if my life depended on it?"

Your mind will probably say, "Yes" causing you to release and let go. (If for any reason you didn't get a yes, I will address that later.) For many situations, this technique works. This inquiry method brings relief and releases your resistance. Resistance is the force you invested into not liking something. Grasping, needing, holding, wanting, struggling, or trying to make something happen are what create resistance. When you let go, space opens around the forces of creation allowing positive action to move your life forward. Repeating this process opens a wonderful spaciousness and peace because it releases much, and sometimes all, of your conscious and subconscious resistance.

This process is not a matter of trying to let something go. Here's what I mean. When attempting to release an attachment, you may find yourself saying something like this:

"It is really, very, very important that I relax right now. I must relax completely right now to get this right. I had better get it right and not get tense. I better relax precisely the right way and not get it wrong because that would be a big mistake."

After reading these words, you would likely find yourself not relaxing because the very wording works against what you want. It would be like telling you not to imagine a pink elephant. For example, do not imagine a pink elephant with a red umbrella in its trunk. Do not imagine a red elephant with a red umbrella in its trunk and standing on its hind legs. You naturally end up imagining a pink elephant even though such a thing doesn't exist because you were trying not to imagine it. The point is that trying doesn't work. In fact, the more you try, the more anxiety you create which causes more resistance to attaining what you actually want.

The process of letting go works when you acknowledge you are willing to let go of the need for the issue and ask a question such as "Could I let it go if I absolutely had to?" The question proposes the possibility, which the mind does not perceive to be threatening and therefore willing to allow. You're not trying to let it go, you are finding out if you could if you had to, and this is a very different process. This establishes what is possible rather than trying to produce an outcome.

Another way to approach this question is to ask, "Does this belief, feeling, or goal serve my true self and nourish my soul? If not, could I let it go?" By asking questions like these, you open space around the issue.

Now once again bring your attention to a situation in your life where you are required to take action. It could be a big decision or a simpler issue. Imagine that situation. Allow yourself to experience a thought about it such as:

I don't know if I can do it.
I don't know if I really deserve it.
I don't know if I am good enough.
I don't know if I have enough time.
I feel stuck or trapped.

Notice whatever comes to mind. Pick a single thought about your situation. As you have the thought notice how you feel. Now ask, "Could I let this go if it were absolutely necessary?"

Now take your negative thought and find the opposite. For instance, if your thought was, "I don't know if I am good enough," the positive opposite would be, "I absolutely am good enough."

- Now, pay attention to how that feels.

- Is it pleasant? Satisfying? Uplifting? Pleasurable?

- Does the issue now have a different quality or texture to it? Notice how you feel in your body now.

- Is there an additional conclusion, reaction, or belief about this situation that you would like to let go?

- If you find something, describe it in words and notice how it feels in your body.

- Again, ask yourself, "Could I let this go?"

- Take a breath now, relax, and integrate this into the body, the nervous system, your whole self.

You will notice that with this process, you are not actually trying to change anything. You are just observing what is present. You are finding what is underneath the stories and perceptions that the mind has created. This leads to a new realization, which is like an awakening. Even through so simple yet this process gives clarity.

Why Some Things Are More Difficult to Let Go

One of the difficulties with letting go is the way you identify yourself with what you want to let go. In most cases, you have held your beliefs, issues, and reactions for so long they feel like these are who you are. This makes them seem more difficult to let go than others. In these instances when you ask the question, "could I let it go," you could get a "no" for an answer because you are invested too much in it.

How do you let go of who you think you are?

The process of letting go can seem to threaten your very identity. You may think, "Who will I be if I let this go?" This can trigger a deep fear. In the same way, a mother who feels needed by her children may feel lost, empty, and abandoned when the children are grown and gone. A man deeply involved with his career can be devastated if something happens to his business or his health so that he is no longer able to identify with the person he thought he was. So when you approach letting go of issues at a deep level, you might sometimes feel threatened by the process. However, the elimination of something you were holding on to, which includes who you thought you were, enables you to connect with a deeper inner truth and essence of who you actually are.

If you feel a pulling back or resistance as you attempt to release and let go, remind yourself that you are safely releasing and opening to your deep true self and soul.

What has been your sticking point or an obstacle that you would like to release? Identify the beliefs associated with the issue that needs to be cleared. Create a simple single sentence describing it. Follow these steps:

1. Here are a few examples you may have heard yourself saying to yourself:

    - Life is hard.
    - I'm not enough.
    - There's something wrong with me.
    - I don't have enough time.
    - I can't have what I want.
    - I attract bad things.
    - Nothing works out well for me.
    - I'm afraid I'll make the wrong decision.
    - Healing is difficult.
    - If I get what I want, I'll just lose it.

Select one and say the sentence twice feeling the charge in your body.

2. What is the degree of charge you feel about this on a scale from 0 to 10 with 10 being the strongest? What number best represents your belief and reaction to the statement?

3. Now make the charge more intense by focusing on it and feeling into its substance.

4. Keep observing your thoughts and reactions. Now give this new level a new number between 0 and 10.

5. Next, focus on your heart center, the area deep in the center of your chest. Say to yourself, "I am willing to let go and release all need for this."

6. Take a deep breath, exhale through your mouth, and let everything go.

When you are willing to feel into an issue, you will find that it evaporates. This is because you open to an expanded presence all around it. This practice needs to be repeated numerous times to clear all resistance.

The "Green Light" to Creating Your Greatest Good Comes When You Release All Resistance

The more you are willing to let go of who and what you think you are, the more you relax into the force that guides your life. The more you learn to surrender and let go rather than trying and doing, the more you open to the underlying reality of your being. Deep surrender releases all resistance and opens wonderful realities. If you have any resistance even around things you love, and you surrender them, your experience of them expands. However, if it is something negative, surrender causes it to disappear to the degree you've surrendered and let go.

Remember the saying, "Whatsoever a man sows, that shall he also reap." This Biblical verse is sometimes quoted in reference to karma, usually in a negative way. Paraphrased it means, "The Universe always says, 'yes,' to whatever you think, say, or do." So, as you keep your attention and awareness focused on the greatest good you can conceive, it will unfold for you more and more. As you surrender and let go of resistance in all its forms, more of the soul's presence comes through, which automatically brings you goodness because it is your true nature.

The mind may try to control the surrender process by raising questions and doubts and then concluding surrender doesn't work. Because of this, surrender must include letting go of expectations about the outcome and any fear associated with them. When you surrender to this degree, you allow the "invisible" forces in your life to manifest the responses and outcomes that bring fulfillment and happiness. You know what to do not by analysis and weighing the pros and cons, but by surrendering and letting go. This opens you to the next phase of the process: opening to receive. When you let go in trust, you open yourself to receive blessings.

How to Make a Decision

1. Reflect on an issue or circumstance where you need to make a decision; a place that requires taking action. Think of a belief, a perception, or a point of view that is influencing that decision.

2. What do you believe about this decision? What does that feel like?

3. Now focus on another belief, perception, or point of view holding influence over this decision and feel its charge in your body. What does it feel like?

4. Feel the possibility of letting go. What would it feel like to let it go?

5. Laying this decision before God, a symbol of a deity, or master in your imagination can often be an effective way to unburden. Feel what it is like when you let go. Feel what it is like when you release the need to do anything yourself. Feel what your inner space is like to surrender any need to do something about a situation. Feel what that space is like. What is it like to relax?

6. Feel the spaciousness of allowing your higher self or soul to take over in the spaciousness created by letting go of your needs, wants, and beliefs about the situation. Let go, release, relax, and open to receive the unfolding of greater goodness.

7. Next, think of something that turned out to be wonderful. It could be meeting a friend or a loved one, making a positive career decision, or completing a project or goal successfully. Most people report that at least some of the positive outcomes in their lives seemed effortless, occurring almost automatically rather than by trying or doing. Of course, some effort is necessary, but an ease and natural flow characterize its unfolding.

   When you surrender, you let go of any form of resistance that keeps you from experiencing your highest inner truth, which can only be for your greater good. Your enlightened presence cannot create anything negative. How could it?

8. Feel what it is like to relax into the space of surrender and let go. Feel the spaciousness and trust opening by letting go of trying and wanting.

One of the paradoxes of surrender is that you don't lose anything you would want. The pain dissolves and is replaced with something so much better.

As you surrender and let go, you will discover the act of surrender is a gift. A miracle unfolds as you touch your own truth. You'll realize the deepest aspects of what you are. You'll feel a deep expansive purity and innocence. You'll feel the deep expansive peacefulness. You'll feel the deep expansive love. You'll feel the deep expansiveness and vastness of eternity.

Remember how many times things have worked out wonderfully in your life, how many times things have worked out despite what you have thought or done at the time, how things have unfolded in some automatic way not because of you, but beyond you.

You have a guiding force beyond your thinking mind. As you let go of all need to control, the guiding force of creation unfolds through you. You will develop a sense that nothing is being done by the small individual you think you are, but rather by an overriding loving and intelligent presence. This enables you to experience life without reaction based on memories, perceptions, conclusions, and impulses from the past. You are able to be alive and fresh in any moment, free of prejudice, bias, or past conclusions and meet events without projecting hallucinations and illusions on what is happening.

The more you release your reliance on your mind, the more you deepen your trust. It gathers force like a snowball rolling down a hill, gradually getting larger and larger. At first you may question and doubt, but then things work out beautifully despite your knowing or doing. The snowball of trust grows larger. The next time you face a crossroad or difficult decision, you realize support you can trust is there.

Day-by-day open your trust a little wider, and say "yes" to receive the goodness waiting for you. Things work out better and bigger than you might imagine, and the snowball of trust grows larger so that even bigger decisions are made for you, even if your mind doesn't have the first clue of what to do, but you can relax and trust to receive.

Isn't this the journey you want to experience? It all derives from deepening surrender and letting go.

Chapter 15

SURRENDER IS THE GOLDEN PATH TO ENLIGHTENMENT

Most people have something they would like to be different in their life, or something they would like to attract or expand in their life. The question is how to release the forces blocking change?

Ultimately, all clearing and releasing methods have an underlying commonality which involves letting go of all resistance and all forces holding the obstacle in place. In a spiritual context, we call that surrender. When you first hear that you are expected to surrender, you might think that is a strange word to use. However, the surrender I am talking about does not mean giving up your power. It is not resignation. It is actually expanding into a greater power.

The process is really quite simple. You have heard the phrase, "Thy will be done." It is part of what is called, "The Lord's Prayer." Most people assume this means resigning to the will of God, which is an unknown mystery because you never really know what God's will is until something happens and then you say with resignation and faith, "It must be God's will." It might even be taken to mean that God's will is for you to be sick and poor for reasons only God knows. Therefore, with this point of view, surrender may not be seen as a particularly fun experience, because it could imply loss and getting into a situation you'd rather not be in.

But this is not what surrender is. It does not mean surrendering to an unknown mystery, nor does it lead to thinking that only God knows what God's will is. When you surrender, you are merely letting go of every possible form of resistance that could be causing you to hold onto something causing you a problem. For instance, you could say, "I fully surrender my anger toward my friend." This means that you are willing to let go of all your strong judgments and emotional reactions to something your friend said or did.

Surrender means letting resistance and obstacles melt while you settle into peace. When you surrender, you are surrendering to more of what life can be.

Do you remember the idea of counting to ten before you react to someone? The idea is that if you count to ten you will not react harshly or irrationally. Sometimes counting to ten gives you enough time to realize that taking aggressive action will not help the situation or get you what you want, thus you calm down. This is a simple version of surrendering. You surrender or let go of your strong reaction.

Surrender is giving up your willpower that wants to make outcomes manifest in specific ways. It is releasing how you thought things should be to make room for the greater good to emerge. Surrendering resistance allows your deeper, creative, pure-soul essence to emerge and begin working in your life.

So if you want your life to be orchestrated by the highest aspect of who you are, then the way you get there is by going through your life and giving up, releasing, and fully surrendering every emotion and every need. What this does is open space in your world. You may at first think you are giving something up, but when you engage in this process, you soon realize that the opposite is true.

The Path to Enlightenment

Consider how surrender can work in your favor. If you surrender and release all judgments, emotions, and resistance around a conflict with another person, what do you think will happen? Space opens in your relationship with that person and healing and enriching of the relationship can happen. If you surrender all your fear and anger concerning something in your work what will happen? You will be able to put your full resources into improving the situation and have the best possible outcomes. Surrendering opens space for greater possibilities to come into your life because you remove the resistance that keeps the goodness out.

You will find that by surrendering and letting go of all resistance around everything in your life, your life gets qualitatively better. No matter what the issue, the best answer always includes surrender. Don't let this statement slip by too fast, because surrender is really important and profound. No matter the question, issue, condition, or problem, the answer is surrender.

When you surrender, you are letting go of any form of resistance that keeps you from experiencing your soul and highest inner truth, which is only for your greater good. Your enlightened soul cannot create anything negative. It does not have the nature or capacity to do anything negative.

By your greater good, I mean greater fulfillment, greater love, greater happiness, greater peace, greater joy, greater fun, and greater expression. In fact, whatever goodness you can conceive can become a part of your experience because you are not in resistance to anything. Your entire inner space changes to feeling wonderful and happy.

Surrender leads to naturally trusting life because through surrender, you let go of controlling how life will manifest for you, knowing that the expression and expansion of good always unfolds. By surrendering you are fully open to receiving goodness because you are no longer sustaining resistance. This internal state brings about the manifestation of what you want even if you don't know what all the details are.

You can begin a practice of surrendering right now, no matter your present condition and refine it over time. The more you practice, the better you'll get until you eventually completely live in surrender.

The Source of Resistance to Surrender

Perhaps one reason many have passed over the subject of surrender is because they haven't known exactly what it is or how to do it. In addition, surrender is particularly threatening to the ego, causing resistance to the process. This makes it seem difficult to put into practice. Any commentary that comes up in your mind when you say you surrender something is the resistance of the ego. The ego is threatened by surrender because surrender releases the defense mechanisms the ego has used to feel more secure, such as fear, anger, and control.

So initially, when you start surrendering, the ego will often perceive the process as making you more vulnerable. But, the opposite is actually true because surrender aligns you with the highest levels of consciousness and your deepest soul presence, which brings the deepest security possible.

How Do You Surrender?

Effective surrender comes from the heart and from being in touch with or connecting with what you are surrendering. It is much less of an intellectual process of repeating words of surrender than one of sincerely feeling into the surrender. You use your senses to move deeper into connecting with the issue and the releasing of all defenses and resistance around it.

The mind tries to analyze and intellectualize the process but you can't accomplish it intellectually. This explains why many people are not effective with surrender. They try to do it with their intellect such as by saying they are surrendering, but find that it doesn't always work, so then they resign themselves to the outcome. This leads to feeling defeated causing them to conclude the defeat they feel is what surrender is. This is not spiritual surrender, but the ego feeling defeated and rationalizing it.

Surrender is a matter of shifting consciousness to let go of all resistance in order to allow yourself to receive the underlying truth of existence.

The Process of Surrender is Filled With Paradoxes

Here is something important to realize about surrender. Surrender is not renunciation. Surrender doesn't necessarily require you to change your positions, give up, or stop doing something you are doing. That's one of the paradoxes with surrender. With surrender, you are letting go of your resistance and attachments to what you are surrendering. You are letting go completely of controlling the outcome. Let me give you some examples of what I mean.

If you are listening to a beautiful peace of music that brings tears to your eyes, you are surrendered to the music. You are not trying to control the music or change the music, nor are you in a rush to get to the end. You are surrendered to the flow of the music.

When you touch deep love or deep beauty, you have a taste of what surrender offers, because those states are only fully accessed through surrender. When you are appreciating the deep beauty of art, music, or something in nature, you surrender yourself to it and even become one with it. When you deeply love someone or some thing you surrender yourself deeply and become one.

Surrender opens the doors to all the wonders of life experience, so when you realize what surrender offers, you will be willing to surrender everything.

What to Surrender

Surrender is the highest and most important practice you can possibly undertake to further your spiritual evolution. Initiating a practice of surrender is not complicated or fraught with difficulty. It is essentially easy and almost effortless. I'll give you some examples you can apply immediately.

Go through your life and release and surrender everything you can think of. In a meditative state say to yourself, "I surrender and release every person, every possession, every feeling, every desire, everything I like and don't like." Include, your body, your need to be right, your dreams, your fears, your gray hair, your fat waist, your anger, your mind, your mortgage, your mate, your children, your friends, your enemies, your debts, your lacks, your limitations, your impatience, your mind, and even your need to be enlightened.

As you sit in meditation, you tune into your body and your inner space and observe what is there. After several minutes of getting in touch with your inner space, you identify sensations, perceptions, or voices, and you say, "I am willing to surrender and release the need for this." Then you wait to see what the inner response is to the statement.

When you start this practice, memories, feelings, or voices will arise within you saying things such as, "This is crazy," "You are not doing this right," "This is silly," "You don't deserve this," "This will never work," "This is a waste of time," or "This is too hard." However, as you continue surrendering whatever arises, the reactions will diminish and you will discover some amazing changes beginning.

By surrendering, you will gradually connect with your soul and spiritual presence more and more deeply, and as you do, your inner being becomes an incredibly beautiful radiance of love, peace, and beauty. With surrender, your life can change dramatically in a matter of minutes and hours. This is very powerful and very fast.

When you are willing to drop all of your attachments, you will become aware of being one with all. At this point the only thing left is unity and oneness. From this place there will be no suffering, no lack, no pain, and no separation; there will simply be the essence of deep love, deep peace, and deep beauty.

When you do the clearing through deep surrender, you are clear of the issues forever.

Your Mind is Your Only Obstacle

While you are trying to surrender all your needs and desires, the mind can become very concerned. It may say to you, "What do I have left if I'm not in control? If I surrender all my thoughts, then what am I to think? How do I engage in life? I am afraid I will cease to exist."

The fear of losing your identity is a projection of the lower ego consciousness, which is not your True Self. You are an individualized consciousness housing lower and higher vibrations of awareness. Your higher consciousness, which is also called your Higher Self, your Soul, your Master Within, your Christ Consciousness, your True Self, and your God Realized Self, is present and living simultaneously with your mortal mind and ego.

When you move into higher consciousness, you do not lose consciousness and wake up as a stranger in a strange land. You do not have a sense of loss because you remain aware. In fact, you become more alive and more aware with more understanding, knowledge, and awareness than you had before you surrendered.

As your thinking and feelings move up to higher realizations, you take on the consciousness of the Higher Self, and the dark energies and fears of the ego are transmuted. On this higher frequency, you are fully aware of your spiritual self, which is your reality. Surrender is what moves you forward on your journey.

Surrender is the ultimate spiritual path that will take you where your heart longs to be. Eventually, you no longer even need to practice surrendering because you will arrive at a state in which you are completely surrendered and acceptant.

Chapter 16

SURRENDER – THE ULTIMATE SPIRITUAL PATH

An almost endless obstacle course seems to frustrate the path of spiritual evolution. Once you start on your journey, you might wonder if it will ever end. Clearing away the illusions and distractions often seem like an insurmountable and endless task. Fortunately, rapid and widespread releases are possible so it is not necessary to enumerate or remember every item to release. You accomplish this through surrender. To become free from the pain and limitations of life, you must release the past, and meditation coupled with surrender is the way.

Many people think they are supposed to be happy with less and think they are surrendering to less. The exact opposite is true. When you surrender, you are surrendering to more of what life can be. Surrender is trust to the highest power—it is letting go of trying to control how life will manifest and of knowing life always flows along positive channels leading to the ultimate expansion of every goodness life can offer you.

Surrender is giving up all control, mental rigidity, and willpower that wants to make outcomes manifest in specific ways. It is releasing how you thought things should be, to make room for the greatest good imaginable.

Enlightenment is a Process of Elimination

Enlightenment consciousness reveals itself through the process of letting go of everything you are not, in order to realize the truth of everything you are. Most of what you think you are is formed out of beliefs you have accepted as true. Your identity is composed of many thousands of these constructs, which are all distortions of what is real and true. The truth is that these constructs are all mental concepts based on conclusions from observations and experiences over lifetimes. The challenge is releasing beliefs that delimit your spiritual progress. At times, this can seem like an insurmountable and endless task.

When you first hear that you need to surrender, you might feel threatened because the word conjures defeat. Remember the common use of that word is in warfare in which the side that loses surrenders. To many people, surrendering means losing what they value. However, the surrender I am talking about doesn't mean giving up that way. It is a process of letting go of your mind trying to control and accumulate.

There is an Art and Science of Surrender

The science of surrender addresses going through the story of your life and giving up, releasing, and fully surrendering everything you remember. Surrender every person, every possession, every feeling, every hope, every desire, and everything you like and don't like. That includes your body, your dreams, your fears, your wants, and even your need to be enlightened. You should also include your emotions, your friends, your enemies, your debts, your lack, your limitations, your impatience, and your life. Once all of these are surrendered, affirm your highest ideals that are the natural unfolding of your soul which is already enlightened. Hold to these ideals regardless of outer circumstances and the world of illusion will melt and a greater reality will unfold around you. Below is a practice I have found to be very helpful in taking your surrender to the deepest levels.

A Surrender Meditative Practice

Surrender is not an intellectual process, but a discovery and feeling process done in a meditative state. Each statement listed a few paragraphs below is to be used like a mantra to help you connect with the pattern in order to release and dissolve any trace of it. I'd suggest using only one statement during each 20-40 minute meditation to explore it fully.

Every pattern the mind holds has a belief that it is needed. Most "needs" are irrational, but the mind wouldn't hold a belief unless it believed it would help keep you safe. The mind will even hold onto something painful because it believes that if it let it go, you would move into unknown territory, which might be worse than the pain it currently experiences. This surrender process brings a soothing, healing trust to the mind, so it is willing to release and dissolve the painful and limiting pattern.

I'd also suggest using a visual imaging method such as vacuuming off the subtle-energy of the pattern and/or disintegrating it as I explain below. This part of the process can be helpful, as often just repeating the statements is not sufficient to eliminate the pattern completely because each memory, belief, and emotion is stored in subtle-energy form and is composed of the lifeforce energy you invested in them. Using a visual imaging method such as I just suggested helps to dislodge the thoughtform from your aura and chakras and releases the lifeforce trapped in them.

This type of imagery increases the speed and effectiveness of the clearing more rapidly than if you just verbalize that you are releasing and letting go.

Vacuum Technique

This is just one suggested variation of clearing subtle-energy patterns. Feel free to modify this method in whatever ways seem the most effective for you. With this method, you accompany your releasing intentions and statements with a vacuum to pull the subtle-energy residue of the thoughtforms off of you. You may think this is merely using a visualization method, but it is actually a lot more than that. In the realm of subtle energy, your intentions are powerful creators. You are actually energizing a created thoughtform to help you remove negative thoughtforms in your field. You do not need to "see" anything visually for this method to be effective. Your intention makes it work.

Using your intentions and the creative power of your imagination, create a vacuum hose with the other end going into the center of creation and move it around you outside your aura pulling off whatever you are releasing and taking it to the center of creation where it is neutralized. For added effectiveness, ask the issue or disturbance to turn a color like bright blue or red and then vacuum off the color; experiment using different sizes of vacuums. Sometimes smaller vacuums work better than larger ones.

How to Apply the Mantra Release Technique

1. Allow approximately 30 seconds or more between each repetition of the mantra you are using in the meditation. Pay attention to any commentary the mind comes up with and say, "Thank you for letting me know, and I surrender and release the need for you."

2. Watch for any follow-up commentary and repeat the process until the mind becomes still. This surrender process brings a soothing healing trust to the mind so that it is willing to release and dissolve the painful and limiting pattern.

3. Use the vacuum technique to remove subtle-energy patterns.

4. Conclude the meditation by asking the soul to merge into any traces of the issue that remain.

Below are the most important releasing mantras that can free you and lead to enlightenment. They are not in any particular order.

I surrender and release the need...

1. For Control
2. For Fear of Being Controlled
3. For Fear of Being Out of Control
4. For Feeling Victimized
5. For Feeling Something is Missing
6. To Figure Things Out
7. To Know Why
8. For My Past
9. To Be Enlightened
10. For Questions
11. For Answers
12. For Confusion
13. For Fear of Making a Mistake
14. For stories and Drama
15. To Know More
16. For Searching, Seeking, Looking
17. For Thinking
18. For The Need to Be Right
19. To Find the Missing Piece
20. For The Need to Believe or Be Believed
21. For Importance or to Be Important
22. To Judge Myself or Others
23. To Struggle
24. To Hold On
25. For Wanting
26. For Fixed Opinions
27. To Resolve What Isn't Resolved
28. To Fear Letting Go
29. To Fear the Unknown
30. To Fear Letting Go of Fear
31. For More
32. Fear of Being Wrong
33. For Explanations

34. To Be Needed
35. To Know How
36. For Solutions
37. For Hope
38. For Expectations

You can select a few at a time of the above and take them into a meditation and keep releasing until you are certain you are free.

Chapter 17
5 WAYS TO QUIET YOUR MIND

For millennia meditators have struggled with how to quiet their mind from racing thoughts. In fact, some even claim that attaining a quiet mind is such an elusive goal that the few who attain it have reached Buddhahood. Once you attain a permanently quiet mind, maintaining it becomes effortless. As a result being mindful and in the "now" becomes automatic and effortless. You'll no longer need to struggle to quiet your mind, nor will you need to use techniques like distracting your mind or willing your mind to be quiet.

Tulku Urgyen Rinpoche states in his book *Rainbow Painting,* "When there are no thoughts whatsoever then you are a Buddha. At that point the thought-free state is effortless." (First Edition, 1995, page 78).

Why Most Methods to Quiet Your Mind Fail to be Permanent

I remember when I was a beginner with meditation I would sometimes take an hour or more just to get my mind to stop thinking so I could have some peace. I often tried many methods such as distracting the mind by watching my breathing, reciting a mantra, staring at a candle, or just passively watching thoughts float by like clouds in the sky. I found that these methods can work in the short term, but they only give temporary results, and as soon as I stopped meditating, my mind would start engaging again.

Why the Mind Re-engages

One problem with mental chatter is the mind is always trying to figure things out. It's always trying to solve some issue, and it grinds away at it day and night. The mind typically does this in several ways. One of the most common ways is by posing incessant questions. It keeps pondering and ruminating over the issues from every conceivable angle. It often rambles away on negative criticism, blame, and worries. The mind wants to know why something happened, and it won't stop until it gets an answer, and then it questions the answer!

Then when you try to meditate, the mind won't cooperate and get quiet. That's why the ego-driven mind is often called the "monkey mind" because it keeps jumping from one thing to another trying to find answers and resolve things.

Your Mind is on a Mission

Your mind believes it has a mission to keep you safe and secure, and it believes that one of the best ways to do this is by analyzing everything. People are trained to do this through the educational system they grow up with, and later in life are rewarded in a career for it.

The very idea that you can put an end to thinking is interpreted by the mind as a threat to its very purpose and to your safety and security. In fact, the very idea of functioning without thinking seems like a crazy and impossible goal, so most people, even advanced meditators, resign themselves to a reality that their mind will gradually re-engage shortly after they meditate.

When your mind permanently stops, you are likely to be startled by the silence and wonder how you will be able to function. After all, isn't thinking necessary to drive a car, pay your bills, go shopping, and do your work? Your mind doesn't have a clue about how to be silent because the only thing it does know is the way it has been trained to function.

Once your mind releases all need to think, you will be able to do everything you ever did and probably do it more efficiently and effectively. However, don't expect your logical, rational, thinking mind to comprehend how this is even possible. The quiet mind requires you to clear and eliminate the many mental programs that keep it engaged. Once cleared, you enter a consciousness level sometimes referred to as "no mind." This is a spacious and quiet expansive level of consciousness.

The Big Question is How do You Quiet Your Mind Permanently?

How do you quiet your mind all the time, not just when you are meditating? Is it possible for your mind to become completely quiet? This does not mean you are unable to think. Of course, you can think if you choose to. What it means is there will be no uninvited thoughts or unintentional thoughts. In most cases, you'll no longer need to think in any conventional way because what happens is a higher level of consciousness takes over, and you automatically operate from awareness rather than from needing to figure things out. When you achieve a sustained, quiet mind, your perceptions will be much more clear and unfiltered, and you'll have more peace all the time.

5 Ways to Attain the Buddha State of "No Mind"

1. Passively observing thoughts is a good way to start quieting your mind. Go into a meditative state with your eyes closed and observe your thoughts with no interaction. One of the most common suggestions for dealing with mind chatter is to think of the thoughts as clouds drifting across the sky. You observe them but don't engage with them and in time, they will diminish. At times I have done this for a long periods without the mind quieting, while at other times, it has quickly worked.

These quieting techniques work because the mind's nature is to be at peace. However, the mind has been trained to be active despite its true nature to be quiet. One reason it is active is because the mind accumulated a lot of mental clutter. With this passive approach, you just relax the mind from engaging by peacefully letting the thoughts drift by without engaging with them until the mind becomes peaceful. This is not a permanent solution, but it helps in the beginning stages to reorient the mind to being present but not engaging with anything.

2. Labeling the thoughts as they come up is another way of letting the thoughts go. Here's what I mean. Mind chatter can come in a variety of forms, so you simply say the one word to yourself that best describes what the mind is doing at that moment and then you let it go.

Here are some labels for your mental activities: Thinking, Judging, Analyzing, Worrying, and Planning. Observe the thought and then say the word that is the best label for what your mind is doing. The mind likes this technique because it is familiar with labeling things, which temporarily satisfies it. When you do this, the mind interprets your stating the label as having dealt with the thought, and so it disengages from it and lets it go.

3. Surrender the need for the thoughts. Peace and oneness are qualities that underlie the activities of the mind. When you attain a surrendered state, you arrive at deep peace and realize your oneness with all there is. This naturally happens because surrender dissolves the obstacles from this realization. To utilize this technique, it is helpful to give yourself permission to surrender and release all need for the distracting thoughts. Some ways of wording effective surrender affirmations spoken in a meditative state include the following:

- I surrender and release the need for this thought.
- I give myself permission to let go and dissolve this thought.
- I surrender and release all need to think.

4. Dis-identify with what the mind is generating. Dis-identification is an essential part of the meditation process and is what ultimately leads to enlightened consciousness. A little known reason why this technique works is because every thought, feeling, and reaction has lifeforce energy tied up in it. This is a subtle-energy component called a "thoughtform."

How I Discovered This Method

You're probably familiar with having a song in your mind that plays repeatedly. This happened to me more than forty years ago around Christmas time with the song *Silent Night*. It had been playing on the radio and in stores, and I couldn't get it out of my head. It was playing day and night for three days. It even played when I woke up at night, and it was starting to wear on me when an idea struck me. I thought to myself, "What if this song is a recording of some sort like a thoughtform made of subtle-energy, and it is not just a function of something in my brain?" I reasoned if that were true then perhaps that subtle-energy thoughtform could be removed with a simple energy-healing technique.

Some people who do not believe in subtle-energy would think this is a crazy idea, but hear me out. I reasoned that if the song were a subtle-energy thoughtform recording, it might be possible to remove it or shift it in some way. So here is what I did. I held the intention to brush it out of my head by making passes with my hand like brushing lint off my head. This is called "aura raking." I made three passes while holding the intention to gather all the subtle-energy in the song thoughtform with my hand and I flicked it away like flicking off water from my fingers. To my amazement the music stopped. This was startling and profound! I was finally relieved. The music stopped and I had peace of mind.

Next, I took this idea further and wondered if it would work with a song, maybe it would work with other thoughts and memories as well, and to my amazement, I found that it did. Those who think everything has to be explained as a function of the physical brain, won't be able to make sense of this. If you are in that category, I suggest you keep an open mind and try it. You don't need to believe it will work in order for it to work for you.

Some neuroscientists will no doubt come up with an alternate explanation, and it really doesn't matter. I just know it works.

Here's a way for you to apply this technique:

This technique works particularly well on strongly distracting thoughts or feelings. Even though this method is called visualization, you don't actually need to see anything in your mind's eye for it to work. In fact, you don't even need to believe it will work for it to work. Your attention and intention are sufficient for this to be effective.

You utilize a creative visualization-imagination technique of putting the distracting thoughts or emotional reactions on a visualized large sponge several feet in front of you. If people are involved in the memory or distracting thought, imagine putting an image of them on the sponge also. The idea of the sponge is to have something that your mind will accept as absorbing and holding the subtle-energy patterns you are releasing.

Once the sponge absorbs the energy of the thoughts, dissolve them with images of an energy beam dissolving the sponge and everything in it. This releases the lifeforce energy back to you that was held in the thought patterns.

Most of the time you'll need to repeat this procedure several times. If the emotion is strong, you'll need to do it many times over several days or even weeks, but each time you do it, the reaction will get weaker and weaker.

5. The fifth technique for quieting the mind is a variation on the above method is **using your creative imagination** to visualize a vacuum hose vacuuming the thoughts and feelings away. When I use this technique, I have the vacuum hose go to the center of creation where all thoughts are neutralized.

These techniques might seem like gimmicks, but after I used them for a few months, all my unintentional thoughts and mind chatter stopped permanently. My mind is now always quiet day and night, so meditation and being mindful in the present moment became very easy. These methods work because the mind chatter is composed of subtle energy and the visualization techniques remove the layers of the energy patterns.

Be aware that this is not a quick fix. Most people require months of clearing out the mental activity before the mind stays quiet, so don't be discouraged if it takes time. I assure you it will work. Many give up before they attain what they want, but I assure you I have helped many attain a quiet mind with these techniques.

Mastery is worth any inconvenience it takes to attain it.

Conclusions on Quieting the Mind

What I have described in this chapter are a few techniques I have found worked for me and people I have worked with. There are other techniques, of course, to deal with the rambling mind, and I am fully in favor of you using anything that works. I know that some meditation purists might denigrate these mental techniques because they believe sitting still and emptying their mind is all that is needed, but for most this is very challenging and an elusive goal.

Techniques are only means to an end. They are ways of utilizing what the mind does to lead to dis-engaging the thinking mind so a person can reach a state beyond mind. When you were learning to ride a bike, you had training wheels until you no longer needed them. The same is true of meditation techniques. Use whatever techniques work for you until you no longer need them.

I have been meditating for more than fifty years and have tried many dozens of meditative approaches and techniques. In this chapter I have distilled a few of the ones that have worked well for me in quieting all analysis and mental chatter. At some point in a committed practice, the mind will not offer anything uninvited and there will be a profound and sustained deep peace, contentment, and love. Knowing it is possible will give you an incentive that you can attain it as well.

Chapter 18

THE FAILURE OF MEDITATION

An article I quote below describes experiences of long-term practitioners of meditation that shocked me! I had to read it several times to be sure I read it correctly. The article reports the results of a study conducted by world-renowned authorities on meditation. The results of this study may surprise you as well, because they are probably the opposite of what you would expect from a long-term meditation practice.

In the *Yoga Journal*, May-June, 2001, page 174, in the article *Standing Psychotherapy on its Head*, by Stephen Cope is the following quote:

> *Boston psychologists Dan Brown and Jack Engler, coauthors with Ken Wilber of Transformations of Consciousness, conducted a fascinating study of yogis at advanced stages of practice. It revealed that, contrary to our mistaken Western assumptions about enlightenment experiences, even very advanced practitioners continue to experience conflict, fear, anxiety, depression, addictive cravings, interpersonal dependency struggles, and so forth...What does change, is not so much the amount or nature of conflict, but awareness of and reactivity to it...[With practice] there is greater awareness of and openness to conflict but paradoxically less reaction at the same time in an impulsive, identificatory, and therefore painful way...[The practitioner] may note the intense desire until it passes, like every other transient mental state; or he/she may act on it, but with full awareness. (174)*

Why Are They Still Living With the Same Issues?

What does this study reveal about "enlightenment experiences?" One finding seems self-evident: Many people must have a limited definition of what enlightenment means in any practical sense. An additional question is what do Brown and Engler imply about meditating even at "advanced stages"? Wouldn't you think that a beginning meditator reading this might think twice before investing thousands of hours in meditation since the results appear to be woefully limited? Their observations, however, describe the opposite of meditation results of many I have taught and meditated with for decades.

Why should our Western assumptions be "mistaken" as the article states? That is not to fault the assumptions, but to question the effectiveness of the approach of the "yogis at advanced stages of practice." They certainly must be achieving some measure of value from their meditations or they wouldn't be continuing, but something is significantly missing from their meditation practice. The results of the study no doubt validate the meditation experiences of many who have meditated for a long time and think they are enlightened. The problem is that they still find themselves living with many of the same issues they had before they meditated for thousands of hours.

How Meditation Can Fail

Something else inferred from this study is that the value of meditation will come from the quality of meditation and not just the quantity. This is reflected in the implications of this study, which is that many people who meditate apparently do not apply an effective method for clearing the causes of basic mental and emotional issues. Herein lays a shortcoming in the approach of many meditators. The approach to meditation they practice is that they should not try to do anything about issues that come up, but they rather be at peace with them and be a neutral observer. This passive approach emphasizes non-doing and is certainly a wonderful state for meditation, but the problem is that while it can lead to sublime states of consciousness during the meditation, it may not clear the patterns very quickly that cause issues in day-to-day life. If it did, the "advanced meditation" practitioners would not have the problems they report.

In their defense, such practitioners might say their meditation practices are not intended to clear issues as much as they are only intended to take a person into refined awareness. In this case, the conclusion would indicate that whatever type of meditation they practice provided the results intended. But this does not address fundamental human challenges. Something else is needed because life involves more than living in transcendent consciousness.

What "Advanced Meditators" Say

Many notable spiritual teachers say, "I'm only human just like everyone else," as if that explains or justifies their issues and lifestyle. I've even heard some give advice to those looking to them for help with problems to "just be patient" or "don't let your mind go there." This is advice from someone who does not have answers.

But, there are answers and effective procedures to clearing the most common mental and emotional issues. Many love the experiences of meditation in peaceful states but ironically they avoid the issues that trouble them in day-to-day life. They do not directly address the issues. Some spiritual teachers think working with issues is not truly pure meditation. They even go so far as to say that working with issues is an unnecessary distraction to spiritual goals and enlightenment. In some cases, teachers have conveyed that "advanced meditation" is all that is necessary because meditation leads to clearing. However, this is apparently not the case with the "advanced meditators" in the study. So why would many teachers teach this? Some teachers are bound by the long-standing traditions they themselves have been taught and practiced.

Enlightenment Experiences or Being Enlightened: What's the Difference?

Before people can legitimately think they have shifted their consciousness into an enlightened state (which includes complete non-judgment and freedom in all ways), they would not only have to experience Self-realization, but they would also need to be mostly free from mental and emotional challenges. Otherwise they are deluding themselves and maybe others that they are enlightened simply because they have had expanded states of consciousness in meditation.

A big difference separates having enlightening experiences in meditation and living in an enlightened state all the time. Because of misunderstandings of this basic truth, many who have thought they were enlightened because they experienced an enlightening meditation were appalled to find that days, weeks, or months later they somehow lost their enlightenment because many of the issues which plagued them returned. Although they had some beautiful and enlightening meditations, they apparently did not achieve a permanent shift in awareness or a clearing of all the lower states of consciousness and patterning that are carried in their consciousness. These very patterns pull them back to where their everyday consciousness actually lives. They are essentially caught in a trap.

I Am Not Attacking Meditation

Meditation is surely the best way to attain spiritual realizations, but most meditation practices do not address the issues causing day-to-day problems that really need to be addressed for at least two major reasons. One, most people's lives have some form of struggle or suffering, and they feel stuck not knowing how to become free themselves. Secondly, the karmic consequences of past choices and actions are likely to perpetuate the issues for lifetimes to come.

Who Am I to Be Making Such Comments?

For over 50 years I have worked to find ways to move through and beyond the "boxes" that most have locked themselves into, and I've taught many others to do the same. I have facilitated hundreds of classes, workshops, and retreats and done more than 50,000 individual clearing sessions with people. I have found ways that lead to transformations of consciousness that actually change a person's experience with mental and emotional challenges. I have discovered that as your mind becomes cleared of low-consciousness beliefs, you are then free to sustain beautiful states of consciousness both in meditation as well as in your everyday experience. This enables you to integrate the beauty of your meditative states into your life in very practical ways. Living in integrity, unconditional love, happiness, peace, and enlightened states then becomes natural and automatic.

The following are a few of the many letters I have received from people who have attended my workshops and retreats. They tell of their experiences in ways that will help you better understand some of what I am describing and reassure you that you can experience all of this as well.

I'M HAPPY, PURE AND SIMPLE

"The inner joy, the heightened senses, the clarity of purpose and the intense love are all experienced in this workshop. Could any amount of money have bought that? I received love and more love, and a direct knowing of my own purpose in this lifetime and what direction to go in order to honor that purpose. I'm happy, pure and simple, and it feels good-- And I'm sharing that happiness with others. Thank you for sharing your lives with all of us." —Frances L., California

RISE ABOVE OBSTACLES

"Words cannot express how much you have helped me pierce many of my illusions. Your words spoken with obvious love in your heart for all others, have enabled me to rise above some personal obstacles in my relationships. Through this workshop I feel I shall approach the rest of my life with a perspective as seen from my heart. I will never forget this experience." —Eileen C., La Mesa, California

SELF-DISCOVERY

"You have changed my life in ways I could never have imagined. You have opened the gate to self-discovery and spiritual awareness that can never be taken away. What I have benefited from you is priceless to me. I feel so blessed to be able to reach the spiritual heights I have so far. Your life's work is very special and I'm sure many have been touched the way I have." —Lisa S., Beverly Hills, California

CLEAR CONSCIOUSNESS

"Tonight I have been sitting in what has been revealed as a "clear stream of consciousness." The purity and fine energetic quality is breath taking, purifying, and life altering. It is nothing short of extraordinary. It is nothing. It is everything. I am humbled by my awareness and connection to this new stream of consciousness. Beyond words.   —Rita H., Iowa

RENEWED

"I felt a tremendous lifting of all things that were holding me back; they just vanished and I felt the ease of relief as they floated off to be transmuted. I was then shifted to a new state of awareness in which I could feel new energy being poured into me on all levels with a spectacularly brilliant white light and a feeling of bliss that accompanied the experience. We resided in the presence of the light and Love which poured over and through us for the next few hours.

"The constant streaming of thoughts that always inundated me on a daily basis just stopped. All of a sudden there was nothing! It is just a blissful place to escape from the everyday madness. Since I have been back home for two months now, the thoughts have all gone away. Also, I now know what it feels like when the soul is one in and with the physical body, the sensation of feeling it is wondrous and lets me know when I am fully anchored. This was just another of the many amazing things that happened to me. I will forever be grateful for all of the ways you have helped me positively change my life. With love and gratitude." —Shawn M., Santa Barbara, CA

Conclusion

I wanted to share those experiences of people I know so you can realize what is possible. This is just a small sample as I have received many hundreds more. I assure you it is quite possible to live significantly beyond what you can imagine. You just need to add clearing practices to your meditations. I know you can do it! However, you do need to be persistent and apply yourself on a regular basis. A higher level of living awaits you. You can set yourself free. Self-mastery and enlightenment are not reserved for specially gifted people. It is your natural state, and it is well worth any inconvenience you experience to attain it.

Chapter 19

YOUR SPIRITUAL JOURNEY THROUGH MEDITATION PRACTICES

The Buddhists and others say that all life is suffering. Some even refer to our existence as composed of a pain body. Certainly as you look upon the human condition worldwide, you see much of both, and you may wonder if a way out of this dilemma exists. Most people seem relentlessly programmed to make choices and decisions that lead to further suffering. Unfortunately, circumstances that lead to pain seem beyond one's control.

You might notice that many different parts of yourself are in conflict with each other. For instance, sometimes you are afraid and sometimes you feel secure. Sometimes you are angry and sometimes you are calm. Sometimes you are demoralized and discouraged and sometimes you are positive and hopeful. And, you undoubtedly wonder why. An insight into factors contributing to the confusion is that you have a higher self or soul and a shadow self or ego, plus a super-conscious mind, an unconscious mind, and an energy body with an aura. The apparent separation of each of these elements creates a perception of separation. Furthermore, the perception of separation is the actual cause of your suffering and pain. The good news is that meditation integrates all the illusions of separation and merges your awareness into the unitive state. At this stage you realize the Absolute underlying infinite principle is both the essence of all you are and the absolute nature of all there is.

The Goals of Meditation Practice

Several phases must be kept in mind as you develop your daily spiritual practice. First and foremost, meditation is not an intellectual process, but rather an experiential process of discovering first-hand what your true self or soul is. This discovery is not revealed as much by thinking about the subject or analyzing ideas about it, as much as allowing the truths to arise from the experience of direct awareness and realization.

When the reality of the unity and interconnectedness of all things becomes your experience, you will awaken to a new way of viewing yourself and all life. You will feel as though you have awakened from the dreams of a deep sleep. Until you have this experience, you may think you are awake and directing your life through your conscious decisions. But when you awaken, your awareness pierces through the images that your five senses mistakenly tell you is reality. You will sense that everything is created out of the same fabric of existence. You will feel more connected with creation and more awake and in touch with everything. You will realize how absorbed in an illusion you were. You will feel reborn as you awaken into a fresh new view of everything.

Meditation Practice

Meditative practices were developed as a means of connecting with underlying reality and the field of consciousness. They also enable you to attune to the still small voice that emanates from the infinite presence. Through meditation, your sense of being connected with and at one with the fullness of the divine will become natural and automatic.

Through each meditative experience you can surrender into a greater realization of who you are, and when you return to your normal every-day consciousness, your awareness will be changed, and with this new awareness, your life changes. You know that you and the rest of creation are not what you always assumed they were, and life doesn't work the way you assumed it did. The only way to know this is by direct experience. It is not known by reading, thinking, or any of the other normal ways you have come to know anything. It is by direct experience in consciousness only.

The Source of Difficulties

The confusion comes from the fact that there are fundamentally two major components to what you think you are. At your core is your soul. It is composed of love and light and has all memories of your experiences from the time of your creation. Much of those memories are only accessible through a refined meditation practice since they are not recorded in the body and brain you have in this life.

The second part of you that you think of as who you are is what has been developed since you were born and which became your ego-personality. The personality is formed from traits you acquired from your parents genetically and energetically and your experiences in this life. Underlying your overall personality are many sub-identities or sub-personalities with traits you have carried over from many lifetimes, and they are mostly composed of beliefs and emotional reactions. This constellation of identities and reactions is what is generally referred to as the ego. The ego is the aspect of who you think you are which was developed over time living with a perception of separation and the resultant forms of pain. Most of the traits considered fundamental to what we think of as a human being are actually defensive characteristics of the ego. This includes your emotional reactions and beliefs, which encompasses judgments, criticism, and blame.

Because the ego is a survival mechanism continuously coping with the perception of separation, all human beings have similar reactions and defense mechanisms. Naturally, each person has developed a unique style and preference for particular defense mechanisms. All of them share similarities. For instance, one main core mechanism of the ego is fear in one of its many forms such as anxiety, panic, worry, and guilt. The experience of perceiving separation from your core nature automatically engenders a number of fears. However, because the underlying reality of existence and your soul is love and light, the experience of separation results in isolating the ego in darkness and void to a degree hard to imagine, and the ego will do anything it can to prevent itself from feeling the terror of this pain of being cut off, isolated, and abandoned.

The ego is terrorized by anything that threatens its survival, so it is driven to cling to as many things as possible to assure it won't go into the deep void of separation or come to its end. This powerful, underlying fear drives people to accumulate, own, attach to, possess, grasp at, or control in an attempt to insulate themselves from the pain of separation and the fear of ceasing to exist. Your spiritual journey includes discovering the many ways the ego mechanisms have been operating in your life so you can experience the beauty and truth that lie within. The best method for this discovery is through meditation.

There Is More to You than the Ego

Beneath the surface experiences of the ego is a deep and aware part of you that knows it is one with the underlying source of love and light. It is present with you now at this very moment, but it normally operates below your level of conscious awareness. This is your True Self or Soul. Your true self is also called the Higher Self, Master Within, God Presence, Enlightened Consciousness, Awakened Self, I AM Presence, and other names.

The perception of your spiritual evolution will occur to the degree your soul surfaces into self-conscious awareness. As it emerges more, it gradually integrates its consciousness, qualities, and awareness into the perceptions of the ego, and you experience a merging of your conscious awareness into the awareness of your Soul.

The ego diminishes the more the Soul emerges and integrates. This process is soul merging. This process continues until the ego traits completely dissolve. The speed with which it does this is both a natural consequence of your evolution and the degree you actively participate in the process. As you merge more deeply with the Soul, you progressively replace the role of the ego. Whatever role the ego plays for you can be replaced and managed better by your Soul. This is what makes enlightenment a process rather than a destination.

It takes time to discover and get in touch with the many overt and subtle aspects of your ego identities, and therefore it generally takes years for the complete dissolution of the ego and the full emergence of the Soul. Once a person becomes aware of these truths, the process proceeds at a much more rapid pace than it did before. Meditation enables you to disconnect from the senses and realize your inner realities and connections in ways the senses could never provide.

Part Four

How to Deepen Your Enlightenment Realizations

Chapter 20

HOW YOUR PERCEPTIONS SHAPE YOUR REALITY

Have you ever felt disillusionment about your life? Maybe you thought you weren't reaching your goals or you had more problems than solutions. Perhaps you may have said, "If I have a destiny and if I'm being led to a positive outcome, it sure doesn't feel like it. In fact, if anything, I have a feeling of being guided from one struggle to another."

All of the above are based on perceptions. That is, they are points of view, opinions, conclusions, judgments, and beliefs. Suffering is formed out of perceptions. This is not to say painful conditions don't exist because, of course, they do, but the way you view them, interpret them, and react to them is due to the filters you create through your perceptions.

One of the main tools of the mind is a perceiving mechanism. The perceiver is the creator of everything you experience. The perceiver is a filtering device that creates identities or sub-personalities composed of beliefs that it projects on people and situations. It uses these perceptions to create your life experiences. The perceiver is similar to having a group of people living inside of your head. It's as if they have a consciousness and life of their own, yet all they do is create and generate points of view and then warehouse them. Your perceiver gives birth to your sub-personalities that are then energized and run like programs in a computer. Identities are components of the ego. The ego is the defensive survival mechanism that uses the five major senses to help you live your life without being connected with your soul.

The ego and its perceptions are all manufactured thoughts and beliefs. The ego creates perceptions to help it know if something is dangerous or not. The ego will then hold onto anything it can to strengthen its perception of security. When you are engaged in the perceptions, they feel as though they are the correct perspective of what is true. Yet, they are merely opinions derived by observing, judging, and concluding. What is so subtle about it all is that even your awareness of this fact does not prevent you from slipping into believing the perceptions are real. That is the power perception has over you. The reason for this is that the perceiving mechanism is there waiting to interpret any sensory input and incorporate it into its experience as reality. As already noted, the ego is a survival mechanism that was created to survive in a physical reality.

Moreover, what is so amazing is that it is cleverly constructed to do all of its work subtly, behind the scenes, totally out of your day-to-day awareness, so you don't even realize it is happening. Furthermore, it will draw conclusions with incomplete information and treat them as if they are fact. Therefore, before you realize it, you are caught with a reaction such as fear, anger, or depression through the ego-mind's perceptions and stories.

What may also seem incredible is that many perceptions are not based on anything that actually exists. For example, any form of worry is a perception of something that does not yet exist, but there is a fear that it might exist, which may drive you to take certain actions. Sales people, advertisers, and governments use this human trait for their own purposes all the time. They tell you what they want you to hear so you will make decisions that support their positions or buy their product. People also do this in relationships. They project their perceptions on the other person based on what they want the other person to be. People frequently ascribe traits and motives to others that may not be true.

The perceiver doesn't really care if something is true or not because its job is to anticipate possible threats to getting what it wants or doesn't want. So the perceiver creates the idea something is there when it is only a shadow or picture projected in imagination. But the perceiver goes one step further and imbues that shadow with the sense of its being real, which triggers a reaction through an emotion or words said. Have you ever gotten upset about something only to find out it wasn't true? Have you ever believed something you later found out wasn't true? You may have even strongly defended the belief. These are a result of the perceiver.

People often take measures to protect themselves from a future possible threat. People react to the perception of a threat in every way as if it were real when there is really nothing there, but your imagination forms perceptions. In other words, the mind constructs interpretations of everything observed and experienced. Then the way you perceive everything determines your reactions, behaviors, and experiences with it.

Perceptions Are All Interpretations

Perceptions influence all the ways you react. Before you react you establish a position. A position is based on perceptions that are really interpretations and opinions. If you take the position that something is real, you imbue it with reality, and react as if it were real. This is why people are so passionate about their opinions; they are convinced they are true and real. In many cases, what people believe are actually arbitrary opinions based on a self-determined belief that may not have any truth at all.

What if you took a position that everything you are dealing with today is based on perceptions? If everything is a perception what does that mean? If you are in a movie theater and involved with a movie, are you really experiencing the movie as if it were real? You only experience a movie in your mind. If you turn on the lights, you are sitting in an empty room with a screen. There is nothing there. It was all a perception that the mind may have interpreted as real. Why else would people get frightened in a horror movie?

The way you deal with life is similar. You project all sorts of stories in the theater of your life. Something inside of you is creating the perception there is something there, and you react appropriately believing it is real. The perceiver is creating illusions out of perceptions! Illusions are stories composed of imagined actions and consequences that are then projected on other people causing actions to be taken.

Everything you sense with your five senses has a perception attached to it. Perceptions are interpretations and mental projections. The question then to ask is if there is a reality to the perceptions. The truth is that all perceptions are distortions. That doesn't mean that some of what the perceptions are based on are not factual; of course, they could be, but the problem is the mind will have a hard time proving what is true and what isn't. The mind can only operate on what it acquires through the senses that are then run through the perceiving and interpreting mechanism in the mind and conclusions are reached. The conclusions then engage reactions.

Conclusions are myths. The way I am using that word a myth is a being or event without a determinable basis of fact. It is an invented story, idea, or concept. Perceptions are imaginary or fictitious projections that are then accepted and used to justify an action. Can you see how life is composed of myths derived from perceptions? In addition, can you see how this can lead to trouble? It wrecks relationships between citizens and their governments, between husbands and wives, between employer and employees, and between friends and enemies.

Here's the razor's edge: You are either conscious or unconscious of this process, and you probably slip between the two many times through the day. You are either unconsciously creating and expressing your experiences, or you are conscious that an unconscious part of you is creating things in your life. The third option is that you are completely conscious of everything going on in your life, and you are fully aware of what makes it so.

Unconscious forces drive most lives. Most of what you experience in a day stems from the realm of unconsciousness as if you are being run on autopilot. You can identify some of the unconscious factors as attitudes and beliefs held in the subconscious that cause you to make certain choices. You can also go deeper and uncover karmic contracts and obligations or promises and commitments from past lives, but the result is the same. Your life is going from one story to another all day long, playing the part, reacting to the script of the story, yet not realizing where the story is coming from. As long as you are in a story, you are in an illusion, which means you are asleep or at least partially unconscious.

I hope that this information will help you to be more awake, but even if you are awake, what about all the other people who aren't? When you are around people who are in a story, it is easy to fall into the unconsciousness of the story yourself and be pulled into other people's unconscious stories.

I'm defining unconsciousness as one of several possibilities such as being in a story and thinking it is real, being at the effect of karma without knowing what is causing situations, or being victimized by your own story or programs. In all of these situations, you are at the effect rather than at the cause because the unconscious story is running your life.

Often others pull you into their illusions and perceptions, and once you are caught, you become subject to the laws of the universe of their illusions. You may also be pulled into all the karmic influences of that universe. You fall into a true deep sleep of unconsciousness where you don't even realize what is happening. You perceive their perceptions to be real.

For example, you can be pulled into the fear or anger universe of another as you listen to people tell their stories. These stories can cause you to join crusades, take political positions, join religious organizations, or other social activist organizations. There is not necessarily anything wrong with any of those choices as long as they are done consciously and not because you are caught in a myth.

Life in the realm of perceptions and illusions is like being in a dream. Lucid dreaming is becoming conscious while you are dreaming. Like lucid dreaming enlightenment is becoming conscious of your unconsciousness. Enlightenment is seeing what is behind the perceptions. The more awake you are, the more freedom and control you have of your life. The process of becoming enlightened is developing the habit of staying awake and being aware.

When you are struggling or suffering, you know you have slipped into the universe of illusions and perceptions. You've heard the saying, "You are in the world, but not of the world." Another way of saying this is when you are going through life awake to all the perceptions and illusions around you, you are in the world, but not of the world. However, when you are pulled into the universe of perceptions and myths, you are then not only in the world, but of the world. That is, you are partaking of the operating system that emanates from darkness and separation that leads to struggle and suffering.

When caught in this cycling of illusions, help is not far to find. For example if you haven't experienced much positive movement in your spiritual or personal growth the past few months, you would probably be discouraged and perhaps perplexed. Feelings of being lost, trapped, or limited might develop. Perhaps you would be angry no one is providing the answers you need. What are you to do? When you catch yourself mired in this trap, you can say, "I am not this. This is not who I am. These are myths and I am none of these feelings or perceptions. They are coming from my perceiver—my myth maker." Then follow through with spiritual practices such as meditations to reconnect with your higher self or soul. The key to success with this is catching yourself in this state and realizing what has happened.

Here's the Life Preserver

The first step is waking up, and you can do this by asking yourself several times through the day if the story you are experiencing and what you are feeling feels like the universe of light or the universe of darkness. Is your experience emanating from your soul or the myth-making ego? Once you identify the source of your experience, then you are well on your way to shifting out of the distortions of perceptions and therefore out of the suffering and struggling.

To do this bring to mind a person and a story that has caused suffering or struggle. Bring the feelings you have about your story to your awareness. Then bring the soul in to merge into and dissolve the reactions to the stories, even if you aren't sure what they might be. The nature of the soul is to know what is unreal and what perceptions cause the issue. The soul can dissolve them to the core by bringing the soul's light to the darkness. To apply this to your situation, you connect with a part of a story until you feel some reaction to it such as suffering or struggle. Then say to yourself, "I call the highest enlightened awareness of my soul to fill my story and all my feelings about this story." This technique takes the pressure off trying to figure out what the source of the problem is. All you have to do is sense what the feeling is. You may sense struggle and suffering without necessarily knowing the cause, which is probably unconscious. Focusing on the feelings enables you to bring the soul's presence of higher awareness to it. Finding all the specifics is not that easy, but with this technique, you don't have to try. You can address anything troublesome or disturbing with this method.

Relationships and Myths

The provenance of perceptions can be demonstrated nowhere better than in relationships. Each person in a relationship of any kind has a collection of perceptions about the other person whether it is friendship, business, or romantic. Each person constructs a story of the relationship with perceptions and myths of what is believed about the relationship. Further, the perceptions, stories, and myths are projected on the other person in an attempt to get that person to become a part of the myth, but it usually doesn't work. Either the person succumbs to the other person's myth, or continues in a state of conflict or disturbance. Hence, partnerships, friendships, and careers rarely last a lifetime and neither do marriages.

Consciousness creates stories and mythologies because without them there is nothing, so the mind is constantly at work creating illusions. A mythology is simply a collection of perceptions and illusions woven into a story. When you are living through a myth, you are usually living unconsciously in the myth. You become mired in the stories and mistakenly think they are real. If you desire a new way of living, you must not be trapped in the illusions of stories. You can't live without them, but you can do so consciously.

You may be surprised to hear me say that you can't live without stories or myths. This is because people define themselves through stories and myths and create their lives around them. Life is just a collection of experiences we assign meaning to, and that is what a myth is. So the next stage would be to choose only the myths and stories that honor who you are and do it consciously. You can especially enjoy them if you play out the conscious creation of mythologies with someone else who wants the same mythologies that you do.

Chapter 21

HOW YOUR BELIEFS CONTROL YOUR LIFE

When your life is going well, taking credit for your good fortune comes naturally, but when things don't go the way you would like, you may be bewildered as to how and why. Difficult times and challenges are often attributed to "bad luck." Conversely, when things go well, many think they have "good luck." But is that right? Does "luck" actually determine outcomes? The answer is a resounding "no." Luck has nothing to do with what happens. The causative force of "good" or "bad" luck lies in the beliefs about the circumstances you face. Your deepest beliefs are what create the reality you experience.

You've probably heard that one of the most fundamental forces affecting your life is that you create your own reality. This can be hard to accept because when things aren't going in your favor, you often don't see the underlying belief behind a condition, so it's hard to accept that your beliefs are creating reality. This is because most of the beliefs driving your life operate at an unconscious level. You might say to yourself, "Surely I am not doing this to myself. It must be those other people doing this to me." Some people even blame God for allowing them to have misfortune. Yet somehow, deep down inside, you probably think you must be a participant in some way in creating your experiences even if you aren't always sure how this is so. If the circumstances are painful, you might think you are being punished for something you must have done in the past. If your life is, in fact, a reflection of your deep beliefs then it would seem to be important to explore and understand what those beliefs are.

What makes this subject more challenging is trying to identify the beliefs that could cause your conditions. This search is clouded by the fact that you can actually believe something consciously that is the opposite of what your subconscious mind believes. When this is the case, the subconscious usually wins. With conflicting subconscious beliefs and programs, you may have a consciously stated goal, but because of your subconscious beliefs, you could actually be unwittingly heading toward a subconscious outcome that runs counter to your stated goal.

For instance, regarding money or relationships you may have subversive subconscious beliefs such as:

(1) Love or money only comes to special or certain people.
(2) Love or money only comes with difficulty.
(3) I don't deserve a lot of love or a lot of money.
(4) If I get love and/or money I'll just lose it.

You can readily imagine how holding any one of these beliefs could contribute to blocking you in those areas. Holding any of these common belief programs in your subconscious mind will likely create the corresponding negative experience or behavior.

How did these beliefs get in some people's minds and not in others? It's not the situation itself that is the entire problem; it is the conclusions and beliefs you continue to hold onto that determine how you direct your energy and lifeforce. If you can orient all your inner belief programs to creating what you want instead of what you don't want, then you can create a wonderful life.

Much of the time, you aren't even aware of what your inner beliefs are or where they came from. These are your blind spots, and they usually form at times and in ways of which you were unaware. For instance, much of what you experienced as a child is long forgotten when you become an adult, yet you absorbed a great many of your childhood perceptions, ideas, and beliefs into your subconscious mind when you were young. These formed your self-image and your views of how your life will work out. As you experience traumas and difficulties or you observe them happening around you, you form conclusions that are stored away in deeper parts of your mind. These then affect your choices and reactions later in life. One of the first and most important steps to take is to look at the conditions you experienced in the past and get in touch with the beliefs and conclusions you have that could be creating the circumstances. Every effect has a cause.

How to Determine Your Deep Beliefs

Examining your current conditions is the first step. Pick one area to work on where you face some lack in your life such as a money issue, relationship issue, health issue, or a spiritual issue.

(1) Next, list one thing about the issue that you would like to change and formulate it into a statement. For instance, if you choose health, you could say: "I'd like to see myself healthy, vital, and full of energy, doing all the things I love to do." Or, if your health is pretty good but could be better you

might say, "I'd like to see myself doing more good things for myself to create and maintain excellent health, including a healthy diet and lifestyle."

Now follow the same procedure with one of these four areas: Money issues, Relationship issues, Health issues, or Spiritual issues.

(2) Next, take the area that you selected for improvement and list one thing you believe about it in your life now. For instance, if you picked health you would want to know something you believe about your health right now. You might say, "I believe I could be doing more things to take better care of myself."

State one thing you believe about your Money issues, Relationship issues, Health issues, or Spiritual issues right now.

(3) Here's another way to ask questions to determine some of your beliefs. Bring to mind what you have going on in your life now with regard to an issue and ask without any judgment: "What would someone have to believe to create or attract what I'm experiencing?" You could have an answer like, "I have bad luck. I don't deserve it. I had the wrong parents. I have bad karma. Apparently something is wrong with me."

Now you should have two or more beliefs about your condition.

(4) Next, ask yourself one more question about the area you just examined: "What else would someone have to believe to create and attract this experience?" When you have time do this several more times. I suggest seven times would be a good number to keep asking yourself to help you uncover the underlying beliefs creating and sustaining your issue. This is the most important part of the process because you can only clear what you identify. If the causes are vague, unknown, or buried, they will keep having their effect. However, when you use words to describe negative beliefs directing your life, you can clear them and replace them with positive ones that manifest what you really want. Beliefs are not static or unchangeable. You change your beliefs all the time depending on what you value at the time.

(5) Go back to what you said you would like to have in your life with regard to the same issue, and ask the same question: "What would someone have to believe to create or attract what I'd like to experience?" This helps you identify positive beliefs you already possess as well as others that would work better for you. You might come up with something like, "I fully

deserve to have this. I'm always in the right place at the right time. I am open to receive blessings of abundance and love. I automatically connect with people who help me attain what I want."

One important key to accepting the beliefs that will bring what you want is giving yourself permission to have it. Rather than granting yourself permission, you might naturally look to others for validation or permission to attain success. Here are a few examples of how many people look to someone or something outside of them for permission:

- Going through an initiation or ceremony.
- Being presented with an award or a certificate.
- Asking people who have degrees for a recommendation.
- Asking a doctor to tell you what to do.
- Asking others if they love you so you feel safe to love them.

In addition, you may have beliefs that limit your success, such as:

- I don't believe I deserve...
- I'm not talented enough...
- That's over my head and beyond me...
- It's not my destiny.

These beliefs limit your efforts to lead a fulfilled life. You can give yourself permission to rise to a higher level even if you look to someone else for validation and to help you reach a higher level.

For instance, you can say to yourself, or even give yourself a certificate that says, "I believe I deserve and have the right to have what I want (fill it in with whatever you need). I give myself permission to have this within six months." Then date it and sign it. Put it where you'll see it every day. This process directly affects your evolution.

Your spiritual evolution gradually dissolves the ego beliefs causing pain, suffering, and lack while simultaneously revealing the beautiful qualities of the soul that lead to happiness and fulfillment.

Where Your Beliefs Originate

All people carry thousands of beliefs about themselves, other people, and the world events they see. Beliefs are often reflected complaints, criticism, blame, and judgments. These all stem from beliefs, which are formed out of opinions and conclusions about virtually everything including how good, bad, or valuable you think you, a person, or something is. Once you have taken a position, you seal your fate to be confined to the parameters of your belief.

Beliefs are the sustaining forces of creation derived from your judgments and opinions. Your judgments reflect the beliefs that form the pillars of creation in your life. Judgments are not the same as beliefs, but they are based on beliefs. Judgments have to do with taking a position about something, whereas a belief is the underlying assumption that causes something to be viewed as real. Beliefs also underlie what manifests or stays in your life. A judgment is a position, and positions are arbitrary points of view based on beliefs. But they are only opinions or ideas, which means they are illusions upon which you base your choices and decisions.

How you interpret what you see and experience is the result of your perceptions. Your perceptions are held in place by your judgments and beliefs. So by releasing judgments, you also change or release perceptions, which change or modify your beliefs, which in truth affects what you create, attract, and experience. By stopping judgments, you change your opinions and therefore your relationships with people and situations.

Your Most Important Judgments

The most important judgments to be clear on are those you hold about yourself. Reflect back to the beliefs I asked you to identify earlier about some condition of lack in your life. Self-doubt, self-criticism, and self-blame are sustaining those beliefs and self-judgments.

The inner judge operates out of your "Belief Universe," which is where you store all your many beliefs about everything. You might also consider this your "causal body" that houses all the forces and patterns that cause your experiences. Your judging mechanism accesses your belief universe from which it forms conclusions. It sets up an arbitrary rating system that always manages to find something that doesn't quite live up to its standards of what it believes is true and important. This is because the ego by nature is incomplete. It knows something is missing, but it doesn't know what it is. As a result, no matter how perfect you do something, the ego will still not be satisfied causing it to project the belief that something is wrong with you, you are defective, you'll never get it perfect, something is lacking with you and your life, and, therefore, you will never be fulfilled or satisfied.

Because the ego is incomplete, it is always searching for something it doesn't have. It always comes from a place of lack and therefore it is always self-critical. To help counter the ego's voice, repeat these thoughts in your mind and make them your own.

- I surrender all judgments that I need judgments.
- I surrender, release, and dissolve all need to judge.
- I surrender and release the need to blame myself.

The ego is composed of your lifeforce energy patterns that have fragmented into numerous identities with beliefs. These are also called sub-personalities and each have their unique opinions, beliefs, and reactions. The ego is a collection of the many independent identities that collectively make up who you think you are.

An effective way to address the ego programs causing pain is by compassionately embracing the beliefs that do not support what you want. This would include the beliefs you identified earlier about certain conditions that are lacking in some way in your life. Because the soul is only capable of unfolding goodness for you as you call to it and compassionately merge its presence and consciousness into your belief universe, only good can emerge. However, it takes persistence to fully dissolve and replace all aspects of the ego. Be patient with yourself as you go through this process because it can seem like it will go on forever. I assure you it won't as long as you persist.

Repeat these thoughts in your mind:

- I invite the soul to merge into all of my beliefs.
- I ask the soul presence to embrace all judgments and beliefs.

The soul merge process reclaims your lifeforce energy that the ego has been using to sustain its distorted beliefs and reintegrates it so that it can be used to sustain beliefs leading to greater goodness and fullness.

If you want to heal a sub-personality or identity that has separated, you can call on the soul's presence as a light of integration. This is an intention like a prayer saying, "Here is what I want to do. I want to dissolve into the truth of my soul and let go of all the beliefs that hold me in a perception of separation."

What happens is that the lifeforce essence of those beliefs comes back and integrates, and the illusions sustained by those beliefs drop away and dissolve. Once that belief aspect of your energy integrates, the illusions it held disappear because there is no longer belief or energy to sustain it. Negative beliefs can only exist in separation.

Hold the intention to reclaim all the lifeforce energy from all the identities that believe something is wrong with you, or missing, or you've done something wrong or bad. The ego believes that you are flawed, imperfect, defective, and therefore deserving of lack or punishment, which is why you have problems and suffer. These distorted ego perceptions and conclusions can lead to accidents, illnesses, loss, and other misfortunes. Acknowledge these beliefs or any of the others you listed earlier that sustain lack or create unwanted circumstances. Pay particular attention to inner voices of questioning and doubt.

Take a moment to bring some of these thoughts and beliefs to mind and verbalize them to yourself.

Once you've done this, say to yourself:

- I hold the pain I notice in gentle mercy and compassion.
- I invite the healing soul to merge into all resistance beliefs.
- I acknowledge all my beliefs embraced with the soul.

By repeating and affirming these intentions, you are engaging a process. The part of you holding the need to believe any form of resistance must surrender and let go at very deep levels. No matter what comes to mind, just acknowledge it and say, "I bless you and surrender the need for you," while simultaneously holding the intention of bringing in more presence of the enlightened soul. Your words are the activating triggers of your intentions.

How the Ego Resists

One way the ego resists is to bring up questions as you engage in clearing negative energies and beliefs. When this happens another part of the mind wants to respond to the questions. If you engage in this dialog, you be hooked by one question after another. Here's what you do: Surrender the need for questions. This doesn't mean you will never have questions, but you want to surrender the questioning and doubting, because the mind uses this to engage you.

Many of the kinds of questions the mind generates have no concrete answers, so it uses this uncertainty to keep you wondering and searching. The antidote is to surrender all need for the questions and allow the soul and presence to fill the need for all questions. So say to yourself, "I am willing to surrender and release the need for questions." By embracing the ego and its need for questions with the fully enlightened awareness of the soul, the ego will never feel threatened in any way, making it more likely to relax its resistance.

As you relax and release more, a continuous opening and expanding into a liberating presence occurs. You'll become aware that you are far more than the little ego ever imagined. The soul knows that what lies beyond the beliefs and perceptions of the ego is something more than the ego could ever believe or imagine. As the soul moves in more, a deepening comfort, a deepening security, and a deepening awareness of peacefulness, completion, and happiness develops. Allow yourself to drift more deeply into surrender and feel yourself opening deeper to the satisfaction and fullness of the love and light that lies at the core of your being.

Say these words to yourself:

- I ask the Soul to merge fully into all stuck feelings.
- I ask the Soul to merge fully into all stuck beliefs.
- I ask the Soul to merge fully into all sensations of being trapped.

As you make the invitation to the soul to come in more deeply, it intelligently penetrates deeply and thoroughly through all aspects of your consciousness as it dissolves the barriers of limiting beliefs and reveals the freedom and fulfillment of the soul's nature. The soul is really the only thing in a position to bring freedom from limiting beliefs and openness to unity consciousness. Without the soul, you are trading one ego belief for another. With the soul, you move into deep realizations of your core truth. All you have to do is ask.

As you work toward clarity pay careful attention to any voices that arise because inner voices or commentaries are one of the clearest means the ego uses to communicate with you, and the voices define what composes the ego. Inner commentary is really the ego's cry for help, and it gives you clues of where to go next with your process of surrendering resistance. Keep surrendering, listening, and sensing what else might come into your awareness as you move progressively throughout all the chambers of the ego until they are all totally replaced with the soul. At this point, the process is under way, so just keep inviting the soul to merge more deeply into all of your beliefs. You want all the separate voices within you surrendered, merged, and unified with the presence of the soul.

You have to invite the soul into all the places where you want it to be. It doesn't automatically push its way in unless or until it is invited. The reason it works this way is because it was pushed out by your unwitting free-will choices in the past. These positions are then automatically maintained at subtle unconsciousness levels with fixated beliefs. Therefore, it takes your free-will choices to invite the soul back in to all the places of resistance. Until you do this, an unconscious intention is in place that keeps the soul out and the ego choices in.

Open your heart to receive the soul's presence into your heart and fill you completely until you are aware of being surrounded with an ocean of the purest light and presence. Receive the soul without conditions. Be relaxed and open, let love and light into your heart. As it fills your heart, let it melt all the beliefs that sustain suffering and struggling. Let it melt them and let them go. Surrender all to the clear healing light presence.

Now say, "Yes, I receive and accept the love and light that is being given to me." This statement is actually an acknowledgement of your intrinsic truth, and this is a very important part of the process. When you say "yes," your heart and intentions become one. You are a being of pure love and light, and all limiting beliefs vanish as you integrate these ideal qualities.

The last step is deepening your acceptance and deepening your surrender.

Say these words to yourself:

- I feel deep, expansive love.
- I feel radiance and presence.
- I feel deep appreciation.
- I ask this all to integrate.
- I feel gratitude for all I have been given today.

Chapter 22

YOUR DAY OF JUDGMENT

In the 1970s the very popular book *I'm OK, Your OK* was something of a phenomenon in the American consciousness and vocabulary for a while. Many were asking themselves if they were OK, and projecting whether others were OK or not. What does it mean, "I'm OK?" How would you know if you were OK? To answer that question you would have to set up some criteria to measure yourself. You would have to have some standard or definition of what OK means. Whose definition would be the correct one?

What if no matter what has happened to you and no matter how people treated you and no matter how down and out you are, you are still OK? In other words, what if you are OK regardless of outer circumstances? What would you be if your life were going along pretty well? Would that be OK too? No matter which way you go with this, you end up having to make some value judgments. What values must you have to be OK if you are OK under all circumstances? The very concept of defining someone or something as OK is something people do all day every day without much thought. It happens pretty much automatically on an unconscious level and most judgments are about what is not OK.

How often do you compliment yourself? For instance, when completing a task, do you often say, "Wow, you did a really nice job on that. You were sure good. You have certainly improved and grown and that is great. I like what you did."

What do you say to yourself about your body image? Do you sometimes look in a mirror and say, "You sure look good standing naked in front of the mirror." On the other hand, how often do you think about the shortcomings you observe with such self-talk as the following: "You certainly could have done that a lot better. You are certainly no saint! Do you think you will ever be able to make things work out well? Will you ever overcome your bad habits? Why aren't you different? Nothing seems to work out well for you."

What is there about the mind that is constantly forming such strong opinions? The country is split between political parties with often widely divergent opinions. Thousands of religions all believe they have the truth. Where do all the opinions come from and who is right? When you meet someone, don't you form an opinion? You look them over, categorize your likes and dislikes, and put the traits that make up that person in a box defined by your judgments of that person. Just about everyone does this. You may even think you can't help it.

Fortunately, the mind's proclivity to judged can be channeled along positive beliefs. Judgments are often subjective. For example, as you go through a store and look over the goods, you make judgments continually about what to buy and what not to buy, and most decisions are made based on feelings rather than objective information. Furthermore, when two people decide to get married, do you think it is based on objective information or feelings? Either way, judgments are involved. Judgments are opinions based on perceptions. Perceptions are colored by prejudices, emotions, and projections from memories and imagination all of which are rooted in subjectivity. For instance if you see a man wearing a beard with a turban, what do think and feel? Do you only see a man whose culture dictates his appearance with no other judgment? On the other hand, do you feel some suspicions about anyone who appears different from what is familiar to you?

Years ago, I met a man like the one I just described. I asked him why he wore a turban, and he simply said all the men wore them where he came from. No particular religious significance was involved. Wearing one was as common as an American wearing a baseball cap, which we wouldn't think twice about unless it had a saying on it we don't agree with.

Another example is a man I met years ago named Pfong Pu who looked obviously Asian. One of the questions I asked him is "Where are you from?" I assumed he might be an immigrant and that seemed like a normal question. He said in perfect American English with no accent, "I'm from New Orleans." Anticipating why I asked him the question, and one which he has undoubtedly been asked many times, he went on to say, "My parents are from Vietnam, but I was born here."

Judgments are usually only opinions formed from fragments of information. They reflect prejudices and preferences, and they usually arise spontaneously from your subconscious mind.

In one respect, functioning without judgments is virtually impossible. Judgments enable you to make your decisions and navigate through life, but many of your judgments probably come with prejudices, which may include condemnation or blame. To evolve and raise your consciousness, it is necessary to develop neutrality and acceptance.

If you tell people involved with politics or religion to remain neutral, they'll probably have trouble because they are convinced their judgments and beliefs are absolute truth. Many people are emotionally invested in their convictions. In some cases people's judgments define who they are and explain their behavior.

Judgments are nearly always distorted for at least three reasons:

1. Sudies show that many people are in a negative state much of the time. You can usually reduce your mood down to one of four states, Troubled, Mad, Sad, or Glad.

> **Troubled** includes fearfulness, anxiety, worry, cautious, desperate, and tense.
>
> **Mad** includes frustration, agitated, anger, regret, impatience, resentment, and insecurity.
>
> **Sad** includes grief, blame, burdened, stressed, controlled, vulnerable, or overwhelmed.
>
> **Glad** includes delighted, joyful, happy, trusting, loving, thriving, and harmonious.

If you are like many people, you may be troubled, mad, or sad as much or more than you are glad. From the positions of being troubled, mad, or sad, what kind of judgments do you imagine you would project that are not positive? Keep in mind that you tend to project on others what you, yourself, are feeling.

2. The second flaw with judgments is their static condition. In other words, expressing a judgment implicitly assumes that the person judged is in that state now and will be for the foreseeable future. A big problem with this assumption, of course, is that the judgment is likely based on a temporary condition or state the person is in, such as simply having a bad hair day or as major as undergoing something stressful. Behaviors affected by a condition don't necessarily reflect the person's underlying character or quality. The truth is people are not their behaviors. Behaviors are temporary reactions to situations. Eventually, all people will evolve beyond their

behaviors and beyond their body, mind, and personality to become their true identity which is the soul or Higher Self, which is beyond all judgment.

3. The third problem created by judgments is projecting the quality condemned on the person being judged while the quality is being held by the person doing the judging. For instance, if the judgment being projected is that a person is selfish, the person judging is focusing on the trait of selfishness and strengthening it by defining it and dwelling on it. So judgments are often dwelling on what you don't want in yourself.

Patanjali, one of the fathers of classical Yoga, said, "Undisturbed calmness of mind is attained by cultivating friendliness toward the happy, compassion for the unhappy, delight in the virtuous, and indifference toward the wicked." (Yoga sutras 1.33. from *How to Know God*. Translated by Swami Prabhavananda) In other words, holding kind, loving, and supportive thoughts and concern for those who are unhappy and by being peaceful and a peacemaker toward those who have done unkind things, your consciousness becomes peaceful.

When you just let the judging mind do what it seems to do naturally, the mind becomes disturbed by the judgments whether they are mad or sad traits, and consequently there is a drift away from the calm, peaceful, realm of the soul and enlightened awareness. So by dwelling on the shortcomings of yourself or others, you are only reinforcing what you don't want.

An outstanding example of how to resist judging others is in the story of Jesus after being beaten and nailed to a cross. He said, "Father, forgive them for they know not what they do." (Luke 23:34) This example is an incredible insight into his being concerned with the welfare and perhaps the karmic consequences of his persecutors, rather than his own suffering. This unconditional forgiveness is an expression of purity of consciousness free of judgment for the behaviors of his tormentors. This also reflects the deep peace within Jesus rather than the "natural" human reaction of anger, resentment, and blame.

If judgments cause you to lose your peace of mind, the cost is too high.

If your judgment or action harms others, it harms you.

Judgment divides and love unifies.

Which would you rather live with?

The Mechanism of Judging

Understanding your judgments is important because they are what form your experiences. What manifests in your life is largely the result of something in your consciousness, usually your unconscious intentions and beliefs. These formed out of the conclusions you made over lifetimes of observation and experiences. Your conclusions are based on perceptions, and your judgments are what hold the perceptions in place.

Your judgments are your positions about behaviors, conditions, or situations. You observe a situation, then form a conclusion about it and attach a value judgment such as good, bad, fun, or horrible. When you attach a value to it, your observation and belief become a judgment. A judgment is a position that stems from your beliefs, and beliefs together with desires and intentions are forces that give rise to what manifests. "Manifestation" is a word that means everything that you experience in your life.

Anything you have your attention on is interpreted and defined by your judgments about it, so you become confined by your judgments. As you let go of your judgments, other opportunities and experiences open before you. Do you realize how profound this is? Once you have taken a position, you seal your fate to be confined to the parameters of the position or belief.

What would your life be like if you let go of all your judgments?

As you release judgments, you continually and progressively open to other possibilities and other experiences. This eventually leads to a full realization and not just an intellectualization. Judgments usually come from fears of not being in control, and without control, the ego believes it will be damaged or even destroyed. Therefore, judgments are desires to control, and control is the main attachment mechanism the ego uses to feel secure.

The need to judge results from insecurity. The judgment puts everything in a defined place by valuing it and limiting it, thereby creating the illusion of controlling it through the judgment. You need to ask yourself, "Who is judging?" Since no judgments originate from the soul or higher self, the only conclusion is the source of judging is the ego. This is a very important because this quite literally affects everything in your life.

When you become aware of judging and what it is, you will catch yourself dozens if not hundreds of times a day doing it. Becoming aware of the troublesome habit of judging is 90% of ending it. I suggest checking in with yourself numerous times through the day, and when you find a judgment, refute it, surrender it, let it go, release it, and dissolve it. As you do this, you will become clearer on the subject.

The Plague of Self-Judgment

One particular aspect of judging that especially causes a lot of trouble is self-judgment. This usually manifests as self-doubt, self-criticism, and self-blame. The self-judging mechanism is a self-monitoring mechanism that watches what you do. In fact, many times it is so diligent that it scrutinizes everything you do, looking to catch you and then point a disapproving finger at you. It may have a voice that says something like, "I told you so. There's something wrong with you. You screwed up again. You don't deserve anything good. You deserve to be punished again. You're not good enough."

The mechanism that I call the "Watcher-Judge" is something the mind has developed to second-guess, evaluate, and instill doubt in you in an attempt to get you to a more secure place. The Watcher-Judge thinks it is helping you because it would say it doesn't want you to be wrong or make a mistake, so it tells you how imperfect you are or how cautious you are about your actions. The critical Watcher-Judge or the Watcher for short, relates to the analytical part of the mind, the part that analyzes everything you say, think, and do, as well as everything everyone else says, thinks, and does. The Watcher is a function of the ego that constantly monitors you and assigns an opinion and a value to everything. It is a mental pattern driven by fear and insecurity that amplifies self-critical, self-doubting, and self-condemning self-talk. It sets up an arbitrary rating system designed to keep you from doing something wrong or bad, but it always manages to find something that doesn't quite live up to its standards.

Self-criticism occurs because the ego by nature is incomplete. It knows something is missing, but it doesn't know what it is, so no matter how perfect you do something, the ego will still not be satisfied and will project the belief and feeling that there is something wrong with you or something is missing. Because the ego is incomplete, it is always searching for something it doesn't have. It always comes from a place of lack or shortcoming, and therefore it is always self-critical.

Judge Not, Lest You Be Judged

The Biblical warning to judge not least you be judged (Matt 7:1-3) has been the subject of much discussion and controversy for over two thousand years. Somehow, we feel in our hearts that we should not judge people, yet there are those who perpetrate heinous acts of abuse and violence which makes it hard not to hold judgments about them. In fact, we have a court system and jury system that is judging people every day and handing out penalties. How are we to reconcile the warning not to judge, lest we be judged with what we find happening every day?

First, being non-judgmental does not mean that you should not censure people who do abusive things or who take advantage of others. Society must have rules for the smooth running of the society. Judgment in the context of spiritual understanding has to do with not condemning the person because of the person's acts. In other words, you are able to separate the underlying soul and the evolving person from his or her behaviors because you know that each person is in various stages of evolution. In addition, negative behaviors stem from ego identities and programs and certainly not from the soul. Negative behaviors trigger negative consequences, which a society needs to insure peace and safety for its population.

By analogy, our educational system contains people at differing grade levels from kindergarten and first grade through middle school and up through high school and college. Similarly, people are at all levels of evolution, and as we would not normally expect a first grader to be doing high school work, the same can be said of not being surprised that those of lesser developed consciousness are not functioning at the same level as someone who is approaching enlightenment.

What we call spiritual evolution is the gradual dissolving away of the ego sub-personalities, behaviors, and belief programs that cause pain and suffering to reveal the essential goodness of the soul that lies beneath those defense mechanisms. Recognizing one's goodness, however, does not mean tolerating offensive behaviors. In some cases, actions become necessary to contain those who display offensive behaviors. We can judge a person guilty of unacceptable behaviors without being judgmental of the person underlying the acts they have done.

To be judgment free means to have space for everything exactly as it is with an understanding that everything is in a state of development or evolution of consciousness. As you evolve spiritually, the soul reveals itself. Unfortunately, in many cases the soul is so deeply buried and the ego so present that the intensity of the fear, anger, hatred, guilt, depression, and rage are intolerable to others and society.

Being non-judgmental in a spiritual sense means you can have acceptance for the soul of the person, but not acceptance for that person's actions if the person violates or oversteps the freedoms of others. This means that you do not need to tolerate abuse in any form. You can create clear boundaries with people, while understanding that factors leading people to do abusive things are due to upbringing and experience and undoubtedly a string of lifetimes that made people what they are. Furthermore, with guidance, help, training and the playing out of the karma, people can eventually evolve to make choices that do not infringe on others and will come to realize that love, kindness, generosity, and goodness are better choices for everyone.

Release Judgments to Evolve

Judgment is a mental practice the ego uses to define itself and to assess the potential threat level of people and situations. Clearing judgment and self-judgment is essential to progressing on a spiritual or self-development path. When you are free of judgments, an infinite space within opens for everything, and you feel infinitely expansive. This is ultimate acceptance.

What does the statement of Jesus mean, "Judge not, lest you be judged?" It means that the position you take on any issue locks you into the energy of that position. Since "like attracts like," you are creating your life experiences by the choices you make about the positions or judgments you make. It is similar to the statement, "Those who live by the sword die by the sword." This statement is not as much a threat as it is an observation. It is like the statement, "You reap what you sow." Your own consciousness creates your reality. The judgments you hold form the pillars of creation in your life.

Why the Ego Judges

The ego runs on fear and insecurity, it assigns a threat value to everything. That is the judgment. Some of the ways it does this is by labeling people with such comments as, "He is a scoundrel. She is no good. I am so stupid." The labels put people in a box constructed of arbitrary points of view and opinions, typically as labels in the form of complaints, criticism, blame, praise, tolerance, or acceptance. These all derive from fixed opinions, evaluations, and conclusions about virtually everything. This can include the choice of clothing you or someone else is wearing, the tone of a person's voice, or how good or bad or valuable you think a person or group is.

Judgment is more than a preference. An example of a preference might be saying you like vanilla ice cream much better than chocolate ice cream. A judgment would be saying vanilla ice cream is good and chocolate ice cream is bad. It could go even further and insist that chocolate ice cream should be banned along with people who indulge in it. Another example uses color to explain how judging works. You can substitute anything you have a judgment about for the colors in this example. You can have a judgment that blue is better than red. This may cause you to paint your house blue, buy a blue car, and wear blue clothing. In these ways, you limit or define your life through the color blue and your judgment about blue limits your life to the blue world. Surrendering your judgment about blue doesn't mean you can't enjoy blue, but it opens you to enjoy red also, and, in fact, all the other colors as well. You can substitute just about any position or judgment for the color blue and you can readily see how your position defines your reality. Your position, however, is an illusion. It is an arbitrary value placed on the color blue. To let go of your judgment on blue, you must first recognize that your position is arbitrary. You must be willing to say, "I'm willing to let go of my position," or at least say, "I don't know if blue is actually better than red."

Why People Judge

Judgment is a rating system projected in an attempt to increase feelings of safety and security. The ego "sniffs the wind" to see where everyone else is in relationship to itself to insure it feels as safe as possible. But to access higher states of consciousness, you must eliminate judgments. Surrender all judgments and you enter the reality behind all creation. Non-judgmental consciousness lets you see deeper realities. Most people have judgments and opinions about everyone and everything, yet the soul is the exact opposite. It has no judgments about anyone or anything. When you fully and totally embody the enlightened awareness, having a judgment about anything is impossible because the soul doesn't judge. In fact, the soul wouldn't know how to judge if you told it to. It can't do it. You'll find life very expansive when you are in unconditional acceptance of everything exactly as it is.

One of the problems judgments create is that they hold you at the level of the judgment. Another way of saying this is that your judgments define your reality. They give definition to your internal experiences, and they define the limits and boundaries of your awareness. The freer you are of judgments the higher levels of awareness you access.

An important aspect of non-judgment is that it opens you to be able to receive. Having any judgment is like having doors that are closed and locked, or at the very least only partially open. So in order to move into the higher states of consciousness, you have to release judgments at all levels.

The Key to Eliminating Judgments is Surrender

A place of no judgment is a place of deep surrender. The place of total and complete surrender is a place of no judgment. A place of no judgment cannot exist without surrender, and surrender cannot exist unless there are no judgments. The two go hand-in-hand.

Perceptions control what is experienced and perceptions are held in place by judgments and beliefs. When you release judgments, you also release or change perceptions, and therefore you change your experiences.

What you experience manifests in your life from your desires, beliefs, intentions, and judgments that you project into your reality. Your creations, manifestations, and experiences are defined and limited by your judgments about them. This means you become confined to experiences defined by your judgments. Once you have taken a position with a judgment, you seal your fate to be trapped by the definitions and parameters of the belief.

As you release judgments, you continually and progressively open to other levels of consciousness. As you surrender and let go of your judgments, other possibilities open before you. Do you realize how profound this is? Every spiritual perspective has a perception about what awaits you in your future timeline or what it will be like when you have evolved into a fully enlightened state. However, no matter how deeply non-attached that perception is, it is still limited by definitions, opinions, judgments, and beliefs.

How to Eliminate Judging

The ego is a collection of independent identities that function with your lifeforce energy. Because it creates pain and suffering, people have a natural desire to stop and eliminate the ego. This has led many people to talk about killing the ego. How do you suppose the ego reacts to hearing that? It uses all of its resources to protect itself and defend itself and it has had many lifetimes to perfect its survival skills. Thankfully, there is a much better approach to addressing the ego.

Since the ego is in pain, you must approach it compassionately offering a way for it to heal. One way to do this is by embracing the pain much as you would an injured child, with tenderness, gentleness, and caring. The ego will then soften its hold and be open to healing. This works much more effectively than viewing the ego as the enemy to be destroyed, an ineffective approach, but nonetheless one that many attempt.

The most effective way of bringing relief and healing to the identities in pain and suffering is by merging the soul into the pain. The soul merge process reclaims your lifeforce energy that the ego has been using to sustain its pain and defenses, and reintegrates it all back into yourself. This brings completion to the fragment that is incomplete because of separation.

When you address the light and presence of the soul as the catalytic presence of healing and integration, you activate a process to eliminate pain and suffering. This is done through prayer-like intentions such as, "This is what I am asking. It is my intention and my desire to heal the painful aspects of separation." The pure lifeforce essence of that fragment then comes back and integrates, and the illusions sustained by painful energies drop away. Because they are not real, they dissolve. Once the aspect of your energy is no longer separate and it integrates, the illusions disappear because there is no longer energy to sustain them. They can only exist in separation.

The goal and intention is to reclaim the parts of yourself that assume something is wrong with you, or you are missing something, or you've done something wrong or bad. The ego's perspective is you are faulty, flawed, imperfect, and defective, thus deserving of suffering and punishment. All these judgments account for why you have problems and suffer. Acknowledge these ideas or any others that come to mind and any inner voices of questioning and doubt. Acknowledge them as they arise and embrace them with light. Say these words to yourself:

- I ask the soul to embrace and heal each pain I feel.
- I wrap pain in gentle mercy and compassion.
- I bring the soul's deep peace to the pain.
- I easily relax and surrender to the Light of my soul.

Repeating these statements engages a process that allows the resistance to feel safe as it surrenders its hold. As you practice this technique, if distracting thoughts arise, do not engage them in a dialog, because they will likely hook you into their level of attention, and you will drop out of the beautiful higher states. Just acknowledge the distraction and say, "I bless you and surrender and release the need for you," while you simultaneously hold the intention of bringing in more light and presence of the enlightened soul.

How The Ego Resists

Fear drives the ego, and when you surrender, you move into unfamiliar territory from the ego's perspective. Furthermore, the ego perceives the surrender process as threatening because through surrender, you let go of its defense mechanisms. For these reasons, the ego thinks if it lets you go further into surrender or more enlightened states, it won't know what will happen to it or how to protect you, and it consequently feels insecure with the surrender process. The ego fears what it has not experienced. It especially fears the unknown, so it is always cautious. This holds you back from evolving, causing you to feel stuck where you are.

The Ego's Search for Spirituality

The ego will let you explore and surrender to a limited degree, but the further and deeper you go, the more threatened it feels. The ego is actually quite happy to have you searching and engaging in religious or spiritual practices because as long as you are seeking answers, it feels safe within the universe of these outer practices that it can control. Ceremonies, rituals, prayers, and practices give the ego a sense of doing something spiritual. This is not to say they have no value. Quite the contrary, but the ego loves you doing outer work because it is familiar with this realm, so it will say, "Keep doing the practices."

The ego's fear is that you will move into areas where it doesn't have control. It considers this dangerous. Paradoxically, as you surrender control, you gain empowerment. This is because as you liberate the soul, you fall into the safety of the soul, and you become one mind with all, and no greater safety is possible. So by embracing the ego and its concerns with the full enlightened awareness of the soul, you never feel you are losing anything or being threatened in any way. There is a continuous opening and expanding into a liberating presence. You become aware that you are far more than the little ego ever imagined. In fact, as the soul moves into the fears of the ego, you will experience a deepening comfort, deepening security, and deepening peacefulness. As you make the invitation to the soul, it intelligently infiltrates deeply through all aspects of your consciousness that are separate. It dissolves barriers that sustain illusions, returning them to unity in the soul's nature.

To facilitate this process, you must pay attention to any voices that arise because the ego uses them to communicate with you, and the voices define what concerns the ego. The inner voices provide you with the clues of where to go next with your process of surrendering resistance. You have to invite the soul into all the places where you want it to be. It doesn't automatically push its way in unless or until it is invited. As you keep surrendering and asking the soul to merge fully through you, you will eventually begin to have a sensation of presence emerging.

Open your heart to receive the soul's light into your heart and fill you completely. Receive the spiritual presence without conditions and let the source of love and light pour that love and light into and through your heart center. As spiritual presence fills your heart, let it melt all the places of suffering and separation. Surrender to the clean, clear healing light. Say to yourself, "I am willing to open myself to deep love and light." Now say, "Yes" and accept what is being given to you. When you say "yes" and open your heart, you become one with spiritual love and light.

Allow yourself to feel deep expansive presence of love and feel deep appreciation.

Chapter 23

THE RELENTLESS CALL OF KARMA

Karma is a word that has a lot of charge for some people. I know a person who is adamant he doesn't believe in karma. He says he's looked into it for years and has concluded that it is all an illusion. I know others who get upset at hearing the word karma in a spiritual conversation because that word is not in the Bible. Regardless of your position on this subject, karma is important to understand. The word karma is derived from the Sanskrit "KRI," "To Do," and means the effects that result from thoughts, words, and actions which includes the effects of past actions and their causes. Another way of looking at karma is that it is energy set in motion. The Bible does say we reap what we sow, and since this is an aspect of karma, it is fair to say that karma is in the Bible in principle if not in name.

All of our thoughts, feelings, and actions set in motion energy patterns that create effects. This is an observation and not a religious issue. The form and direction of what has been set in motion continues until another force changes the motion or the energy dissipates. This is karma.

Impressions are made from everything you have done, including every choice you made, conclusions you came to, beliefs you held, trials you suffered, what you love, actions you are ashamed of, and events you took credit for. Every feeling you have and every judgment you've come to have made their impressions. These impressions work as a force of attraction to bring favorable and enjoyable experiences, or to attract things that you would rather not have to deal with. Everything in your life is derived from energies you have set in motion in the past, and, therefore, everything, by definition, is karmic. And most of all of these factors are occurring at unconscious levels. That is, you are usually not aware of what is causing your situations.

From my experiences counseling tens of thousands of people, I estimate that at least 80% of the causes of situations are below a person's conscious awareness. Sometimes people can figure out about 20% of how they are causing their life situations to be the way they are, but large blind spots are usually a factor. An insightful quote inscribed on the Temple of Apollo in Greece says, "Know thyself and thou shalt know all the mysteries of the gods and the universe." The deepest truths are hidden from conscious view as you become enmeshed with life, so self-discovery for most people is a life-long process.

The Laws of Balance & Continuance

While growing up you accumulate many conclusions and beliefs that structure your personality; they define what you identify as yourself. What you identify with today is the result of past and present thinking. This includes past lives as well as the past in this life. For example, if a person were a shipping merchant from Spain exporting goods to the new world in a previous life, that person may find they are living in another country in this life involved in some sort of business dealing with Spain or other Spanish countries. A continuity of energies initiated in the past continues until altered by new energies or until they have run their course and come to completion or exhaust themselves. The law of continuance says that a force in motion continues until something happens to change it. For instance, if you loved music and played an instrument in a past life, music may very well play a big part of your life in this lifetime.

Another way the law of continuance works is that some people make promises to people in one life that follows them to the next life. For instance, if you tell someone, "I love you so much. I want to be with you forever. Even death will not separate us," the person might be attracted to you in a future life. Alternatively, the opposite is also true, causing animosity in future lives if you harbor ill will telling someone, "You beast, I hate you and I will follow you into hell and seek revenge on you." If the energies were negative such as lying, cheating, stealing, hating, judging, fearing, hurting, or in any other way going contrary to one's soul, natural balancing forces will come into play that will cause the person to try to compensate for or balance out the negative.

For example, if people brought suffering to others or harmed someone with their hands in a past life they may have a deformed hand in this life, or the opposite might be true. They might compensate by using their hands to bring healing in this life. This is only an example. Many people are using their hands in constructive and healing ways that are applying the law of continuance as they continue to express love, kindness, healing, and support, and they may have been healers of various sorts over many lifetimes.

Differences in the results are dependent on the attitude of those who put the energy into motion. This is the law of consequence. For example, it is one thing to accidentally bring harm to another, but it is quite another to do it intentionally with hatred. These are examples of the laws of balance and continuance that are aspects of karma and shed light on how it all works.

Your Actions Have Consequences

Even though you may release the energies associated with a negative past, in some cases you may find that some of the scars remain. This is sometimes true of conditions of the physical body. If part of the compensating and balancing energy includes a disability such as deafness, blindness, or a deformity, it may not go away when the energies are cleared. You will, however, stop the energy from going any further and carrying over into other lifetimes, and this knowledge may also prevent future compensations from plaguing you.

The ego has an inherent belief that pain and suffering pay for wrong doing or being bad, so if you have violated your inner soul's goodness by causing suffering or loss to someone else or even to yourself, you may generate a pattern that causes some form of loss or suffering even if you deny the reality of karma. It all operates unconsciously whether a person believes in it or not, or whether a person knows about it or not.

Everything is Karmic

Everything experienced is karmic because by definition karma simply refers to forces of creation set in motion. As long as ego exists, karma will exist. If there were no physical forms, no thoughts, no vibrations, no desires, no movement, and no intentions, then there would only be a quiet, calm, and waveless ocean of consciousness, but in that calm awareness, desires and intentions do arise all the time.

Patanjali's dualist description of reality is the movement or force of creation and the will behind the force. This is what creates and sustains duality. Patanjali's explanation was based on the direct experience of literally thousands of advanced yoga adepts. Their experience suggests that this goal of freedom, awakening, and enlightenment can be achieved in one lifetime through certain practices. These practices include purification of the body, mind, and spirit along with surrender and nonattachment. However, desires create waves of intentions that divide into many other waves, which appear as causes and effects. The reality we experience every day is the force of creation with the intentions behind the force. This is how all of our experiences are created and sustained.

The Karmic Snare

One perspective is that karma is an illusion. In one way this is true because from a transcendent consciousness, everything is an illusion. However, that doesn't negate the effects of gravity and inertia on the person who is experiencing the transcendent state of consciousness. Inertia states that energy in motion tends to stay in motion and something at rest tends to stay at rest. The same is true of karma. Karma is simply energy that has been set in motion in the past and continues its effect until something alters it or halts it.

Saying that either inertia or karma does not exist or saying that they are illusions doesn't make them automatically go away, but some would like to believe that denying their existence negates their effects. However, disbelieving in something doesn't mean it will not affect you. Unless you are proactive in releasing yourself from karma, it will continue its cause and effect impact until it either naturally wears itself out or is balanced through whatever is accepted as sufficient compensation.

Karma is About Good News Too

Everyone lives under the umbrella of karma, which is not all bad news. Karma also refers to the continuance of what you like and love, but if thoughts, words, or deeds violate a person's integrity or alignment with the soul, the karmic force of compensation may interfere with the full realization of the positive energies. Whenever something is done that is counter to the nature of the soul, a conflict occurs that will play itself out through a need to balance or compensate for it.

When a person is not in integrity, natural consequences follow. Ego reactions create mental and emotional energy patterns that have creative and attractive forces. In the realm of subtle energies where these patterns reside, like attracts like, and so the patterns which are out of integrity with the soul will create and attract energies inconsistent with the nature of the soul. This leads to negative and painful experiences. The creation or attraction is not usually immediate, which gives the person who is uninformed about or denying karma the illusion that person has escaped it, but once the forces are set in motion, they will find expression unless a shift in consciousness occurs and the energies are cleared.

The soul is an embodiment of essential goodness, not in a moralistic sense, but rather as an acknowledgment and description of the nature of the soul. The soul embodies every wonderful and admirable trait and virtue. Lying, cheating, stealing, and harming others are all out of integrity with the essential nature of the soul and, therefore, by the natural law of the universe, they bring consequences whether a person believes in the forces or not. This is called the law of consequences or cause and effect.

An inherent problem with the law of consequences is that everyone's inner guide operates from deep beliefs that determine karma. You are never quite sure when sufficient suffering has balanced or compensated for a past "mis-deed." The problem arises from not being objectively able to quantify the value or lack of the "mis-deed." For example, if you stole some money from your mother's purse when you were a child, you might harbor guilt that could lead to certain consequences. Perhaps someone would steal something from you, but suffering by having something stolen from you would not necessarily relieve you of a deep-seated guilt over your actions of having stolen something. Consequently you could continue to suffer in a vain attempt to pay a karmic debt for your guilt.

In most cases, a person never consciously makes the connection with suffering as a consequence for a particular action from the past. When you include the numerous past lives everyone has had, the process becomes even more tangled and difficult to figure out.

Your Karma Reflects Your Consciousness Level

Karma operates through your consciousness level, which by its very nature, creates and attracts what you experience. You are a composite of energy fields with a particular frequency, and you are able to change the level by making choices. Since you can change awareness level, you can change your karma. If your consciousness drops to a lower level of thinking and activity, you create a lower level of karma that is usually called "bad karma." As you spend time thinking positively and doing acts that are positive, you raise your level of attention and the lower negative conditions naturally drop away.

Karma Isn't Really Cause and Effect

Karma appears to work as a law of cause and effect, but this is only an external view of what happens and not an explanation of what actually occurs. Karma has to do with your field of attention, or consciousness level that is determined by your thoughts, beliefs, emotions, and actions. Karma really defines your level of awareness. You fluctuate up and down in the level of your consciousness as a day goes on, but you have an overall level of consciousness that attracts circumstances.

Karma reflects the type of energy you allow in your life and therefore what you become. You can rise as high as you want or sink as low as you can imagine. The qualities you hold within are the determiners of your future. If your reaction to situations is love and kindness, you will be happy and fulfilled, but if your reactions are anger and blame, you will perpetuate situations that trigger those responses.

Karma is Your Way of Escape

Karma is not bad news. It is actually your way out of suffering, and a key to changing your consciousness level. For example, wouldn't you agree that being nice and kind to someone puts you in a very different state of awareness than if you are hateful and cruel? A good action temporarily raises your consciousness and puts you at a level where you will attract circumstances of like kind. When a negative circumstance happens, you have a choice of whether to give it energy or allow its energy to simply flow away from you, while you hold yourself in a finer frequency or higher state of attention. When you are in a higher level of attention, you have greater peace, fulfillment, and happiness.

Essentially every issue and circumstance in your life has an antecedent of patterns you energized in the past. They are reflective of where your consciousness level is.

Your Past Comes to Haunt You

A person may have difficulties today because of what was done in the past. For instance, someone who overworks in this life may have been in poverty in a past life, so that person now works to avoid the trauma of poverty. Insomnia may be the result of having had a bad experience while sleeping in a previous life. Headaches may result from having had head injuries in past lives. Other causes could account for these things too, of course, but I've seen patterns like these repeat in people's lives, sometimes for many lifetimes. You are the living product of your past, and even if you cannot identify specific memories, all of your past lives are affecting you. All talents, fears, attitudes, likes, and dislikes are rooted in your past.

None of this means a person is doomed to a life of misery in some future existence because of mistakes in the past. Consciousness can be raised, negative patterns cleared, and a more peaceful, happy, and fulfilling life attained. Usually, all the circumstances in life were attracted, created, and accepted at unconscious levels. In most cases, they were created to continue or balance something from the past. If you established a pattern of doing something that you either really liked or hated, this could be sufficient to continue it into other lives. Often people attempt to balance or compensate for past actions by doing good things now, or by suffering that is taken as payment for causing suffering in the past.

3 Ways to Become Karma Free

Another word will help you understand karma a little more is "Dharma." Dharma means truth. It has to do with being true to yourself, which means being in integrity. Your dharma means following a course of action that is congruent with your inner truth. When you follow the truth of your soul, you create good karma because you are aligning your consciousness with the higher or highest aspects of consciousness.

Three major ways can free you from negative karma and align you with your dharma. Undoubtedly, there are more than three, but these are three main ones that I'll mention here. You may want to apply whichever feels the most comfortable for you and is compatible with your orientation.

(1) The first method is a particularly beautiful one of having deep devotion to God or a higher power. This will create a field that will release and dissolve karmically created negative patterns. If you have never been a devoted person, you don't know what you are missing. It feels wonderful, is supportive, and helps to clear you.

(2) The second approach is to utilize a recognition, acknowledgement, and removal of each karmic pattern through releasing techniques such as forgiveness or energy-pattern clearing techniques. This methodical approach requires that you specifically identify the karmic pattern and either express deep self-forgiveness or remove all the underlying beliefs, judgments, and emotions.

(3) The third karmic releasing method is perhaps the most elegant and complete approach. It is through deep surrendering. In a spiritual context, surrender is about releasing all forms of holding, all forms of resistance, and all forms of attachment. Ultimately, all spiritual paths converge and agree on the surrender approach, although the methods of implementing it vary.

How to Apply Becoming Free

Because everything is created with free will, it takes a dedicated choice and will to acknowledge and release all attachments to what has been created. This is why the ego doesn't just disappear automatically if we merely ask it to. You are a powerful creator and when you put the force of your will and intention into a choice or decision to live through an ego trait or defense, you empower it with a tremendously persistent creative force. To let go of what you have previously invested great energy and emotion in creating takes time, attention, decisions, and deep surrendering of every aspect of yourself that sustains the pain or struggle.

In addition, the surrender process offers a hidden bonus. When you reach a state of surrender, you will not judge, emotionally react, or resist anything, and therefore you will not hold onto or create negative karma. When you reach this level of consciousness it is as if karma no longer exists, not because it never existed, but because you are so deeply surrendered that you no longer sustain it for yourself in any way. This happens when surrender ceases to be a process and has become a state of being. At first, you practice surrendering the causes and effects in your life. This is the surrender process. You may say, "I surrender all causes of struggling," and you may feel some relief. As you continue deepening into surrender, you eventually arrive at a new, higher level of consciousness.

An example will demonstrate the process for you. For instance, you are having financial stress, and have feelings of being unworthy of abundance. Take the words describing what you are feeling and experiencing and plug them into a surrender intention while connecting with the emotion behind the words. For example, one sentence I recommend for this issue is, "I am willing to surrender and release the need for financial stress and feeling unworthy." As you repeat this process, each time reaching deeper and deeper into the belief patterns, you will eventually reach the core, and when you surrender and release that core, the issue will be gone. During your surrendering practice, continue releasing all the things that come up one by one, until you release the core that generates them. The generator is what is called the ego.

As strange as it may seem, the solution to the ego does not lie in destroying it as many people think, but in integrating it fully into your deepest, true self. This is where surrender applies. When all aspects of the perception of separation are integrated into your deepest, true self, separation vanishes, the belief sustaining the limitation or suffering disappears, and you live from an awakened and enlightened state. Reaching this state emerges naturally from a process of reconnecting with your soul's core through surrendering.

After you have practiced surrendering every issue and resistance, you enter a *state* of surrender in which you experience complete liberation and freedom from the tyranny of karma. This is true enlightenment.

Making surrender an ongoing practice is important because many things exist in the blind spots out of your conscious awareness. You may even be in denial of issues. To become aware of them so that they can be acknowledged and released takes time. Many months or even years may be necessary to delve the depths of the surrender process, but the rewards are called liberation, self-realization, and enlightenment.

Clearing Karma with Love

Love is the force that neutralizes the sting of karma. Following is a method that combines the three main ways of clearing karma: devotion, clearing techniques, and surrender.

Love is the most elegant and effective way to clear karma and make life what you want it to be. The key is being able to receive love without placing restrictions on it. In other words, you want all the areas of your life to be filled with love that are not currently integrated with it. This includes struggle, suffering, confusion, feeling stuck, blocked, or any other area that isn't working in a positive, flowing experience. Sometimes people are afraid to receive love because of past experiences. This causes them to shut down to receiving it. In addition, few have received love the way they want it or as often as they want it. This is just a fact.

A place to begin opening to receive what you need is through the heart center because through the heart center, you can access most of the issues that are blocking you, as well as access the healing soul. Therefore, the heart is the place to begin receiving love and healing because as you clear issues and blocks there, everything can open up.

Put your attention on your heart center in the center of your chest and acknowledge the presence of the highest enlightened awareness of your soul.

By making the request and holding the intention, you begin to open a door that has always been there, the door to your deepest self, the door to inner space and to a deeper reality. What enables you to open this door is your willingness to surrender all attachments to resistance in the form of conclusions, beliefs, emotions, perceptions, and projections. You release the grip your mind has on them as if they are absolute truths. The mind will only do this if it is shown a better way, and in order to do this, you must be willing to open yourself to another experience than what you have had up until this point.

Every mind ultimately believes it has truth. It believes it is right. If it thought it were wrong, it would seek something else to replace what is wrong, and then it would think where it arrived is right. The problem comes when the mind is fixated on fear of making a mistake or getting something wrong that will lead to pain. So you must be gentle and show it another way can bring it what it seeks. The mind doesn't know how to look within because it primarily operates externally through the senses. This is where your free will and conscious choice enters. You make the request to begin turning inside to sense and feel what lies within the core of your being. Love and peace reside here.

So to find peace, love, healing, fulfillment, and happiness, start by being willing to let go of the things you aren't that the mind thinks you are:

- You are not your emotions.
- You are not your judgments.
- You are not your perceptions.
- You are not even your thoughts and beliefs.

All these thoughts form what you have previously identified yourself with, which have prevented you from experiencing the deep love and the realization of what you are.

Pay particular attention to what you want to hold onto. These places are the ones that have been wounded in the past. When something difficult comes up, such as a condition, a situation, or a painful memory of someone who let you down or hurts you in some way, turn and face it. Face the difficulty that is challenging you. Acknowledge that events happened, and hold it in your heart presence.

A natural tendency is to avoid looking at pain, but to heal from pain, you need to address it. So choose an issue now that you want to address.

Have mercy and compassion on yourself for what you went through, and hold the intention for healing in your heart. Recognize that whatever initiated the event or issue is past and acknowledge you are willing to let go now. The key is to:

(1) Face the pain and acknowledge it.
(2) Have compassion on yourself.
(3) Forgive yourself for your part in causing the pain.
(4) Be willing to let go of the pain, judgments, and conclusions around the issue and people involved.

You may think you are certainly ready to let go, but there must be some part of you invested in holding it, so say to yourself, "I am willing to let go of the need for this."

(5) Stay in your heart and call to your soul to embrace you. Take a deep breath and release anything that comes up, and be present with yourself.

(6) Call to your soul to merge with and embrace the issue. Say, "I ask the highest enlightened awareness of the soul to integrate fully and deeply into this issue."

Be willing to let go of all the people, events, and experiences that have caused you pain and to shut down. Look for places that have been shielded and protected by defenses such as anger, resentment, fear, worry, revenge, hatred, depression, blame, and other negative reactions. You put up these defenses when you are afraid of being attacked, criticized, blamed, judged, betrayed, violated, or hurt. You then make your reactions and judgments to be your reality. A key to healing is through letting the love and light presence of your soul dissolve into what you have created. Healing and clearing the path to an awakened and enlightened life is the art of learning to open yourself to the pain and struggle that covers the deep love within. The fear and anger are blocks in the doorways to the deeper essence of who you are.

As you hold your attention on the issue call to the highest enlightened awareness of your soul and to God and the realm of the angels if you are so inclined. You can also call on all enlightened beings, ascended masters, and other archetypes to assist you in washing away the illusions of the self-created perceptions of pain and struggle.

Notice any feelings associated with an issue and any beliefs you have about it. Acknowledge them and notice anything emerging.

What do you believe about this?
What conclusions have you come to about this?

Next, repeat in your mind,
"I call to the soul to merge into all these perceptions."

"I call upon the peace and love of all the angels and archangels to clear away my limiting perceptions, beliefs, and reactions.

"I call upon the peace and love of all enlightened masters and ascended beings to wash me free of my limiting perceptions, beliefs, and reactions."

Notice what is actually in your heart as you make the requests. You will begin to receive the awareness of a new presence emerging that has space for every reaction and perception that comes up.

Notice the response to your requests. Sense the awareness of a deepening presence that merges into your issue.

Observe what is happening in the emerging presence of light and love.

Generally, beliefs are attached to every perception. These are inner voices holding judgments, opinions, and conclusions about all of your experiences. They may sound something like, "I'm not good enough. Don't trust this. You're making a mistake. I'm not worthy. I'm afraid. Nobody is there for me. I'm stuck." These are some of the most common voices, but there are thousands of others, as well as those that are unique to you and your circumstances. Just make note of them when they come up and let them release and dissolve. Verbalize to yourself that you are letting go of the need for the voices. Just say to yourself, "I'm willing to release the need for that voice now." Take a moment to do this now.

Healing occurs when you allow your soul to dissolve your own creations. This is all you are doing.

Most problematic beliefs were created unwittingly and most likely you don't remember when or how it was created. Your ego created your reactions automatically and instinctively out of a need for more security and safety. However, what the ego doesn't know is that the soul can take care of you better than any coping strategy, judgment, emotion, or position it can create. So make the commitment in your heart right now to let go anything negative or limiting you have created that is not from your highest enlightened soul awareness.

Apply This in a Meditation

From this point on read the rest of this chapter like a self-directed meditation.

Take a deep breath and release anything that comes up.

Be willing to let go of situations or people who have made you angry or upset. Yes, it may have hurt, but why keep hurting yourself over and over by continuing to own it?

Be willing to surrender and let go of any thoughts about your past.

You ultimately want to let go of any grasping after thoughts or concepts.

Get in touch with what this means: a total letting go and releasing of every thought and feeling in order to receive the deep experience of the underlying reality of all existence.

Now you can bring love to parts of yourself that have been holding pain. Embrace the pain by calling your soul to merge into any dark or troubling places. Say to yourself, "I forgive myself for holding pain and struggle."

Allow the natural love and light that is the truth of your soul to permeate you completely. You've made requests; now allow yourself to receive the gifts.

When you make the request, the answer is automatic. You find relief in the form of greater peace and presence.

You may feel a good feeling inside. There are many ways to experience happiness. Allow yourself to receive what is being given to you.

Say to yourself, "I accept the deepest peace at my core. I receive the expansion of my awareness into the ocean of consciousness."

You are setting your attention to receive the support of God, the universe, all creation, and all goodness.

Just relax and trust you are receiving all you have requested. Deepen your trust in receiving.

You are approaching the clearing in three ways.

(1) You identify with something that needs transforming, which is the ego. The ego identifies you with something that is only a concept, a thoughtform, a created identification with a projection of consciousness that isn't real. This process of identifying and describing the issue or pain is a starting place, but then take it a step further.

(2) The second part of the process is the way of surrender in which you allow yourself to open your awareness more fully to receive and embrace your reality. This is purification of the self through merging with the light of the soul so that you can become the soul. This opens your heart causing you to feel the devotion of the soul emerge and dissolve everything other than love. No thinking is required. Only observing what surfaces so you can bring the light and presence of your soul's healing love to it. Let the love of the soul be your friend and wash away anything that gets in your way. Say,

"I ask the full enlightened presence of my soul to merge into me and to fill me now."

Notice how the love and light of the soul works their way through you deeper and deeper until they clean the places that you didn't even know existed.

This process requires no action on your part. It is all about receiving in response to your requests.

The love is its own light and its own intelligent force as it moves where it is needed, and what you have been holding relaxes in its presence, allowing you to let go and receive its gifts.

Move more deeply into places within you now and release the beliefs, concepts, judgments, and emotions that have been holding you in illusions.

Let the deep soul love release you and take you out of your prison.

Let yourself receive the deepening presence of your soul to bring light and presence to the areas of darkness, clearing you deeper.

Sit in the presence and allow yourself to receive clearing and healing deeply within.

Say "yes" to receiving very deeply now.

- Become pure and radiant with the light of truth.

- Recognize true enlightenment through God realization and the embodiment of light in your heart, mind, and soul.

- Say, I open my heart to accept the full essence of my soul.

- I embrace the divine reality in all creation.

- I surrender and release, all thoughts, beliefs, and feelings.

I lift up all aspects of myself to be purified and returned to oneness.

- Feel into your heart and see what has happened to you.

- Merge with beautiful light in your inner sanctuary.

- Notice more peace, more beauty, more light, more love, and more presence within you and all around you.

You feel lighter, cleaner, brighter, and more radiant inside your heart.

This is your sanctified self.

You are the holy jewel that carries this precious light inside of you.

Receive the light transmission so that the divine radiance within you can diffuse all through the inner sanctums of your being like a beautiful fragrance.

Just feel, watch, and witness.

This is who you deeply are. This is your true nature.

You are opening doors that have long been closed, and the soul presence spreads through your whole being with pure beauty, love, and light.

You are being blessed with words of love, beauty, and joy written into your heart to enrich your realizations and bring more and more good things to you.

Express gratitude for what you have been given today.

Make the internal request now to integrate all you have explored.

Know and allow this integration process to continue day and night.

Feel into the subtle surrender around you.

Enjoy the presence of these energies.

Chapter 24

HOW TO APPLY HOPE & TRUST IN YOUR LIFE

This chapter is about two qualities that bring nearly as much fulfillment and enrichment to your life as love: positive hope and trust. Hope, the way I'm using it, is the willingness to believe in positive outcomes and to implement what is necessary to create them. Those without hope tend to lack motivations to achieve goals, and they often lack strategies to overcome obstacles when challenged. On the other hand, those with hope have positive goals for their life.

False Hope

Often the idea of hope is used as a form of denial or avoidance. For instance, while feeling discouragement, despair, and defeat, you might say, "I hope everything works out for the best." This is false hope that robs you of the energy and motivation to do something differently. Positive hope might use the same words, "I hope everything works out for the best," but in this case you are positively expectant about the future and take all the steps necessary to create that positive outcome. Recognizing this difference can help motivate you to stay in the positive form of hope.

Positive hope and trust are not like tossing a coin in a wishing well and hoping for something good to happen, as in the case when people sometimes use hope and trust as false crutches. "I trust things will work out, and/or I sure hope we get out of this jam we are in." Sometimes people say, "I trust it will work out if it is for my highest good." This expresses false hope and worry and does not come from a place of positive expectancy. False hope is based on a fear that something might not work out the way you would like it to, so besides actually being a form of worry, it is a blind wish without basis for a positive outcome. It's like a superstition because false hope is not owning your power and precludes being deeply in touch with real positive hope and trust.

When you say I trust a person or a situation, you acknowledge the essential goodness within the core essence of a person in relationship to you. It indicates that you have positive expectancy that person will come from a positive place. That is what positive hope offers.

Positive hope and trust bring out the excellence in other people in regard to you in the areas they have knowledge and expertise. For instance, you trust your dentist has the necessary skills, and is capable of performing the dental work you need, regardless what else might be going on in other areas of the dentist's life. As a result, you are able to have a high degree of positive hope everything will be resolved in a satisfying way. Positive hope and trust become the underlying basis of how you can live and experience life.

All you ever really have is the present moment, and every moment is absolutely new. The past is gone and the future isn't here yet, so in the present moment you hold a commitment to create a better future. That commitment creates positive hope. This is the power of positive hope. If you don't hope and believe in a better future, you are not likely to create one. Being positively hopeful is living with the feeling that the future will bring you opportunities for more happiness, fun, and fulfillment.

Spiritual Presence Creates Positive Hope

Bringing the spiritual dimension into the positive hope process is acknowledging a higher intelligence that is ever guiding and moving your life forward. As you relax into your connection with the awareness of higher guidance, you open yourself to receive the guidance, the gifts, and even miracles from the spiritual world. Positive hope also carries with it a deep trust that a presence is operating in your life that can override any form of darkness. If you have had a mystical experience yourself such as miracles or answered prayers, or circumstances working out wonderfully, these can reinforce your trust in the underlying forces of goodness operating in your life.

How to Develop Positive Hope and Trust

Answering a few questions will reveal ways to live in positive hope. As you reflect on your life, think of two things that have brought you fulfillment in the past or which you think would bring you fulfillment if you had them now or in the future. Or, other possibilities for this self-analysis include the following questions:

- Where would you like to be in the future?
- What would your daily life feel like in the future?
- What do you hope to be doing in the future?
- What would your life be like in your positive future?

Next, consider one way you can devote more time to pursuing something that brings you fulfillment. While engaged in this kind of self-examination, you may hear some inner dialog or self-talk, or you may feel a response in your body. Notice any inner uncomfortableness or tension. Then imagine you are in a place where you feel relaxed and recognize how that would enable you to experience living with positive hope and trust. If you feel positive hope and trust, do you see how you would be relaxed in nearly all situations?

Self-examination along these lines, is an important step to opening yourself to the power of positive hope by releasing and letting go of thoughts that are not totally hopeful and trusting. All you have to do is surrender all the rationalizations that you may have told yourself when disappointed. What sometimes makes positive hope seem out of reach are the unhealed wounds of past disappointments, broken promises, and shattered dreams. To reveal the light under the darkness requires that you become aware of the wounds and disappointments. When you recognize what these are, you can bring healing light to all those places and replace them with spiritual presence and awareness.

Maybe a situation that happened to you years ago didn't bring what you wanted. It may have deeply hurt or angered you, or you may have thought, "There must be something wrong with me, I'm not good enough, and I don't deserve what I want." These conclusions might have taken you away from positive hope for a time. Say to those places within you, "I ask for the pure light of truth and the enlightened presence of my soul to fill those memories." Simple statements like these reconnect you with the deepest part of who you are.

Even though you are asking the pure light of truth and presence to fill you, the truth is that it already does. You are already filled with the light of truth and the light of your soul. They are there even when you don't put your attention on them, you just aren't aware of them. If you live in a cave with the door shut that doesn't mean the sun isn't shining; it just means the door is closed, so the cave seems dark.

Some of your life disappointments probably stem from childhood, from what you experienced or what was lacking. You have probably thought of these things numerous times. Remember and acknowledge these memories and feelings and say these words from your heart:

"I embrace my memories and feelings with deep caring and healing from my heart and soul for what I went through."

"I send deep love and light to those memories and feelings of being wounded and disappointed."

"I call from the deepest part of my being to the sacred and holy presence that lives in me."

"I bring the fullness of divine presence forward to merge into all my memories and feelings."

The space that was occupied by disappointment is now being replaced with positive hope and a reality that expands from unconditional trust and divine presence. This is what resides with your true self. Expand your spaciousness for trusting divine presence to emerge more and more fully. When you live with the experience of this presence, you go beyond an intellectual acceptance or believing, and you will realize that you deserve all the goodness life can offer. This automatically brings positive hope and trust for all you aspire to.

This process connects with your soul. Remarkably, by simply addressing the soul, acknowledging it, and putting your attention on it, the divine presence emerges and replaces the pain. Say to yourself, "I open to receive divine presence and I feel presence, in my heart."

As you become more aware of this truth of your being, you will experience a natural coming home to your true self, which is your soul. You are not trying to create a mood, but rather an awareness of spiritual presence as a living force within you that carries deep trust, positive expectancy, and hope.

How to Apply Positive Hope and Trust

Bring to mind an area in which you have some doubt, concern, or worry. Maybe bring a fear or worry about how somebody has treated you, or how you reacted to a situation or how you may have been treated by a business, friend, relationship, or government. You could also focus on a money issue or a worry about an aspect of your life, such as a health issue. Choose something that creates concern or has been troublesome.

Now to embody the quality of trust say to yourself, "I am willing to surrender and release the need for this, and I trust." You could also say, "I feel trust. I live in trust. I am trust."

You don't have to do anything except extend the invitation to trust to embrace the situation. Notice you are not trying to come up with a solution, but rather a shift in awareness that positive hope and deep trust bring. Positive hope and deep trust are states of consciousness. They are traits of the consciousness of your enlightened soul.

Connect your consciousness to the energy of the issue you brought up a minute ago and then again say to yourself while feeling into it more deeply, "I am willing to surrender and release the need for this and I am trust." Allow yourself to relax into the soul's presence where hope and trust live.

Let yourself experience the stability and foundation that surrender opens and receive the hope and trust that come in naturally.

Surrender, hope, and trust take the edge off fear, doubt, concern, and worry. This happens automatically without even coming up with an answer or solution. This process creates an upward shift in your awareness to an inherent quality of who you truly are. Your enlightened state lives in the quality of surrender, hope, and trust. Notice how this process gives you more space. This is far more than a mental or psychological openness. It is a shift in perspective that occurs causing a shift in the way reality is experienced.

You will also notice something else that this does. You are more open and free, and your consciousness has more room and is more receptive to the full emergence of the soul and presence. Divine presence is the basis of who you are and this realization brings transformation to any shadow side of yourself.

Only the mind comes up with judgments and only the mind fights and struggles. Whatever questions or fears come up are simply thoughtforms asking you to release them and create space for trusting your own soul to express through you. As you surrender the struggles and questions, the soul presence emerges naturally.

As you surrender and open to hope and trust, you create an environment with the creative flow of life essence through you. This helps you open to the next step in awakening to your potential. Whatever the outcome, positive hope and trust put you in the space that the outcome will be something important to your continuing evolution. Since there is always a need behind motivation, by surrendering to positive hope and trust you bring higher guidance to your life. Your inner spiritual essence automatically works on your needs, and when you do this consciously, you accelerate the process. Surrender, positive hope, and trust can completely change how you live in all situations and with every concern. Feel the power of this!

Chapter 25

THE ENLIGHTENMENT PATHS OF FAITH, HOPE, AND TRUST

Faith is something you probably have heard a lot about if you attended church. Faith is also brought up when a person is going through a crisis. The word "faith" is used in a number of different ways, which is probably why it is not usually found in the context of enlightenment. For instance, one way the word faith is used is in a question such as, "What faith are you?" This question means what church do you belong to.

A second way the word is used is in saying, "I have faith everything will work out." What this really means is the person hopes it will work out but the person has no way of knowing for sure, and might have some doubt.

A third usage of the word faith is in the New Testament of the Bible in Hebrews 11, "Now faith is the assurance of things hoped for, the conviction of things not seen." Faith in this context is similar to the second way the word is used noted above which is holding onto a belief and that the future will work out positively. The phrase "things not seen" imply there is no visible evidence or proof. The words "faith" and "hope" are often linked together in a future context that something you want will come true for you.

A fourth way the word faith is used is an attachment to a belief based on someone else's testimony or on someone's opinion regarded as an authority. An example of faith used this way is when someone holds on to a belief without evidence to support it but because someone said it. People either arbitrarily decide to believe something or have given power to someone else to tell them what to believe. This is "blind faith" which is like saying, "I choose to believe it, just because that is what I choose to believe. And I'm willing to die to defend my belief." Many who have died as martyrs took this position.

A fifth definition of faith is foundational to attaining enlightenment.

A Fifth Definition of Faith

As we grow up, trust often becomes replaced by doubt, confusion, and cynicism. Yet when properly understood, "trust" encompasses a deeper aspect of faith.

Often when people lose trust in one belief system, they quickly embrace another that seems to offer more security. People have a strong need to believe or trust in something. This is what leads to searching for the latest self-help suggestions. As newborn babies develop, their trust morphs into faith and belief systems where their beliefs become their truths. Their doubts, uncertainties, and disillusionment with people are replaced with new hope. This ultimately leads a person to abandon trust in people who don't live up to expectations and, therefore, not surprisingly, faith and trust are difficult to adhere to.

Trust is more than a nice idea or a spiritual sounding word; it is a most practical way of living. Often life brings the unexpected as well as circumstances beyond your control and knowledge, but through trust, you are able to live in the moment without fear or anxiety about the future. Trust in a spiritual context relates to your relationship with your soul, which is directly related to how surrendered you are. In other words, trust reveals to what degree you are surrendered and therefore awakened to your true nature. Your truth is who you are beneath the emotions, beliefs, and judgments.

Surrendering is an extremely important subject for anyone serious about spiritual evolution because it releases all resistance. Deep surrender brings deep trust, and deep trust means you are in deep surrender. As you continue to surrender, you will reveal the beautiful, peaceful, happy, loving core of yourself. The deeper you trust the surrendering process, the deeper you will discover who you are, and the more you will live in faithfully trusting.

Surrender really means you are awakening to whom and what you truly are. Surrender guides you to the next step of your life and navigates you through the rough waters of whatever life brings to you. Trust is an evolving awareness that stems from surrendering and releasing blocks that prevent you from trusting. By deepening your awareness in truth, you discover your core essence or soul that knows only trust.

Applying Faith, Trust, and Surrender

What kind of reaction do you experience when facing conflict or disappointment? How do you react when you don't understand why people are treating you the way they are, or you are frustrated with a relationship or a project? What goes on inside of you when you face uncertainty on a health or financial issue? Is there an aspect of you that is not in complete trust? Do you get frightened? Do you get irritated, angry, and defensive? Do you retreat, get quiet, withhold, or get depressed?

People react differently to negative situations depending on how they grew up and how they faced these challenges, whether they successfully confronted them or not. To know what really does go on within you may be best understood by your relationships with others. In what ways do you react that are different from believing that you are treated fairly, with respect, and support? If your reactions were negative, you will likely worry, retreat, or react in some way problematically. The areas of your life that need acknowledging and addressing are those where you feel despair or discouragement.

Tuning into your body will help you discover areas where trust is an issue. Your body can be a key to moving into trust. Feel and observe your chest, stomach, and throat. If you notice any tightness or discomfort this can be valuable clues where trust is missing.

At this point forgive yourself for each way you reacted negatively instead of trusting. Say to yourself:

"I forgive myself for my reactions"
"I forgive myself for lacking trust."
"I surrender all need for being frightened."
"I surrender and release all need for being frustrated and angry."

Now ask yourself, "Does my inner life reflect a belief that I am taken care of and safe? Do I really believe in trust?" Feel any responses in your body or mind caused by fear or insecurity. Now say to yourself, "I give myself permission to be at peace with that part of myself that is frightened." You can be specific if specific situations come to mind.

These are important steps to opening yourself to the power of trust. You first start by acknowledging aspects that react in any way that are not totally trusting.

Secondly, be willing to put aside all rationalizations about disappointments and have mercy on areas that feel the lack of trust. Maybe a person didn't deliver what you hoped for. Or, perhaps a venture didn't live up to your expectations. Maybe something was offered to you as a child that didn't provide what you needed, causing frustration and anger. You may have even thought, "Something must be wrong with me, or I'm bad or not good enough."

Be present with these memories and feelings without judgment and as a neutral observer of yourself. You must listen to inner voices, memories, and feelings because the conclusions you have formed sabotage your efforts to attract the people, abundance, and spiritual breakthroughs you seek.

If you find incompleteness instead of fulfillment in any area, underlying conclusions and beliefs are responsible, and you can address them to be healed. Be a gentle supportive friend to that part of you that is scared of not getting what you need and is operating from fear. Say to yourself,

"I embrace that part of me that feels disconnected and afraid."

"I merge mercy, compassion, and love into the part of me that doesn't have answers."

Feel into this merging process and allow it to come to you.

The answers are all inside of you because your soul lives in trust. The soul doesn't have to learn to trust or practice trust because the soul is pure love, trust, peace, and every other reflection of goodness there is. Just observe yourself relax all defenses and resistance in the presence of your emerging soul. The lack of trust exists because of unhealed wounds of past broken promises, disappointments, and shattered dreams. In your movement to create more space for trust to exist within you, you simply request and invite the healing light of truth of your soul into all the places that reflect disappointments. Some of these disappointments may be rooted in childhood experiences when things didn't happen the way you wanted. It is helpful to observe and acknowledge these memories and feelings and bring a healing acceptance and soul presence to them now.

Call from the deepest part of you to the sacred and holy presence that lives within. Repeat the words in your heart that bring the fullness of the divine presence forward. Words such as, "love," "trust," or, "I feel divine presence in my heart." This opens more space to receive more trust. The space occupied by the disappointments is replaced with the truth of the unconditional trust the soul possess.

Trust is a consciousness of surrendering all resistance and obstacles. Let trust reveal more of itself to you. A deepening, emerging trust comes from a place beyond all your problems. It resides within your soul. Expand your space for trust to emerge and deepen within you. Say to yourself, "I give myself permission to live in deep trust."

"I give myself permission to feel deep trust."

Trust is an acknowledgement of the inner goodness, wholeness, and completeness of who you are. It is an awareness of the truth of you, which is your spiritual nature. Trust knows you deserve goodness in your life, and it is a power of itself that spontaneously leads you to that goodness. Give yourself permission to feel the truth of the consciousness of deep trust. All you have to do is surrender everything you feel that is not trusting.

Goodness is at the core of what you are. You deserve to give yourself a relationship with your divine nature not as intellectualized knowledge or as instructions from others of what is true, but as internalizations because it is your own experience. Not all your issues have to be resolved before you become aware of your soul's perfection and purity. Invite your soul's presence to emerge more fully and acknowledge it is who you are. Be very still and listen to the resonant shining star of your inner presence. You can sense it as you tune into it.

The soul is you and it responds to your requests, intentions, and invitations. So just open yourself to receive it. Sense and feel peace, comfort, and quiet. The feeling of the soul's presence will transform your mind and clear your thinking. Acknowledge to yourself, "My soul's presence is the core of who I am."

This is a basic yet extremely important realization. From this realization comes the ability to transform any shadow side of you. There is nothing to do. There is just willingness to open to let the truth of who you are emerge while you receive and observe it emerging without judgment or expectation. Notice how your whole body experiences your soul's presence as you attune to the subtleness of presence emerging within you.

Most people live in thoughts, beliefs, and analysis that keep them in separation from their soul's presence. However, spiritual realizations arise from consciousness rather than from mental analysis and rationalization. Analysis is a defense mechanism the mind uses to keep you from areas where the mind can't control. However, you can overcome this by recognizing that questions and fears that come up are efforts to logically resolve issues blocking you. Realizing they are merely opinions created by the mind releases them, and as they are surrendered, you move into trust as your soul expresses through you.

As you surrender and open to trust, you create an environment with the creative flow of the soul's essence through you. This process opens you to the next step in awakening to your higher potential. Whatever the outcome, trust puts you in the space that is important for your evolution. The need behind why you want something is often unconscious and usually stems from the ego-mind feeling unsafe. Your inner soul essence automatically works on those needs, and when you keep surrendering, you accelerate the process of clearing the illusions and distortions that the mind has created.

Surrender, positive hope, and trust completely change how you live. They change your perspective in all respects, in all situations, and with every concern.

Chapter 26

YOUR SOURCE OF VIRTUE

All the words associated with virtue reflect such wonderful qualities that I love saying them, reading them, and taking them into my meditative reflections. Words such as love, joy, peace, patience, gentleness, kindness, faithfulness, and trust. As you read this chapter connect with the virtuous words and notice the positive effects they have on you. Taken in a broad sense, virtue refers to excellence in a wide array of qualities, all of which is essentially good. Therefore, we can say that virtues are traits valued as being good.

Virtues relate to discovering your core truth. Of course, some say that virtue is merely a psychological construct and are baseless fabrications and unattainable quests. Others argue that virtues are merely words to highlight the flaws and shortcomings all people experience. However, I think you will come to recognize virtues are none of these.

The ancient Greeks referred to virtue as "habitual excellence" as opposed to an occasional situational excellence where a person rises to special action for a special situation. Rather the Greeks viewed true virtue as something displayed at all times. They saw virtue as a reflection of a person's character and therefore must be present continuously for any person to be considered virtuous.

In addition to the traditional Christian virtues of faith, hope, and love, the Christian Bible lists what it calls "fruits of the Spirit" in Galatians 5:22-23. They are love, joy, peace, patience, gentleness, kindness, faithfulness, humility, and self-control. To understand virtue you must include many words but that still is not a complete definition of virtue. Virtue encapsulates a wide range of traits that describe the heights of human consciousness, and, therefore, all words and definitions are somewhat lacking.

I am well aware that as soon as I say that virtues are traits valued as being good, some would regard this as a dualistic label and therefore an illusion. However, virtues are really an exploration into the nature of the soul. Virtues are all traits that I have found that are natural outgrowths of merging with your soul or core essence. In addition, nothing that is your soul's essence is a myth or metaphor because it represents a real quality of what you are at your core. The list of words considered to be virtues are merely pointers to underlying intrinsic qualities of your existence.

It may be that some project judgments on these core traits; however, virtues are the basis of your fundamental reality. Some things such as virtues cannot be divided into dualist interpretations. This will become more evident as we continue.

The words I associate with virtue are the traits I have observed naturally expressed from those who are connected with their inner spiritual essence that I call the highest enlightened awareness of the soul. Sometimes you will feel the virtues are more evident than at other times. However, when you experience them or observe them in others, you know you are connecting with a deep inner core truth of goodness that lives within. Furthermore, you may be inspired when you find these traits expressed in others, even if only as random acts because they tap into and reflect essential goodness.

You will recognize, as I have, that they are not traits normally seen in movies or on TV. They are also certainly rare in politics and the business world. Nevertheless, when you understand what they are, you thankfully do find them in many people.

Of course, I will naturally start my list of virtues with love but not the normal emotional love that most people experience. Love in all of its forms is what nourishes life. It is the substance and sustaining force behind all creation. It is what makes your very heart beat and what makes you feel alive. You can touch on that love when you take a moment to connect with the presence of life and love within you.

Within your heart, say to yourself, "I open my heart deeply to merge into Divine love. I feel love presence deeply in my heart." As you express those words with deep sincerity, you will feel the presence of your own inner essence formulated from love and designed to express love. As you repeat that intention a few times, let the sensations that arise fill your body from head to toe. As you tune into your inner space, notice what you are sensing and feeling. In whatever way you experience these sensations, request to merge your consciousness into them throughout your body as you hold the intention to move deeper.

When you connect with your inner spirit and the love that is your soul's nature, you then begin to find gladness and an uplifted spirit emerging. In some cases, it is felt as peacefulness, contentment, happiness, and sometimes blissfulness. These are also virtues. Virtue is being connected to and one with your soul. Such a connection encompasses a wide range of additional qualities, such as:

- forgiveness and acceptance
- altruism and unselfishness
- freedom and flexibility
- openness to receive
- innocence and purity

The Divine States of Buddhism

Buddhism has four (brahmavihara) "Divine States" that can also be regarded as virtues in the sense I am using the word. They are as follows:

1. Loving-kindness toward all. The first divine state encompasses the hope that a person will be well and it is the wish that all beings, without any exception, will be happy. This is a natural and automatic extension of connecting with the deep inner essence of love that radiates from the soul. As you connect and merge your awareness with your soul, you naturally and automatically feel loving kindness. This is a most wonderful consciousness from which to experience life. You feel in love with everyone and everything. What could be more fulfilling than that?

2. Another of the divine states is altruistic joy in the accomplishments of oneself or another and sympathetic joy that rejoices in the happiness of all. This state warms your heart and fills you with deep satisfaction at all times.

3. The third divine state of Buddhism is (Karuna) compassion, which is the hope that suffering will diminish for everyone, and the wish for all to be free from suffering.

4. The fourth state is equanimity or becoming very deeply acceptant of both loss and gain. One does not distinguish between friend and enemy but regards everyone as equal. The state of equanimity is what I am calling peace as a virtue. Peace in this case means deep inner peacefulness that is actually a by-product of being virtuous. For instance, "Right Meditation" is defined as a state of clear-minded tranquility. From this point of view, you could say that peacefulness may be considered a virtue.

A final virtue subsumed by the four divine states is Patience. As the mind becomes peaceful and one is rooted in deep soul love, patience naturally emerges, which includes it corollaries of mercy, tolerance, flexibility, and perseverance.

People seem to have an instinctual understanding that a higher path to journey through life exists, as evidenced by the fact that virtually every culture on earth has recognized the value of aspiring to a virtuous life. For instance, the Buddhist practice as outlined in the noble eightfold path can be regarded as a progressive list of virtues. It includes:

- Right Values: A commitment to mental and ethical growth.
- Right Speech: A non-hurtful, non-exaggerated, truthfulness.
- Right Actions: Avoiding actions that would do harm.

You can recognize these as essential goodness that is the highest aspect of the human spirit.

Other traits of the Noble Eightfold Path are kindness and goodness. Goodness is a word broad in scope, but it reflects a deep attitude of trustworthiness, integrity, truth, and honesty with oneself and others. These words are really gateways into the exploration of the nature of the soul and the higher non-physical nature of our being.

Danger lies in relegating these virtuous qualities as unattainable. If they are unattainable, one's inherent nature reduces to only an opinion with no reality or value other than the arbitrarily assigned to it. Therein is a trap. Under the guise of being open-minded or intellectually logical, such a view debases the very nature of being and provides justifications for following lower instincts and drives.

Transcendent Virtue

Transcendent virtues include appreciation of beauty and excellence, gratitude, hope, humor, and spirituality. These are somewhat self-evident and are the essence of the human spirit. They emerge from realizing the underlying unity of existence that we are all interconnected in many ways and share and value these virtues. A simple way to know if you are operating with virtue is if you express loving-kindness in your actions. Your honest intentions of expressing love and kindness are the virtues of essential goodness connecting you with the divine source. Your willingness to release obstacles to virtues opens the door that to your inner soul-nature that is composed of virtues.

How to Be a Virtuous Person

You are spirit and I want you to feel that reality as you deepen into your inner realms and connect with your soul. Reflect on how much you have grown and how much you have already let go. Acknowledge all you have gained, places you've traveled, people you've spent time with, what you learned, all you've done. Be nice to yourself. Give yourself some credit. Thank your body, thank your mind, and thank your soul. Give yourself love and appreciation.

Now think about this. How enjoyable do you want to make your life in the next year? The key to connecting with the miraculous presence is opening to receive with devotion through your heart. Your life can be as enjoyable as you make it. Pause, sense, and feel the presence of your inner essence within and all around you. Say to yourself, "I am open to receive the divine into my heart and my life."

All thinking is just an accumulation of data downloaded into your mind. All thinking is just a collection of thoughts riding on the surface of your peaceful consciousness. Let go of all you think you must do. Be willing to release blocks, limiting patterns, doubts, and other limitations including the unknown unconscious ones. If you open to receive, you really do not need to do anything else to reveal virtues. All you have to do is relax while recognizing the spirit that you are. Let this all be as easy, effortless, and as enjoyable as relaxing in a warm bath of liquid love supporting you.

Imagine you are surrounded by the golden-light radiance of your soul. It fills your aura and all the space around you. You are light and love, and you radiate the purest, most beautiful golden light of your soul. Sense the purity that emerges from your surrender.

As you fill with love and light and deepen into releasing and dissolving all need for resistance, any thoughts of limitation dissolve. Issues and difficulties are automatically dissolved from you for they are not your truth. So much of everything is available to you, and you are worthy and willing to receive it all. Feel the openness and expanded willingness to receive as you open your heart center to receive the soul presence and its virtues.

Follow these words and make them your own:

"I open to receive eternally expanding goodness and abundance into my life."

"I feel gratitude for all I have received and am continuing to receive."

"I integrate all this wisdom and awareness into my present reality."

Feel energy radiating from you in all directions like the sun. Acknowledge the divine presence within, bringing all goodness to you. Remember these words and connect with your virtues and desires for all good to manifest in your life.

Part Five

Elevating Your Consciousness to Enlightenment

Chapter 27

4 LEVELS ON THE PATH TO ENLIGHTENMENT

Spiritual teachers have made many attempts to describe differences in consciousness levels. Distinguishing differences enables you to understand where you've been, where you are, and where you are headed. In this chapter, I'll describe four major levels of consciousness and the stages in each.

LEVEL 1

The first level encompasses the darkest aspects of self and progresses to a much more integrated, congruent, and genuine self. For example, when a person hears an inner voice saying, "Lie, cheat, and steal," and that person acts on these urgings then that person is tuned into to the lowest frequencies. When a person responds, "I don't think I should do that. I don't think it is right," the person is operating out of a higher consciousness level. When that same voice says, "Lie, cheat, and steal" and the person responds, "I know that isn't right; I wish to live with honesty and integrity. I won't do it," that person is in an even higher consciousness level. As a person awakens and evolves, he or she attunes more and more to the soul's voice and spiritual presence.

LEVEL 2

The second level includes opening to the soul through the heart center. This is a level of deeper communion with the spiritual nature within. When the heart opens, there can be sensations of bliss and peaceful happiness that cause many to believe they have reached enlightenment, but as beautiful as this is, it is not yet enlightenment.

The second level requires a greater commitment to live in integrity. This means being honest, consistent, and congruent with your deepest soul truth. When you reach this level, you have a dedication and commitment to the path that elevates you to higher levels of wisdom, love, and enlightened consciousness. This may seem simple enough, but it requires a commitment and resolve to be on your spiritual path and do what is necessary on a daily basis to attain your enlightenment goals. You are no longer living for satisfaction of the ego-personality. You are living with surrender and deeper levels of love and awareness of divine presence. In time, if you continue on this path, you will come to quantum jump into the third level that deepens your awareness further into the soul.

Once you experience this, you are ready to merge into a state of completion of your whole being. I refer to this level as the Soul Merge. I use the term "soul" as an equivalent term for the Higher Self or true self. This is the real you. It is the truth of who you really are.

You will discover the precious purity with which you were created as you reach this state through deep surrender. This means you have released all holding and attachment to everything that has kept you from connecting with your deepest truth. This is your beginning of enlightened levels of consciousness. You will experience peace, contentment, comfort, completion, equanimity, and non-judgment. This is a very peaceful and beautiful level to live in, and it prepares you to expand into higher levels of consciousness that are yet to come.

LEVEL 3

Each person has unique qualities, purposes, and vibrations. As you deepen into merging into the soul, you experience the disappearance of separate identifications and you integrate a deep spiritual presence.

In these levels of opening the heart further, you will discover the "still small voice" of true spiritual guidance. When you reach this level, you will know you are hearing a clear inner voice not of your subconscious mind or your spirit guides, but of the voice that comes from the Divine Spirit within you that is all in all. This requires a deeper level of commitment to purify your heart and mind. Your intentions guide you from level to level, enabling you to enter refined states of being. They help you heal and clear yourself which opens doors to higher levels of consciousness.

In deepening into the Soul, the individualized soul merges back into the ocean of all awareness. This movement is described as the extinction of the separate self and the movement back to unity. The East calls this Nirvana. Nirvana means emptiness. It is the releasing of separate identifications. This is a challenging stage because it is one thing to say, "I'm going to give up all of my ego wants and needs" and another, to be actually willing to disengage from and dissolve identifications. The ego can be terrified at this event because it is driven to survive and desperately cling to what is known, yet at this stage of evolution, you must be willing to surrender everything you have known yourself to be.

The goal of all spiritual paths is enlightenment which includes the realization of being one with all. When reaching this awareness, which is called unity consciousness, a person may believe that full enlightenment has been reached and the path to enlightenment has ended. While this is certainly a level of enlightened awareness, this stage is not the finality.

Sometimes you will encounter some who seem to be very aware and enlightened, but have an air of arrogance or are still struggling with some issues. This may be due to having attained awareness of unity consciousness (the awareness of being one with all existence), but without having risen to sufficient spiritual realization to be free from karmic forces or all traces of ego. To go further, one must go through the heart center. The heart leads this process and brings another dimension to the enlightenment experience.

Enlightened Experiences or Enlightened?

Many emotions and reactions are connected to the heart and lower chakras, and many spiritual paths don't employ adequate systems for addressing the issues held there. In fact, I've even heard teachers say to ignore them or "just don't allow yourself to go there." This approach usually teaches transcendent meditation practices in an attempt to rise above the pain. The problem with this approach is that by not identifying, releasing, and clearing the emotions, reactions, and judgments, they can end up being repressed and recycled. You may feel OK while you are in the retreat or meditation, but the old issues come up when you return home, or situations arise that challenge you. This is what causes people to say they have lost their enlightenment. This reveals the difference between having enlightening experiences and being enlightened.

Typically, when a person experiences a transcendent state for the first time, some would say the person is enlightened. Sometimes transcendence happens as a "flash realization" or shift in consciousness in which the person experiences jumping to a new level of awareness in a relatively short time, perhaps in one meditation or in sitting in the presence of someone who is enlightened. But this is only a beginning and signals the person is ready to progress to yet higher realizations.

The initial enlightenment experience is only a beginning on a beautiful journey in which life begins anew now that the person is more fully awake for the first time. When the awakening occurs, people feel they are starting life anew. Now everything they have ever perceived is seen with new eyes, and after the initial awakening, a gradual unfolding of greater realizations occurs as long as the person continues with practices that lead to further realizations.

Further Enlightenment

Eastern terminology includes a stage of enlightenment called "sahaj Samadhi" or "bakah beelah" in the Sufi tradition. This means that from the crown chakra the light of consciousness has fully integrated throughout the heart, mind, body, and soul. At this level, there is complete integration into God realization that is stabilized and consistent. To reach sahaj samadhi, one must go deeply into the heart and continue to meditate until all issues and blocks are cleared and the ego dissolves. Generally, at this place on a spiritual path you enter some form of service to humanity. This means that whatever you are doing comes from a motivation to serve, and in every person you meet, regardless of outward appearances, you see the divinity within.

LEVEL 4

When you cross into level four, you enter the world of non-duality and full unity. At this point, you can now say you have reached enlightenment. "You" have disappeared now and are non-dual. You are not just feeling cosmic, not just knowing and understanding spiritual truths, but you are living in the awareness of the deepest underlying reality of emptiness, oftentimes referred to as nothingness.

This level is reached through a continued commitment to live in the elevated realizations of the purified heart and soul. You experience illumination with light and love and radiate it to all. As you enter the illumined life, you bring the clear light of consciousness through you and you see everything as one.

From the third level and below there can be struggle, difficulties, and problems in increasing amounts the lower you go. At the fourth level, a person no longer experiences most of the types of problems that people encounter at lower levels. To reach the fourth level requires a deep dedication to becoming completely clear of all lower vibrations, beliefs, and emotions. This is usually done through considerable meditation practices and a commitment to living a pure and respectful life.

What Enlightenment is Like

When you experience a spiritual awakening, your mind changes and works differently from before. Because the ego is gone, the your past, negative emotions, memories, judgments or attachments no longer exert control. Your reactions change. You enter a new and higher state of awareness. You no longer perceive as you did previously, and certainly much different from the rest of the world.

People around you may have no idea of your internal changes, for you look the same externally, but perhaps with a bit more happiness on your face and have a more quiet and loving presence. You absolutely feel very different internally, and, in fact, you are quite different. Deep stillness, purity, clarity, expansiveness, unconditional love, awareness, knowing, and profound peace dominate your new state of being.

As you reach the progressively higher states of consciousness, you will find that you become more peaceful, life is more fun, and you sense a deep inner strength and know that you can face anything. As you move further on your path, you will sense a deepening of love and unlimited clarity, expansion, and oneness with everything. You will be in love with everyone and everything. Life will take on a harmony and fullness beyond what you can imagine. Eventually, your mind becomes completely silent all the time as you have no unintentional thoughts or need to think. At that point, you'll operate from awareness itself.

What the Process is Like

As you surrender daily, you will be returning to your true nature as the ego issues progressively melt away. In this state, there is only love, beauty, and peace. Life takes on a higher, deeper, wider, and fuller expression of these qualities that is far broader and deeper than you could ever imagine. However, as long as your heart is veiled with ego distortions and illusions, you can only know these qualities in small measure.

Wanting, desiring, trying, searching, and attaching are all sources of struggle, pain, and suffering. Once you release these hooks and dissolve through surrender, you will experience only peace, beauty, and love of spiritual presence.

Your life journey presents many things that cause suffering and struggling that you must release, and it often seems like an insurmountable and endless task. Fortunately, a way exists to affect rapid and widespread releases. The way forward is through surrender, soul merging, and meditation.

Chapter 28

HIGHER STATES OF ENLIGHTENMENT

Clearly, some people seem to be more evolved than others, and have moved beyond the normal human experiences of pain and suffering. They may also have profound experiences and capabilities on an ongoing basis. This is because there are states of consciousness far beyond what most people understand as enlightenment. Indeed, there are states of consciousness that very few have experienced and therefore there is little mention of them or how they attained their capabilities.

For those who keep applying themselves, continuous new levels open and this means enlightenment is a relative term. That is, no "absolute" state defines it, but rather enlightenment denotes a change in consciousness with regard to understanding and experiencing life.

Vertical and Horizontal Enlightenment

One way of addressing enlightenment is through what is referred to as horizontal and vertical enlightenment. If a person has completely disengaged from attachments and the ego, non-duality has been achieved, and that is as far as anyone can go with letting go because there is nothing left to release. There is no more enlightened state beyond this. This might be defined as horizontal enlightenment: going to the outermost expansion of consciousness into pure awareness and emptiness.

However, vertical enlightenment takes a different trajectory. Since you exist as an individual being, even when you have attained non-duality you can continue evolving without the illusion of separation or having attachments to anything. This may seem contradictory from a non-dual view, but it is another very real aspect of existence.

For instance, you might want to continue vertically expanding in such areas as service, sharing, generosity, love, exploration, and participating in creation through many dimensions. In addition, with this model, you can continue developing in the areas that interest you the most.

Many people would say this qualifies as being ego-driven as if "ego" is a bad word; however, ancient Sankhya philosophy uses the term "Ahamkar" to refer to egoism that is a sense of self or individuality that is not negative;

it is neutral. It emerges from the "Mahat" or Universal Mind Intelligence into diversification and identification, but it is not negative. The so-called negative aspects of ego develop through the senses, judgments, and attachments, depending on the frequency of the choices a consciousness makes utilizing "sattva," "rajas," and "tamas" through the subconscious and sensory mind. Sattva, Rajas, and Tamas are the three main qualities of Prakriti, or Nature, which serves as active, passive, and balancing forces of nature. They are all essential for anything to exist.

As you look at nature and the universe, you find everything is evolving or changing, including you. For those who prefer dissolution into non-duality and who call that enlightenment, that is an option. Others may seek a movement into vertical expansion that may go on for a very long time, perhaps for eternity. In higher dimensions, beings who share consciousness engage in creation and service. You could say all the higher dimensions are filled with enlightened beings enjoying individualized lives.

Finding Freedom from the Ego

Knowing only the realm of the ego subjects you to the physics of that reality, but as you continue on the path, you will find that ego realm is not as large or as formidable as it appears. You have an intrinsic soul existence that is continually evolving. When you rise out of the ego, you will discover how it was constructed from a very limited view of reality.

The difficulty with escaping the ego's grip is that it continually causes you to cling to anything that seems to give support or security. People will cling to their perception of reality as a drowning person clings to a life preserver while floating in the ocean. They cling to it for dear life and are afraid to let go and reach for the lifeguard on the boat who can save them. When people are willing to admit they are clinging to fear and feeling cut off and are willing to surrender and let go of those perceptions, only then they can be helped. The lifeguard is the soul waiting to be embraced, but you cannot embrace it fully until the ego is completely released.

The ego drives people to keep doing, trying, striving, seeking, building, learning, accomplishing, acquiring, controlling, possessing, and owning, but never achieving lasting fulfillment or completion. Often people possess a frenzied feeling that if they keep going, somehow, someday, they will attain total fulfillment, ultimate safety, and full completion, but this will never occur in the ego universe. Running and seeking are the ego's traps. The ego believes the answers lie just over the next hill, so people immerse themselves in business, hobbies, relationships, spiritual seeking, sports, careers, or other pursuits that they think will bring fulfillment. Ironically, they do not realize they have turned their backs on their own soul, which would bring the fulfillment, completion, and happiness they seek.

The answer is so simple yet so overlooked. Your spiritual truth and nature has been with you all the time and to discover it, you need only turn your attention to it with the intention of reconnection. As the soul emerges, it automatically dissolves the ego defenses that arose from separation, providing a completely new and different way of experiencing life. The soul solution is what brings completion and lasting fulfillment along with all the beautiful qualities and virtues that are the nature of the soul.

How Can Spiritual Awakening Become a Continuous State of Being?

As long as the negative ego exists, it will pull a person into its web. Therefore, for the awakened state to become continuous, the ego must be completely let go. The challenge is that the ego has so many overt and subtle expressions that no simple or single formula will accomplish this. Some suppress their negative feelings and reactions and therefore may appear to be sustaining a state of peace or even bliss, but ego traits that lurk below the surface will eventually express themselves.

Denial is an interesting trait nearly everyone has to one degree or another. Denial is refusing to acknowledge something that is present, typically a condition or a fact. The denial pattern pretends the situation or circumstance is not there. Why does anyone do this? Denial is a natural defense mechanism attempting to protect you from pain in any form, but it really can't. It is like pretending that everything is all right while ignoring something is destructive, unpleasant, or unfortunate.

Denial is not always about something outside such as a tragedy or unfortunate circumstance; it can also respond to inner tensions, such as fear, anger, or any other negative emotion or reaction. Denial declares something is definitely not true and therefore you do not need to accept it.

Denial is actually the ego's version of refutation. Refuting something is a good process because it declares truth and acknowledges the soul or true self that does not attach to or identify with negative traits. Refuting is acknowledging what is deeply true while denial ignors or refuses to acknowledge a truth. Refuting works because it is a form of dis-identification that enables you to subsequently surrender and release the causes of pain and suffering.

In your spiritual practice, refutation is a useful tool because it declares what you believe and know to be true about your essential core nature, which is complete love and light. For instance, if you are feeling fear or discouragement, you can acknowledge the sensation and then declare that you know these are not emanating from your soul or core truth. Therefore, these emotions are not who you truly are, but rather ego reactions tricking you to thinking these negative reactions are you. Why is this distinction important? Because releasing troublesome beliefs is difficult if you believe they define who you are or are part of you. But if you acknowledge and declare they are not you, dis-identification begins to dislodge and distance them from being accepted. This makes it much easier to let it go and dissolve them.

Dis-identification is fundamentally important to becoming totally clear of all issues and obstacles. It is an essential part of the journey to mastery and enlightenment. By being observant and mindful of your inner reactions and then surrendering the attachment and investment in them, the pain of the ego reduces and the awakened state is experienced for longer and longer intervals.

Levels of Consciousness

Would you like to have a map so you can identify where you currently stand in your pursuit of spiritual growth?

In his book *Power vs Force* as well as his other books, Dr. David Hawkins describes in detail the many characteristics of various states of consciousness, and even provides a means of determining a person's relative position on a continuum from zero to one thousand. He calls it the Scale of Consciousness. Everyone falls into a place on this scale and each number represents certain characteristics. Most people fluctuate levels throughout the day depending on what they are experiencing. For instance, when meditating a person's consciousness will be at a higher level than when a negative experience triggers negative emotions. Dr. Hawkins claims that each person has a unique baseline number that describes an overall level of consciousness. Below is a brief summary of how it works:

Below 200 are negative emotions such as fear, anger, guilt, and shame. 200-300 is living in integrity and being honest and respectful. 300-400 is forgiving, friendly, and contributing to society.

400-499 is the level of increased intellectual development.
500-599 is where love becomes the dominant principle.
600 is the enlightenment threshold.
850 is where the ego completely dissolves.

Above this level are more full integrations of non-duality. The higher up one goes, the more fulfilling, happy and beautiful life is.

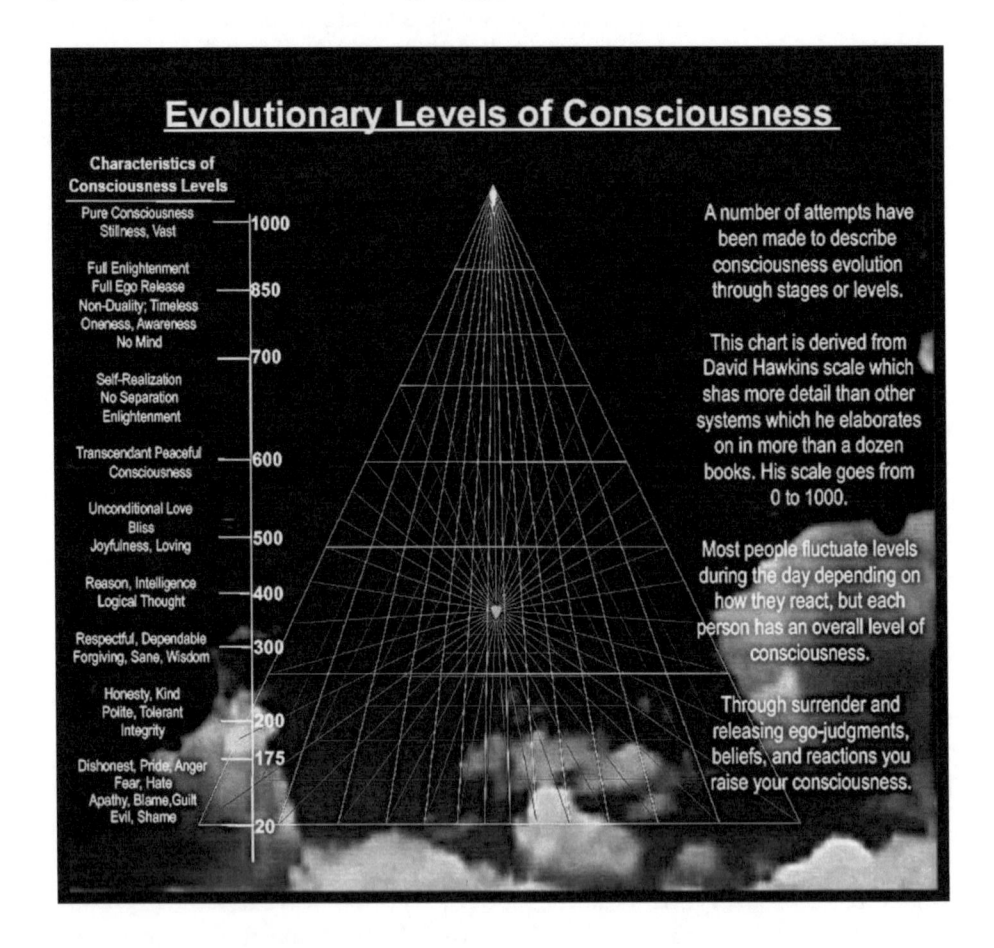

Evolutionary Levels of Consciousness

Characteristics of Consciousness Levels:
- Pure Consciousness, Stillness, Vast — 1000
- Full Enlightenment, Full Ego Release, Non-Duality; Timeless, Oneness, Awareness, No Mind — 850
- Self-Realization, No Separation, Enlightenment — 700
- Transcendant Peaceful Consciousness — 600
- Unconditional Love, Bliss, Joyfulness, Loving — 500
- Reason, Intelligence, Logical Thought — 400
- Respectful, Dependable, Forgiving, Sane, Wisdom — 300
- Honesty, Kind, Polite, Tolerant, Integrity — 200
- Dishonest, Pride, Anger, Fear, Hate, Apathy, Blame, Guilt, Evil, Shame — 175 / 20

A number of attempts have been made to describe consciousness evolution through stages or levels.

This chart is derived from David Hawkins scale which has more detail than other systems which he elaborates on in more than a dozen books. His scale goes from 0 to 1000.

Most people fluctuate levels during the day depending on how they react, but each person has an overall level of consciousness.

Through surrender and releasing ego-judgments, beliefs, and reactions you raise your consciousness.

One Way to Raise Your Consciousness

One way to raise consciousness is through the daily application of the simple Polynesian practice of Ho'oponopono. The best part is you can start this practice right now. You don't even need to say anything aloud or to anyone else. You can do it in the privacy of your own mind.

Here is the way to do Ho'oponopono. Hold a person or situation in mind that has caused you any kind of pain, misunderstanding, struggle, or suffering. Then you repeat these sentences several times.

1. I'm sorry.
2. Please forgive me.
3. Thank you.
4. I love you.
5. I bless you with every blessing of health, prosperity, and happiness.

Does this seem too simple? Maybe so, but the beauty of it is that it really works! Regular use of this practice will make you more mindful automatically and change your world.

Chapter 29

THE SOUL'S MIRACULOUS LIGHT

This chapter contains details concerning one of the most amazing discoveries and revelations I have had that can directly and profoundly affect every aspect of your life, including relationships, finances, health, and spiritual evolution. This chapter contains information on this topic not in my book, *The Soul Solution*.

Since the beginning of history, people have wondered about those who have the powers to perform miracles and heal simply with a thought, a look, or a touch. The stories persist of individuals who are said to have performed unexplainable healing feats and other miracles, and we are left to marvel at the accounts of what is said to have taken place. To most people, the keys of how these things were accomplished were largely unknown and often thought to be myths or special gifts of only a few. In the past, the secrets of how such things could be done were passed on only by word of mouth to devoted disciples and students but never explained to the masses.

In my life-long dedication to seeking spiritual discoveries, I too have heard and read these stories and tried to find answers that would unlock the mysterious, hidden secrets. This is not an easy endeavor, since many of the answers are not usually found in books or any other written sources, and those purported to have such abilities say little about how they are done. Over the centuries, the keys were often purposely masked with stories, parables, or allusions. While there are certainly stories of masters and others who have done miraculous things, the inner secrets of how they were done have not been revealed.

An Astonishing Healing Light

A number of years ago I made a discovery that was new to me but which is quite ancient. This discovery revealed something that people can use to make amazing changes in their lives. This is the story of a subtle-energy experience that can be used for great good and even potentially make miracles possible, and it is accessible to everyone.

This energy or presence is not like any other energy I have ever encountered, such as pranic healing, therapeutic touch, mana, Reiki, magnetic healing, shaktipat, psychic surgery, or other forms of energy healing. The range of experiences that people have with this energy is truly amazing. Some people have been healed virtually instantaneously of illnesses. Some have had heightened extra-sensory perceptions opened, and others have told me that their creativity and income have dramatically increased within a few days or weeks after being introduced to it.

If I told you all that I have seen this light presence do, you might have trouble believing it is all possible. The various results read like fiction, but later I will share a few letters from people who have written to me about it. In short, I can say this energy is one of the secrets behind miracles.

Perhaps the most important aspect of this light and energy presence is that it can have a significant effect in helping shift your consciousness to amazing and beautiful levels. Some people have had enlightened states of awareness open. Some have had visions and dreams of angelic realms. Some feel a deeper communion with God and their divine nature. I have found that this light and energy presence can be a dramatic help in achieving all of those things. What is wonderful is that this energy presence complements any other system of healing, clearing, or spiritual practice a person may be following. It can also change a person's life by opening the way to new opportunities for prosperity, health, and happiness.

Numerous people have written to me describing their experiences. Here is what one person wrote about its healing effects:

Some wonderful results are showing themselves. One person is relieved of pretty intense hip and leg pain which had been with her for a couple of years. Her quite noticeable limp is now almost gone. Also, as an anorexic, taking in adequate nutrition had been a problem for her. Not only has she started eating twice a day, but she is also receiving intuitive messages as to what nutrients she needs! She is about the fourth person I know of whose higher communication has been positively impacted.

A woman wrote telling me of an "immense joy" she experienced:

When I was sitting across from you, I was at first "waiting" for it [the light energy] to come to me. Once I let go and just "was," it sort of clicked into place, sort of like when you put a battery into its position. It was like a groove that was waiting for the perfect fit of energy. (There really aren't words to describe this). Then, instantly, when it clicked into place I remember that tears of IMMENSE joy fell. It was a feeling of connection, like a pipeline to the Divine. As I sit here now, I can feel a STREAM of energy straight through me, almost from below my feet straight through my head and up beyond my head, connecting me to the Source. I feel so truly blessed and am extremely grateful.

These two examples demonstrate that this is not just a healing light energy, but an intelligent transformational energy which can deeply affect a person's awareness and consciousness. The best part is that you can easily access it once you are aware of it because it emanates from your very soul.

How I Found It

The story of this amazing energy began with a miraculous discovery on Mt. Shasta in 2002. Although I have been on a dedicated spiritual path now for over 50 years and have discovered many profound truths, this experience was unique. It is well known that Mt. Shasta, located in northern California a little south of the Oregon border, is regarded as one of the sacred mountains of the world. Many books describe the spiritual experiences people have had on this mountain, and thousands have felt its special energy many miles away. Years ago I conducted dozens of retreats, workshops, and classes there myself.

The combination of being in the remarkable energy of this area combined with two weeks of meditating with a group at the base of Mt. Shasta opened me to this remarkable experience because I specifically wanted to find a way to help more people with their physical, emotional, and spiritual issues. I held the intention of wanting to be shown how miracles could be done to help people, and specifically how to be connected with the same miraculous source that the Bible describes as happening 2,000 and more years ago.

On one particular evening, I had an incredible vision in which I saw the Universe being opened. I was sitting on a couch with my eyes closed relaxing and thinking about the previous day, when I saw a bright light. I thought someone had come into the room and turned a light on, but when I opened my eyes, I realized that was not the case. I could see this light with my eyes open or closed, and I thought that was remarkable in itself, so I opened and closed my eyes several times trying to figure out what was going on. It became obvious to me that this was no ordinary light.

The light grew brighter and brighter and blazed into and all around me. This light filled me from head to toe, putting me in a remarkably euphoric state. I saw the heavens opened with thousands of angels beside what appeared to be a huge opening much like a rip in the fabric of the universe. I also saw a beautiful being in a golden robe standing next to the opening in the universe who was holding it open allowing the light to shine through. At the time, I thought this being was Jesus, or at least a representative of the Christ consciousness.

My inner knowing was that this was an opening to the divine Source to enable direct access to the light and power of creation and transformation. I came to understand and realize that this is the light and presence that underlies all appearances. It is the very fabric of the soul.

This experience burned a lasting impression into my mind that is so clear and powerful that years later, I am still fully aware of it, and I can still see it in my mind's eye as if it just happened.

What Happened Next

The next day after I experienced the vision I was doing a counseling session with a woman who had been attending the retreat I was hosting at Mt. Shasta, and she commented to me that my energy felt in some way stronger to her. She was experiencing emotional turmoil and I was helping her through it when she felt a spontaneous release and lightness.

At that time, I didn't fully understand what happened to me during the vision, but the experience with this woman made me realize that indeed something significant had taken place. Over the next several weeks, I did many counseling sessions, and many people reported similar experiences. I realized that what had happened to me because of the vision on Mt. Shasta was having a significant impact on others.

Here's the Important Part of the Story for You

Over the following months, I realized that by telling people the story of my vision and asking them to be open to receiving the light of their soul that they were also having profound experiences. Describing the vision and the energy seems to activate it in others.

This energy has been called different names such as "Christ Consciousness energy," the "Holy Spirit," the "light of truth," and "God Force Energy." While all of these references are true and good, I recognize this light as the light of the soul and the divine presence that lives in all of us.

Because of the results that many have reported to me, I have sometimes referred to it as "the miraculous light," a term heretofore not used. Using a new name that doesn't have a history behind it as do most of those mentioned above has its benefits. Since it is a new name people can avoid prejudices and preconceived ideas and thus view it in a new light.

The nature of the light energy and presence, however, is more important than the name, especially because it helps attune a person to a deeper inner truth that ignites the spark of God within. The soul and its miraculous light has an intelligence within it that creates spiritual awakenings and growth in every aspect of a person's life, including how a person works, learns, treats others, and relates to spiritual matters. Awakening to this light creates an inner transformation that brings a deepening presence of love and light.

What I see actually happening when a person experiences this process is an opening to a deeper connection with the soul. Everyone already contains a divine soul presence, and all that is happening in what I have just described is that the soul presence is coming to the surface of awareness. The light that radiates is an inner light of healing and transformation that is the light of the soul.

It's Available to You Now By Asking it to Emerge

Since this light is really the reconnection to one's soul, anyone can access it and experience it. Once you know about it, you can begin to have your soul reveal itself to you by putting your attention on it, acknowledging it, and inviting it to emerge. It then automatically begins raising your frequency and making changes in your life. Light, energy, intelligence, and love essence are accessed by holding attention on the soul's presence and requesting and intending that it awaken, emerge, and initiate transformations. This is a huge key to raising your frequency for ascension. Ascension is about raising your consciousness and ultimately only the soul can do that.

This miraculous presence works by holding your intention for your connection with it to deepen, and it automatically does. You may not notice it for a time when you begin meditating on it, but don't become discouraged. As you continue, it will emerge because you are just calling to your own inner soul nature, so it is a very natural process.

I know that many people have had awe-inspiring experiences, but they may not know what to do after the initial awakening. In many cases, they may feel as though they lose the experience as time goes on. This does not need to be the case. My practical side has always said, "How can I apply this to everyday life?" As you will see, I will show you many practical ways to apply the soul-awakening process to the challenges and concerns of day-to-day living.

An Experience for Everyone

What's exciting to me is that this awakening seems to be able to work for just about everyone. Some people will feel it more than others, especially at first, and each person will have a unique experience with it. Because the soul is composed of a very pure spiritual light, it contains high frequencies and qualities within it, and therefore brings about whatever healing and transformation a person needs. As you begin calling to your soul's miraculous light and presence, you may notice you feel more peaceful and relaxed. Over time, you may see light or feel a vibration in your body. Some people feel heat. Some feel tingling and/or waves of energy. Yet others experience euphoria and bliss. There is no right or wrong experience. Whatever you experience is right for you.

As I see people filling with this energy, I can watch the pure, divine light radiating from them growing brighter and brighter. This experience helps me understand even more fully the many biblical accounts that link spiritual people to light, and the "light" in these instances is the light of the soul depicted in many paintings of saints as halos and glowing auras.

Pain Relief

Several people have been able to use this soul-light energy to reduce their level of pain. One person reported this to me:

My friend had high-level pain which she reported to be at 9 on a scale of 10. After thirty minutes of sitting with the miraculous light swirling through her, the pain level dropped to 0 and she said if it comes up again, she knows how to use the energy to relieve her pain. Another person with foot pain found that the energy eliminated the pain. Three days later, the pain returned, and she said, "I just told the soul to go fix my foot and it did!

More Than Healing

Needless to say, healing is a very important aspect of the miraculous light, yet the effects of the light extend beyond healing the body to causing spiritual transformations. In this connection, one person wrote to me about how she experienced a deeply felt spiritual "love" through the miraculous light of the soul:

I want to thank you very much for all you have done for me. The experience of the energy transfer that you gave me on Saturday was awesome and amazing. It felt to me like love was embracing my whole body. I have felt more awake and alive ever since then. I thank you for this amazing experience!

The effects of this process on spiritual transformation are, perhaps, the most amazing and important. One man wrote the following:

It seems so other worldly, yet so simple. I am certainly changed. I feel a calmness never before experienced, a quiet thought that all is well and I need not keep beating my head against the proverbial wall. The clearing of negative debris has had a felt effect. I do feel the lightness of being that you predicted, but much more, a deeper sensitivity to nature, as if I look around and all is, as Wordsworth would say, "appareled in a celestial light," yet a light radiating from within that shines on the world around.

The result is a state of being with such feelings of love and unity; words prove inadequate. I've experienced a little of this before in moments, but not as intensely or profoundly as today. I look around and see, as it were, through new eyes as if all is somewhat etherealized. I'm deep into a honeymoon of consciousness; the world is a different place. God bless you for your work and your generosity to share it.

A Few Words in Summary

I do not want to imply that everyone will have the same or similar experiences. I have found that everyone is unique and therefore responds differently. Some do not notice much of anything externally in the beginning of accessing it, while others experience dramatic changes. For some it takes months of meditating to notice the effects. However, even if you don't have profound experiences, making the inner connections with the divine light and soul that radiates within you is still very important. Let me explain why this is so.

When I first started working with the soul and other subtle realities, I often didn't notice or feel anything. In fact, in the beginning I did not see any visual images. I suspect that my four years in college studying chemistry and physics conditioned my analytical mind to only acknowledge the most tangible and measurable effects. Over time and through meditation practices, I awakened to the subtle influences that normally lie beyond the five major senses.

Here's Some Good News for You:

Your soul already has the many wonderful and beautiful qualities admired in saints and revered teachers, and as you deepen your relationship with your soul, these qualities will automatically emerge in your life. In fact, connecting with your soul and spirit is the key to all miracles you have read or heard about. No doubt, your commitment to ongoing spiritual practices affects your progress. Eventually, everyone will experience all there is to experience. All will be realized and experienced through future shifts in consciousness.

Chapter 30

6-STEP MEDITATION INSTRUCTIONS

With so many approaches on how to meditate, it's time to learn a simple process that works for beginners as well as more advanced practitioners. Many distractions and stressors are in everyone's life these days, and meditation is perhaps the most effective way to deal with all of them. I've personally used this "how to meditate" method, and I continue to benefit from it.

You will need to set aside at least 15-20 minutes, but dedicating 30 minutes or more will be especially helpful.

6 Phases of How to Meditate

Select a place where you can be comfortable and not disturbed or distracted by people, animals, or phones.

PHASE 1 - PREPARATION

Spend a few minutes just in this phase of your session, as sometimes it takes a little time to quieten the mind from the distractions of the day and turn your focus to your spiritual work.

To learn how to meditate effectively you'll need to relax physically, emotionally, and mentally. You'll do this by letting go of anything distracting.

Physically: To remove physical distractions, you need to be comfortable. Find a comfortable position that you can hold for the duration of your practice. Sitting rather than lying down is more advisable to keep you from drifting off. Meditation is not an endurance trial. Yes, you can scratch your nose if it itches and reposition yourself if you are uncomfortable.

Mentally: The media these days relentlessly stirs up worrisome thoughts and troubles. Once you've been exposed to this type of information, you can find your mind fixating on subjects you can do little about resolving, but that doesn't stop the mind from processing the input and grinding away on it.

Most people experience mental activity in the form of repeating thoughts and inner voices. A number of ways can reduce this activity, but a simple way is to accompany your breathing with a soothing visual image such as a quiet and restful natural setting near some calm water.

Emotionally: Your emotions are your reactions to things happening in your life or people around you. People often say or do things that are upsetting, and to successfully learn how to meditate, you'll want to settle those feelings. Here are some ways to do that:

Generally, some form of controlled breathing is helpful at this point. For instance, measured breathing works well to settle your energies.

Here's how it works:

Inhale and exhale to the same slow count from one to five. Actually, any form of slow connected breaths will bring you into the state of greater mental stillness from which greater clarity will emerge. Do this for two or three minutes.

Grounding

The next thing to do that helps is grounding yourself in a very specific way that I have found to be very effective. Grounding helps you to settle your energies and quiet your mind. The way I suggest you ground yourself is by directing your attention to form a connection from the base of your spine to the center of the earth. This works far better than imaging little roots coming out the bottom of your feet, which is what many people do. It is not necessary to "see" this connection in your mind's eye even though I use the term "visualize" to activate it. Many people simply hold an intention and conceptualize the image.

The image that I find that works most effectively is to imagine you are sitting on a tree stump (the color of wood) three feet in diameter. This will serve as a grounding connection. The trunk of the tree and its roots go deep into the earth all the way to the center. Keeping the diameter of your grounding connection the same all the way to the center of the earth is important.

Your first chakra is located at the base of your spine. Its energies move downward into the column of energy you have created with your intention, and it has a wonderful stabilizing effect on your whole being. You will find that when you are well grounded that your thinking and memory improve, you are more focused, you feel more stable, and you have more ownership of your space and therefore you are not as affected by others.

This form of grounding does two other important things. It helps to keep you in the present moment, and it gives you a way to release anything distracting. Here's what I mean: It is natural to collect subtle-energy and thoughts from other people, organizations, and places you have been. These subtle energies affect your feelings, thoughts, and reactions. Think of your grounding connection functioning something like a drain in a shower or bathtub; it gives what you are washing off and releasing a place to go. You can imagine what a shower would be like with no drain. Now imagine that you have no outlet for the accumulated energies. Without an easy escape, they will condense and settle into your organs and systems and stay resident in your body, aura, and chakras.

Once you establish good grounding, declare your intention that it stay in place at all times. You will find it helps you all through the day. In fact, if you turn your attention to it a few times throughout the day, you will always be in a grounded state. Then when you are in your meditation practice, it will only take a few seconds for you to turn your attention to your grounding and hold the intention that it removes any energy that isn't yours or which doesn't positively support you. This simple grounding process, which only takes a few seconds a day, can be of immense value to you in both meditation and everyday life.

PHASE 2 – CENTER YOUR AWARENESS IN YOUR HEART

The second phase of your meditative practice is to center yourself in a place where you can have more clarity and begin your connections with your Soul or True Self. Everyone's consciousness has a point of focus. If you pay attention to yourself right now and tune into your inner space, you can become aware of where your awareness is focused. It is usually focused on an area that is holding your attention. For instance, if you have a pain in your shoulder, you are likely to find your awareness at least partially focused somewhere near your shoulder. If your mind is active your awareness is probably somewhere in or around your head. In some cases, it can even be outside of your body, in front of you, in which case you are likely to feel a little spacey, unfocused, or forgetful. If you are feeling stressed or tense, the tension may be in your abdomen near your solar plexus. You've no doubt heard the expression, "What does your gut tell you that you should do about a situation?" When you are tuned into your "gut," you will find your awareness focused somewhere around your abdomen.

Another area where your attention can usually be found is in your chest or heart area. Some people carry grief, sadness, regret, and feeling betrayed in the chest area. Of course, this is also the area where love and compassion are felt. Your chest area has an important value in how to meditate because your Higher Self and Soul are most easily accessed through the heart center. So put your attention on your heart center in the upper center of your chest. It is usually helpful to gently place one hand over the center of your chest and reverently say to yourself, "I ask the peaceful soul presence of love and light to emerge in my heart."

Sit quietly with that for a minute or so to allow yourself to connect with the words and the inner presence. You can repeat that request several times, and each time deepening your connections with what the words represent. You may not notice anything other than feeling more relaxed and peaceful.

PHASE 3 – CONNECT WITH YOUR HIGHER SELF & SOUL

As you learn how to meditate, you may just feel a quietness come over you, but in time a felt presence emerges. Repeating some statements in a mantra like process helps. Some suggestions are, "I feel my Soul. I feel Divine love in my heart. I am peaceful." Alternatively, you can repeat a name of God such as, "Yahweh, Allah, Alleluia, I Am that I Am, Amma, Baba, Adonai, or simply, I am love." The idea is to repeat something that helps you make an inner connection with a peaceful, inner essence. Repeat your mantra softly to yourself while moving your lips and be silent for about 15-30 seconds between each time you repeat the mantra.

As you repeat these statements for several minutes, you will find yourself connecting more and more deeply each time you repeat the words. You will sink more deeply into your experience of discovering your true nature that is an expression of infinite love and light.

Attuning Deeper to Inner Guidance

Intend to deepen the connection each time. After a number of minutes, you may notice that a shift takes place within you. This can take anywhere from a few minutes to 30 minutes or more. In the beginning weeks of meditating, you may not feel very differently, but if you stay with the practice you will eventually feel supported, comforted, and spiritually awake. At this point, compare how you are feeling with what you were feeling in the past before you meditated.

The meditation itself will guide you in where and how to explore next. You will be taught from within. Once you feel you have reached a nice state for the meditation through the repetition, practice sitting in peaceful stillness and attune yourself to the subtle impulses that arise. Be willing to stay out of judgment to allow the new awareness to arise.

Be Patient and Understanding with Yourself

Meditation is an ever-improving skill the more you do it. In time, you will find yourself attuned to your inner spiritual connection nearly all the time. It can become a continuous inner communion with your divine connection throughout the day. You will begin to feel a harmony and congruity as you align with inner guidance and you will feel "off-track" when you are not. Step-by-step the controlling mind relinquishes its grip as it realizes you are guided through an inner direction that heals fear, struggle, and suffering.

In the early stages of this practice, you may not be seeing, feeling or hearing much of anything and assume you are either doing it wrong, or something is wrong with you that prevents you from success. Neither of these conclusions is true. Judging yourself, becoming impatient, and having doubts will prevent deepening into the meditative state. Continue with your daily practice, for no matter how long it takes to open your receptivity, you will succeed if you persist, and the rewards are well worth everything you put into your practice.

PHASE 4 – INTEGRATION

The fourth phase is integrating your experience before you bring yourself back to your normal day-to-day world. In this phase, you relax your mind, let go of any questions, and become still. Sense and feel the peacefulness and expansion. You will want to rest in this phase for at least five minutes and maybe longer. Give yourself permission to fully surrender yourself and merge into your deepest truth. You may rest in this phase for a little while or a long while, depending on what feels appropriate.

PHASE 5 – GRATITUDE

The fifth phase is to express gratitude for your session, regardless of your perception of your meditation's nature or quality. Gratitude is a form of surrender that opens you to higher awareness a little more each time you express and feel it. Say to yourself, "I am grateful for all I have received today from my meditation. I bless my life with love and light."

PHASE 6 – RECONNECT

Very gradually reconnect awareness to your five senses Notice sounds, feelings, and sensations.

Take several deep breaths before opening your eyes, savor the air and notice the feelings in your body. Relish the way you feel as you begin to stretch your body.

Be mindful of not contracting or tensing at the thought of returning to your normal day. Hold the intention to maintain the peaceful space from your meditation.

As you return to your normal activities, you may think you are losing what you experienced in the meditation, but know that your awareness has stretched from where it was to a new experience of yourself and your spiritual connections.

As the day goes on, you may find that you "pop" in and out of the awareness gained in the meditation. This indicates that you are changing. Notice how the new insights live in the back of your mind throughout the day providing a fresh experience of whatever is before you.

The more you meditate and connect with the inner you, the more you realize that your outer perceptions have been limiting and confining, as the inner truths of love and light begin to emerge from within. Your awareness gradually awakens to reveal your inner core essence of love, light, and beauty.

Chapter 31

OPEN YOUR HEART TO YOUR TRUTH OF LOVE

If you hold the intention to receive, you can experience a significant leap in your level of consciousness. The only obstacle is your mind because it always engages perceptions through the senses.

Self-discovery is about discovering an expanding awareness of love because love is the core of your nature. It is the nature of what you are below the traits of the ego. Therefore, what is needed is to deepen your realization of love, and that is your path home to enlightened awareness. Your core soul essence is made from a fabric of love. Humans are somewhat unique in their capability to be creative and innovative. They also have the capability to feel, give, and receive love, a true miracle.

When you feel love, you are feeling your soul and spirit. This is the purpose of your existence, and therefore the direction of your evolution. To feel love is to remember who you truly are. That is your true essence and the gateway is through the heart center. Your heart center is the entry point that enables you to reconnect more easily and completely with your divine essence.

Everyone talks about love being the way, but the love I speak of is not just an idea, a feeling, or a platitude. It is a frequency and realization that transports you to another level where you become love. You become an embodiment of love in total surrender to love. I'll describe a way for you to apply this in your life right now.

Self-Guided Love Meditation

Sit back, relax. Let go of any distracting thoughts. Feel a relaxing wave of peace move through you as your entire physical being is becoming calm and relaxed. Give yourself permission to tune into the nature of the soul, which is the real you below the personality traits. As you relax, open your heart to allow the soul to emerge. Open yourself to grace, spiritual presence, and love.

Imagine the soul is a beautiful angel wrapping its wings of love and light around you. Merge with that feeling and enjoy it.

Open your heart as if you are stretching and opening your capacity to feel and receive love. As you breathe out, let go of whatever has kept you from feeling love and peace. Open to receive more grace, love, and divine presence. Let your body and mind be a pure vehicle for that love.

What excuse is your mind using to keep you from connecting with deep love? Let it go. Let go of whatever doesn't serve you. Let go of anything keeping you from deep love. Say to yourself, "I'm willing to surrender and release the need for this block to love."

You have the ability to receive deep love because you are made of love. You only need a willingness to surrender and open all receptors to the full expression of love.

- Open every cell of your body to that love.
- Be like a sponge to soak it up and embrace it.
- Dissolve into the healing feelings of love.
- Let yourself go and enjoy the feelings.

Allow the love to deepen and expand the feelings of love and being loved until you become conscious of love as the fullness of your nature.

Feel your heart open to receive effortlessly.

Repeat the following statements silently to yourself and make them your own:

- I am willing to surrender all my past where I have not seen myself as love.
- I am willing to surrender my need for all thoughts and beliefs that I am not worthy or capable of deep love.
- My purpose is to know love and be love.
- I am love.
- I feel love.

Relax now and become totally filled, saturated, and transformed with deep love.

By surrendering all that you think love is, you embrace a deeper experience of love.

One of the differences between the love you have known and the deep love of which I speak is that the love many talk about is associated with an emotional feeling. You've probably used the phrases, "I feel love," or "I feel like I am in Love." Deep love, however, is not just something you feel on an emotional level that comes and goes, but it is more inclusive, expansive, experiential, and permanent.

The heart offers you the path to enlightenment, not the mind, so open your heart completely to receive the presence of your soul's nature. It is easiest to experience deep love presence through your heart center in the center of your chest. Put a hand over the upper center of your chest. This helps bring your focus there and opens you to the soul's love. Merge into the feelings as you move deeper and deeper into the frequencies and feelings coming in.

Let love in and continue to notice the sensations throughout your body.

As you practice deepening your awareness of love, you will become conscious of being a source of love. It is not you the person, but it is you, the essence, the soul, which is love and light and the essence of what you are. This process awakens you to your connection to the Source of all. No other comparable force exists in the universe.

Imagine your heart space growing, your soul expanding, and your love increasing. Surrender any objections. Melt into the feeling. Let yourself go. Observe your feelings and breathe into your heart. Feel love flowing through your body.

When you become the resonator of love, your presence activates it in others because they too are love but may not know it yet. Deep love is what you are, and it is an important part of self-discovery. As you surrender to deep love, you will discover an awareness of your soul's essence made of love. Invite the Soul's essence to embrace every atom of your being. Say these words to yourself:

"I invite and open myself to receive the deepest love into every atom and cell of my consciousness."

Love is the ultimate power in the universe and no effort is required to experience it. You are a divine incarnation of love. Surrender to become the embodiment of love. Each day open to love a little more.

Many people try to get love from other human beings, but when they are connected with the deep love of the soul, it doesn't' really matter whether another person is able to give love or not because everyone has it within. Deep love has always been the greater part of you, your core essence. It is who you are and it will continue to flow through you naturally and automatically as you surrender to it. Deep love is the key to moving to the next step in your evolution. Request that it permeate all levels of your consciousness. Be like a sponge and totally saturate yourself with deep love. Feel it, experience it, know it, absorb it, be it. Be Love! Carry with you the full awareness that you are always and continually will be an open-hearted, radiant source of deep love for everyone and everything.

Chapter 32

SELF-INQUIRY TO DISCOVER YOUR TRUE SELF

The essence of Ghana or Jana (pronounced: ghee-ah-n) is a path of self-reflection, self-inquiry, and direct awareness. It is more correctly pronounced ghee-ah-n or yahn. It relates to self-discovery, which is rooted in thousands of years of study on the nature of the self.

The Bible, which although it has many valuable and inspiring lessons and teachings, doesn't go into the philosophy of the nature of the self in the way that some of the ancient documents of India do. These are among the oldest documents ever recorded. They contain the oldest continuing lineage of thought that has ever existed, and they certainly contain some of the deepest and most profound insights into the nature of reality, the self, God, and humanity. Among these are the Vedas that are considered the oldest scriptures ever discovered written by the Rishis who were the holy ones living somewhere around 5-8,000 years ago. The Rig Veda, considered the oldest of the writings covers the nature of the self, the nature of God, and the purpose of existence. Several Vedas make up what are called the Upinashads and later the Vedanta, which means the sum of the Vedas or the sum of wisdom of the ancient yogi writings. This led to Advaita, which is transcending the known and entering non-duality.

Ramana Marharshi from south India was one of the teachers of non-duality to bring self-inquiry into the forefront of meditative practice in the late 1900s. He is the one who modern westerners became aware of who taught the practice of inquiring into the nature of the self with such inquiries as "Who am I?" as a way of coming to know the self. Another teacher of non-duality was Sri Nisargadatta Maharaj who wrote the book, *I Am That*. It is a deeply transcendental book and has profound wisdom and is among the best works written on the topic.

Self-inquiry leads you to know yourself and the nature of reality through self-reflection. This is an effective approach to transcending cognitive mental processes and delving into consciousness itself. It is a way of bending your stream of attention away from the mental activity of the mind which causes your attention to look upon your own consciousness. All self-inquiry eventually leads to a state of consciousness beyond mental activity or analysis and even beyond belief or perspectives. It leads to a suspension of any sense of self where the meditator disappears in what is called Samadhi. All that remains is an awareness of a stream of consciousness. In this state, you experience a profound understanding of all life and a total sense of being one with all existence. No amount of thinking or analysis can prepare you for this experience or lead you to it. As you let go of the mind and all its workings, an automatic expansion of consciousness takes place.

True Samadhi creates an awakening that recognizes that prior life was a life of deep sleep. There is a sense that you were just going through the motions of life without fully participating or being aware of who you are or what was taking place. A vastness without thought characterizes the Samadhi state, an emptiness full and complete, and a sense of not just being one with all existence, but also being all existence. This is why it is called non-duality: a state with no differentiations or sense of separateness.

Many states of consciousness exist. You might even enter Samadhi thousands of times experiencing peace and unity. Then, one day, you never fully return to the "normal" human state. You enter a continuous state of being one with all there is. When this occurs the pain and suffering experienced previously melts away. The ego vanishes and circumstances are no longer experienced in the same painful context as they once were, and for this reason one is said to be liberated.

How to Reach Samadhi

Samadhi is generally, but not always, accessed through meditation and especially through self-inquiry and what is called witnessing or observing the mind, the body, the breath, sensations, and thoughts.

To be effective, meditation must be engaged in regularly. Therefore, setting up a program and a schedule to meditate is important for furthering your spiritual evolution. It doesn't really work effectively to try to squeeze meditation into your life or catch a few minutes on a lunch break. It's just too easy to find something else you think you need to do more.

The morning has advantages for meditation because you are rested and the mind is not stimulated. Most people find the morning works well, but the evenings can also be quite good, especially later in the evening. I would also recommend trying the middle of the night at least on occasion, between 2 and 4. A deep stillness at that time helps you achieve remarkable clarity and a sense of deep presence.

The question then becomes what you do when you meditate. Listening to a guided meditation is certainly an easy way to approach it, but meditating apart from a guided process is also valuable and important.

One form of meditation particularly helpful is Self-Inquiry. This method is especially helpful because others have defined you early in life by giving you your name, dressing you in certain ways, teaching you how to behave, telling you what is important to know, defining for you right from wrong, etc. At some point, you come to realize that the ways you have been defined and identified by others no longer works for you. So you seek to define yourself. This often happens by analyzing your successes, and failures, and feedback from other people. Typically, at each new stage of life, you reach new definitions and descriptions of yourself. As life goes on, you continue to redefine yourself based on your changing likes and dislikes and what you value and cease to value. Self-inquiry may lead to consciously or unconsciously asking yourself "who am I, really." The question "who am I" can be expanded by asking, "What do I really want?"

Everyone is seeking something. You may think, "What I want is the right mate; I want to be happy; I want to live on a tropical island; I want to have a great job. I want a red sports car and millions in my bank account." Many people have these desires, but the follow-up question needs to be, "What will they give me?" If you have the perfect mate, job, and living location, what will these give you? If you answer satisfaction, fulfillment, happiness, and peace, I would reply, "You can have all of these right now," because all external searching is really for something internal. Moreover, a way to arrive at that internal state is through self-inquiry. Self-inquiry can provide what you really want and lead you to discover who you really are.

The person you think you are is the personality operating through your mind, and it needs to become an observer rather than a doer.

Mental activity such as analyzing your questions and answers contracts your awareness and blocks realizations which is why most never awaken. They are busy trying to figure it all out mentally, and they become lost in the myths and analysis their minds create.

Start Your Self-Inquiry Here

Get in touch with the part of you that is looking to evolve yourself and ask what is it seeking?

A place to start self-inquiry is to ask, "Who is wanting? That would seem logical, but if you say, "I want," you aren't going far enough with the question. The "I" you have believed you are is a constructed personality. What it wants is driven by emotional reactions and programs created through desires. If you define yourself by desires, personality, and possessions, you ignore your deeper history of the many lives you've had as well as who you will come to be. All concepts of self actually cloud your experience and mask the realization of your true identity.

Thinking that your personality defines you is problematic because your personality is always changing. You certainly are not the same personality you were when you were five years old or in high school. In fact, most have gone through any number of personality changes over the years. Your personality can even change somewhat from day-to-day, depending on what kind of a mood you are in. Each mood can be called a sub-personality. This includes being upset, having a down day, or experiencing anxiety. The opposite could also be true. You might suddenly feel unexplainably happy or giddy.

You might also think you are your character and values, but these are also constructed personality traits that drive you and define your nature. Yet, there is something about who you are that transcends personality and character. It is an inner essence that you intuitively sense that is difficult to define.

When you are in touch with your inner essence, you sense a deeper truth. This is your true self, and it is always present under the personality and character traits. It is below who you imagine yourself to be. You discover this through natural revelations, through meditation, and especially through self-inquiry. Self-inquiry reveals your true self and the nature of reality. All you have to do is reflect on yourself. If you want to know what you look like, you look at a reflection of yourself in a mirror. No effort is required just as no effort is required to discover what you physically look like looking in a mirror. Self-reflection is an inner mirror that reveals the true self.

To understand your own nature, you reflect on yourself through inquiry. This approach transcends analytical reasoning and delves into consciousness itself. It diverts your attention away from analysis in order to observe your own consciousness. All self-inquiry eventually leads to a state of consciousness that is beyond mental activity or analysis and even beyond beliefs or perspectives. It leads to a suspension of any sense of a separate self where the meditator disappears in an expanded awareness. This leads to a profound understanding of life with a total sense of being one with all existence. No amount of thinking or analyzing can prepare you for this experience or lead you to it. The opposite is actually the case. As you let go of the mind and all its workings, an automatic shift occurs and an expansion of consciousness takes place.

When a spiritual awakening occurs, you recognize that life prior to it was one of deep sleep. There is a sense that you were just going through the motions of life without fully being aware of who you are or what was taking place. Before the shift happens these words may not make sense to the analytical mind because most people think they are awake in every sense they understand the word to mean. However, the spiritually awakened state encompasses a vastness without thought, an emptiness that is full and complete with a sense of not just being one with all existence but also actually being all existence. This is why it is called non-duality or God realization. It is a state where no differentiations or separateness exists. It is a state of unity consciousness and dissolution into emptiness.

Many states of consciousness exist, where you might enter transcendence and experience deep peace and oneness. But, then one day you have an ultimate experience from which you never fully return to what is regarded as the normal state. This is an enlightened awakening in which you enter a continuous state of being one with all there is. Sustained peacefulness and joy occur at this level. You feel complete, satisfied, and happy. Of course, this is actually what most people are seeking in their external lives, when ironically all the time it is found living within them. When this consciousness shift happens, the suffering experienced before melts away. Circumstances are no longer experienced in the same painful context as they once were, and for this and other reasons one is said to be liberated.

Take Your Next Inquiry Steps

Attaining this state is generally, but not always, through meditation and especially through self-inquiry and witnessing. Witnessing is an inquiry process of neutrally observing. Witnessing or observing is relatively easy if you follow these instructions:

Be fully present in the here and now. The clearer your mind, the clearer you will be on knowing who you are and why you were born. You have come to a pivotal point in the evolution of your consciousness where you are ready to remember more fully who and what you are and what your purpose in life is. A part of you already knows this, so now just acknowledge the part of you that senses it is ready to evolve itself further and wants to awaken more fully. Relax and enter a meditative state and do the following:

- Witness and observe the mind and body.
- Witness and observe the breath.
- Observe and hold attention on the heart center with the intention of opening and deepening.
- Observe and hold attention on the crown chakra with the intention of opening and expanding.

Whenever you find yourself in emotional pain, mental activity is creating conflict, analysis, judgments, and conclusions, but you are not the body and not the mind. Realize that who you are exists beyond the mind.

Sense yourself in the state of awareness where you are just feeling what is present. This helps you disassociate with what the mind and body have been identifying. You are not trying to make anything happen. In fact, you are not trying at all. You are mostly observing yourself and your feelings, and becoming aware of realizations emerging out of the inquiries such as "who am I?"

Acknowledge the part of you that senses it is ready to evolve itself further and wants to awaken. For instance, you know that whenever you find yourself in emotional pain, mental activity creates conflict and analysis, judgments, and conclusions. What if you realized that you are not the body and not the analytical mind? To help you awaken more, ask yourself some questions about yourself such as:

Who am I when there is no activity in my brain?
Who am I when there are no thoughts?
Who am I without a body?

If you are not the body and not your thoughts, then who are you? Could it be that you are consciousness and awareness beyond the physical experience? Realize that who you are exists beyond the mind. What is left when you let go of what the mind thinks you are?

Sense yourself in the state of awareness where you are just feeling what is present, and say the following words to yourself:

- I am not my body and I am not my mind.
- I am the consciousness observing the mind.
- I am the consciousness expressing through this body.
- I am the expression of consciousness flowing through this body and causing this body and mind to operate.
- I am what is observing the mind.

These affirmations help you acknowledge you are more than the physical body and more than the brain and mind. You disidentify with what the mind and body have been identifying themselves with.

You are not trying to make anything happen.
You are not trying at all.
You are observing yourself.
Observe your feelings.
Become aware of realizations and awakenings that emerge out of the inquiries. Continue with more inquiries.

What part of you wants to know who you are?
What is it that draws you to inquire?
Why do you want to know?
What draws you to a spiritual path?
Go to the source of that.

These inquires remind you of what you already know deep within. They trigger an awakening awareness of a deep truth that lies at the core of your soul. As you hear the words and connect with the consciousness behind the words, you'll notice a ring of truth and a feeling of coming home.

What part of you wants to know all of this?

Be conscious of the part of you seeking ways to be conscious of itself.

Be conscious of the fact that there is a consciousness evolving you.

As you continue inquiring, you will rise to your highest potential. It is a path to enlightenment, one of allowing and not doing. Quit trying and allow what is guiding you to reveal itself.

Analytical thought contracts your awareness and blocks understanding. This is why many never awaken. They are busy trying to figure it all out, and they become lost in the stories and analysis their minds create.

The key is not about understanding information, but opening the heart and awareness, thus allowing the presence of consciousness itself. When you connect with the source within, you feel peace and love.

To fulfill your life's purpose, you must first become conscious of the self that has a purpose to fulfill, which is the part of you that is aware of itself as the real you. A part of you can feel the depth of these words. This is your consciousness and your soul, which are already enlightened. You have only to wake up and self-consciously connect with them. A part of you would like to evolve itself to its highest potential and uncover and realize the truth of its own being. Put another way, your inner being would like to awaken from the diversions of the mind in order to experience the purity of its own nature. This is the ascension of your consciousness and enlightenment.

Chapter 33

HOW GRACE OPENS THE DOOR TO ENLIGHTENMENT

I consider surrender to be not only the most important path to enlightenment but the only path to enlightenment. You will not attain enlightenment as long as you are attached or holding onto any person, place, thing, or concept. Every thing must eventually be surrendered. That is why I return to this subject time and time again. There are two other words that need to be linked with surrender and they are trust and grace. If you are deeply trusting you are also deeply surrendered, and if you are deeply surrendered, you are in a deep state of trust. I covered this in some detail in chapters 24 and 25. Grace comes into the surrender and enlightenment picture because nothing of value can be discovered without grace.

Grace is one of those words religion uses and yet it has a meaning far beyond what most people think. First of all, Western religion doesn't really address or even seem to know about the state of consciousness known in the East as Enlightenment, but it does have some inkling into part of the process that leads to enlightenment, and this is where grace comes in.

Grace is like a gift because it is something you receive, but could not from any person, and not even from yourself no matter how hard you tried. It is a gift that only comes from the creator, the source of all, and it couldn't come from any other source. The reason is because grace is a gift of awakening to an awareness of the truth of your being that underlies all perceptions and judgments. This is a profound statement, and I don't want to go past it too fast. In other words, grace is what leads to your awakening to the highest aspect of your soul and to your enlightened awareness. I know this is not the usual definition of grace preached in traditional church services. In Christianity, grace is defined as "unmerited favor" from God, and it is certainly that. There is nothing a human being can do to pay for, bargain for, work for, or strive for to cause enlightenment. That would be equivalent to the ego's trying to enlighten itself, which is ridiculous. On the other hand, you must take action to arrive at the place for the gift of enlightenment to occur.

In order to become enlightened, which means to release the ego needs and drives, something beyond the ego must come into play. Beyond the ego is your divine source, soul, and deepest truth.

Grace is traditionally described as a gift from God for development, improvement, and character growth without which there would be limitations, weaknesses, flaws, and impurities which humans could not overcome on their own. In the sense that these perceptions are all ego characteristics, this would be true. It takes grace or enlightened awareness to transcend the perceptions of the ego which is composed of limitations, weaknesses, flaws and impurities. In another sense, however, even this is not exactly true since those are all illusions. None of the limitations, weaknesses, flaws, and impurities are actually real or true, but perceiving them to be true makes them true to the perceiver. This is where grace comes in because grace is about transcending illusions.

The well known parable of the Prodigal Son (Luke 15:11-32) is traditionally understood as containing the teachings of Jesus on grace. (The word Prodigal is not a word we use in day-to-day conversation, but it means spending money or substance with wasteful extravagance). In this parable, a son demands the family fortune and then goes out and wastes it. Then humiliated he returns home expecting little in the way of good treatment, but his father welcomes him back with open arms and a great celebration over the objections of his other son who stayed at home and was a good son. The older brother resents the favored treatment of his faithless brother and complains of the lack of reward for his own faithfulness.

But the father responds, "Son, you are ever with me, and all that I have is yours. (This is a metaphor for being in unity and at one with God). It was the right thing to do to be happy and have a celebration because your brother was dead, (living through the ego) and is alive again; he was lost, and now he is found." (Came back into unity).

Many throughout Christian history have perceived in this parable that the grace of God is something that upsets human reactions about what is deserved and what is due as payment and consequence. This goes to the common ego "instinct" of justice and fairness.

Grace comes through being surrendered. By letting go of all judgments and all resistance, you release all need to be in control and discover that you don't have to be. Grace is completely letting go of the past in every form, at every level, and in every way. In the parable the son living with ego surrenders the ego life and in returning home finds the door open. When you are surrendered, something beyond your conscious awareness takes over and by being surrendered you stay open to receiving the gifts of liberation from illusions to awaken and realize the truth of your being, which is your enlightened soul.

How to Receive Grace

1. First Prequisite for Receiving Grace. In order to receive the gifts of grace it is necessary to surrender and let go of the ego and all of its attributes such as fear, shame, guilt, anger, and persistent feelings of being unworthy, which is the self-judgment of not being good enough and feeling that you are a mistake and your life is a mistake. Grace doesn't work in the field of these kinds of perceptions so they must eventually be surrendered. Once you've successively surrendered all these things, a sense of awakening and liberation opens and carries you into an awareness of truth.

All the gifts of grace emerge as a result of surrendering and letting go of everything that separates you from your divine truth. You can't earn grace. You can't control grace and you don't even have to deserve grace. You just have to surrender what you think and believe in order to realize who and what you are, and then you automatically return to your real home in unity with God.

Grace operates outside of certain very natural human ways of doing things. For instance, people want to believe they are in control. In fact, people feel like they need to be in control in order not to feel out of control. People assume they can do specific things to ensure that they are rewarded. So since everything in life is earned through hard work and effort, it is natural to assume and expect that they need to do something to rise to the top spiritually. Most expect the gifts of God to be given out according to some recognizable plan that entails rules, conditions, prerequisites, and effort. To a certain degree you certainly have a role to play. You must be honest with yourself at a deep level, surrender and let go of whatever you have been holding on to that gives you an identity that you value.

2. Second Prequisite for Receiving Grace. A way of practicing surrender, in addition to the obvious, is to practice gratitude by saying "thank you" for both happy as well as challenging experiences. Gratitude offers you several gifts such as relaxing and releasing resistance, and

gratitude opens the doors of acceptance making you available to receive. So you can practice gratitude by saying:

- Thank you for all the people in my life.
- Thank you for all the plants and animals on earth.
- Thank you for art and music.
- Thank you for all experiences, memories, and dreams.
- Thank you for all blessings, and all goodness in my life…
- I appreciate everything and everyone I encounter.

Now I know this sounds simple enough, but gratitude is not always as simple as it may seem at first. For example, often instead of being happy and content with what you have, you may find the ego-driven mind greedily wants something more, better, or different; however, the ego can't be grateful while it is making comparisons and wanting and desiring more. For this reason it takes practice to be grateful all the time for all things.

3. Third Prequisite for Receiving Grace. Another aspect of receiving grace is to be open to receiving with effortless effort. Most people go through life working hard at what they do, yet some seem to be continually moving forward with amazing ease while others appear to be fighting a daily grind. "Effortless Effort" is a Taoist concept although it is also a basic way to approach life.

Effortless effort describes a state in which the world seems to be working for you rather than you working for the world. It is a state in which you feel calm yet alert, focused yet receptive, and immersed in an energy stream that flows with ease. In this state you are not disturbed by the storms surrounding you because you are standing in the peaceful eye of any storm. In other words, outer conditions and circumstances do not control your inner space. In this state hard work does not feel like hard labor. Effortless effort is not inertia, laziness, or passivity. Rather, it is like swimming with the current or *going with the flow*. Effortless effort arises from a sense of being connected to your soul, others, and the environment.

In the words of Chuang Tzu, a Chinese philosopher from the fourth century B.C., we must learn "detachment, forgetfulness of results, and abandonment of all hope of profit." This is just another way of saying be surrendered. By allowing the Tao or Divine Presence to work through you, all your actions truly flow naturally and effortlessly. As a result you flow with all experiences and feelings as they come and go.

The approach of effortless effort is related to the concept of non-doing which is a difficult idea for Westerners to understand because people are conditioned to action, control, and doing to make anything happen. Westerners who contemplate Effortless effort often ask, "How can we not do when there's so much to do?"

This is not at all a contradiction, as it at first appears to be. There is the acknowledgement that some effort is required to exist. You get up in the morning, get ready for the day, eat, and do what is before you for that day. That takes effort, but the energy behind the effort has an ease and flow to it because you are surrendered and not in resistance to anything. Therefore, you are automatically in a state of harmony and synchronicity.

You become aware of a deep reality when you are not doing anything, all the ripples of the mind have subsided, and your whole being is simply silent. All desires have left and there is deep peace, quiet, and stillness. In that moment of total surrender, the totality of wholeness, completion, and unity comes to you. You are accepted by grace. Without any effort, you just float in the ocean of consciousness. You can practice developing being in the flow of life by being a neutral observer, open to ideas, experiences, people, the world, and the sacred without judgments. Openness is an ability to go with the flow, as Taoism puts it, without expecting predetermined outcomes. It means being receptive to new possibilities without prejudging them. It is an ability to make yourself available to all opportunities. The contrast to openness is a mind that judges and has a narrow view. It is characterized by a rigidity of mind. For instance, pessimistic people who have armored themselves against preconceived disappointments are not open, and dogmatic and stubborn people are often inaccessible.

How flexible are you with regard to your beliefs? How interested are you in people, especially those whose beliefs are quite different from you? How firmly do you hold your opinions? How willing are you to try something new? These are the questions to ask to assess your non-resistance and openness.

The Final Threshold

Now let's get back to the most important subject of all: the final ego release and enlightening experience. Grace applies to all the steps leading up to this culmination as I have been describing, but the final and most important one is the final release. This is the one where all resistance in every form lets go. This is only achieved through deep, complete, and total surrender. All ideas, beliefs, fears, perceptions, reactions, and desires must be released.

At that point, something truly incredible happens. The idea of letting go to this degree creates thoughts that everything would be lost, yet this never happens. What does happen is completion: The complete dissolution of separation and complete merging back into the realization that your awareness is the awareness of all there is. There is only one awareness and that is what is called God, the Tao, Brahman, The Absolute and undifferentiated awareness that underlies all existence. The experience is beyond words. To even say there is a sensation and a realization is not quite accurate, because it is truly beyond words and impossible to put in words because as soon as you attach word symbols to the experience in an attempt to define it, you lose it.

Everything is understood, fulfilled, and complete through grace. In other words, you do all you have to do to get to the threshold through surrender, and then you automatically awaken through grace. The experience is a little like opening your eyes in the morning to experience a reality quite different from the dreams you have been dreaming.

Grace is the awakening or enlightening of your awareness to the truth of your being that underlies all your perceptions and judgments. Surrender leads you to the place where you can receive the grace that awakens you to the enlightened state of your inner being, your true self, and to God Realization.

Chapter 34

NON-DUAL ALIGNMENT

The path to an enlightened state of consciousness is all about entering a fully surrendered state. Most people experience day-to-day duality, which means perception of being distinctly and profoundly separate rather than unified with all creation. In the dual state, the senses define reality. On the other hand, surrendered awareness or unity consciousness is experienced as a transcendent state disengaged from what Socrates referred to as the world of "sensual pleasures" that like leaden weights drag people down and turn awareness of their souls to things that are below.

Duality can perhaps be understood through analogy. Imagine a chalice made of gold. The gold and the chalice are not two separate things. The gold is still as much gold as it ever was before being made into a chalice. What is the difference? The gold has been given form. Previously it was a lump of gold. Once it has form, we give it a name. We call it a Chalice. This is called dualism, which is assigning form and name. If you put the chalice in the ocean, seawater fills it and is all around it. The water inside mingles with the water outside and all the water becomes one and indistinguishable. The form of the chalice is what kept the water inside separate from the water outside, but the water in the chalice and the ocean are the same. You are like the chalice maintaining a form but filled and surrounded with the same spirit essence that permeates everything.

The form is a concept with a label and a description, and the conception is a name called a chalice. It can change form and be remolded into something else. If that happens, the form of the chalice ends even though the gold is still there. This is birth and death: birth of a chalice and death of a chalice. In both conditions, the gold remains gold throughout. In all creation, the underlying intelligent spirit of creation remains the same. The chalice is made of spirit with a particular form. The universe is made out of spirit essence or intelligent essence.

What makes anything distinct or different from the underlying intelligent spiritual essence behind all appearances is dualism. The distinction is formed through labels, definitions, judgments, and beliefs in the labels and definitions. The essence and emanation of the underlying intelligent essence behind all appearances will always remain the same whether the form changes or not. This is the phenomenon of birth, death, and rebirth. Only forms, conceptions, names, and definitions change. They define something as distinct within the ocean of divine essence.

An enlightened perspective focuses on the underlying spiritual essence behind all appearances and not the form. People tend to identify with the chalice or form, which is not permanent. It can change form and when it does, this can lead to disappointment and unhappiness because all form is always changing. By virtue of being in a physical universe, we inhabit an existence composed of form, but we have the amazing capability of simultaneously also experiencing unity awareness.

What is The Practical Use of This Information?

There is a very practical side to all of this. When you integrate the surrendered state, you can utilize this awareness for healing and clearing issues usually addressed with limited effectiveness by other methods. Your surrendered reality can be used as a means of attaining an incredibly clear state from which to experience life. Most people seek techniques trying to fix what is wrong. This approach offers some usefulness of course, but the surrendered approach brings a shift in consciousness to a higher state of awareness that transcends conflicts and difficulties.

A surrendered way of clearing and healing acknowledges the healing power of the deep inner self or Soul, or the *un*conditioned mind. This refers to a higher aspect that is not conditioned, affected, or changed in quality by personal history. This is the key to accessing the underlying truth and essence of what you really are. This process awakens and anchors you in the ever-present experience of pure and peaceful consciousness.

The marvel of the unconditioned mind, or the non-attached, surrendered mind, is that it leads to completion, happiness, and fulfillment. When you bring this consciousness to any condition or situation, an inner shift happens and you no longer view it in the same way. If you have been meditating for a while, you undoubtedly have noticed that you feel very differently when you are in meditation and for a while when you come out of a meditation. After meditating for a few months or years, you will notice that you do not react to situations the way you used to. There is much more equanimity. If you have experienced this, you are experiencing your surrendered truth.

The surrendered consciousness is the consciousness not fixated on the form or experience. It has the awareness that nothing needs to change externally in fact, your experience of everything changes because you are oriented to it differently. Emotions, reactions, and perceptions may still arise for a while, but you are no longer enslaved by them. You become much more of an observer of your reactions. The more you live in this state, the less you find yourself being pulled into the whirlpool of reactions, judgments, and emotions that formerly engaged you, and therefore you create more peaceful and healthy experiences. A surrendered state of awareness is so wonderful because your outer experiences no longer determine your inner experiences. Your education, finances, history, or even physical conditions do not limit the quality of your life. Additionally, the surrendered state enriches your relationships. You will find yourself at peace and intimately connected with everything within and around you. You will sustain a state of contentment and happiness. You are also likely to find your relationships enriched as you become aware of the interconnection you have with each person and everything else in your environment. In Buddhism, the experience of the *un*conditioned mind is called the "ultimate medicine" because it is universally healing, whereas other more conventional therapies have limitations. When you rest in this state, also called resting in presence or in the enlightened awareness of your soul, it is impossible to worry, be angry, or have fear. You no longer battle your conditions.

Resistance melts and you experience satisfaction with life and existence. Life assumes an effortless quality and harmony. An additional benefit is that this state opens natural channels for healing qualities to emerge and flow through you, bringing you progressively into more balance and health. The experience of residing in this state gradually merges through all layers of your conditioned mind and emotions and changes the very structure of your habitual thinking, perceiving, and feeling. This process is sometimes described as the transformation of the very structural foundations of your being. Through connecting with the state of pure being, the energies and mechanisms that condition your life lose their power to distort your experience and cause pain and suffering.

The soul merge process expands surrendered presence of the enlightened soul and integrates it in and through all aspects of your being. It focuses on enhancing the qualities of your soul in the present moment rather than struggling with the past or what might happen in the future. This process focuses on what you are rather than what you think you are. It cuts through stories about what happened, what should have happened, or what might happen, while bringing a presence of love and light through all fixations and resistance. The soul merge process is not denying anything, but embracing everything with a new surrendered presence. It is not about disconnecting from people or life, but about bringing newness to every experience and relationship.

No effort or struggle is needed with this approach since your soul is your unique expression of the divine or the transcendent through your life. Therefore, no conflict occurs between your physical life and your experience of spiritual transcendence. In fact, you can embrace the physical with your transcendent nature.

Where Are You Aligned?

The soul merge approach requires you to identify a disturbance and then disidentify from it. First you must acknowledge you have perceived a disturbance. Describe or define the experience. Then shift into the surrendered state to acknowledge that your reality is not the form or perception of the issue, but the presence of essence beyond all form. Surrender all resistance to the experience and release all resistance to whatever you are experiencing. This de-energizes the forces creating and sustaining the disturbance, making them disappear. As a result you will feel more at peace and fulfilled.

One of the big challenges to the surrendered approach to life is the characteristic of our modern culture that keeps us busy and active. Simply "being" is interpreted as being unproductive. I know people who can't even sit still for an hour and listen to music or watch a movie unless they are also doing something else, such as reading a book, doing some writing, talking on the phone, or sending texts.

If a problem arises, the standard response is that it must be addressed now. The surrendered approach however is different; it is about letting go of all effort and struggle and resting in the peace of the moment. Letting go in a surrendered way means you need to do nothing. You are free of being driven or having compulsions. The concept of resting in the surrendered state can trigger both positive and negative associations in the mind.

While the surrendered approach comes bundled with ideas of expansion, freedom, and liberation, you might think you will lose touch with the real world and become less interested or capable. It may sound like transcending desire and accepting life as it is implies life will be bland, boring, and uninteresting. You might be inclined to conclude you will not be motivated. These, however, are just mental projections and are not true.

To the unenlightened the surrendered state can seem like a vast, empty expanse of non-attachment without life or humanity in it. The ego fears this perception and regards enlightenment as an enemy to avoid or defeat. One of the deepest fears of the ego, operating in a realm of the senses and separation, is that it could end up in eternal separation, which it interprets as abandonment, darkness, and void. The ego therefore concludes it must avoid the surrendered state at all costs. However, these are all false conclusions and constructs of the ego-controlled mind projecting what it imagines the surrendered or enlightened state is. These are all constructs of the mind conditioned to analyze, judge, compare, blame, and fear that results from operating totally in a realm of separation. Ironically, the things that the ego fears the most are some of the very things that dissolve away as one enters the surrendered, observant state. As a result, the surrendered state that the ego fears turns out to be the very condition it wants most—deep peace, safety, fulfillment, happiness, and completion.

In actuality, as you enter surrendered states of consciousness, you continue to think, feel, see, touch, and experience much more richly. Experiences are heightened. Happiness and fulfillment become your natural state. Once you have the surrendered experience, you find that you want more and more of it in your life.

Since you are always aligned with something throughout the day, you can make a choice to bring more and more of the surrendered state of consciousness into everyday experiences. You can be attuned to looking at the stock market tickers go by, stirring your vegetables as you make a meal, mowing the lawn, or any other activity while also being attuned to your inner expanded self, your soul, and your heart. It is possible to do both simultaneously. Alignment in this context is attuning to your inner being, and connecting with your expanded soul through your intention. You attune and align with your inner truth and open and surrender to it. This means being attentive to your heart space and aware of the subtle worlds within while interacting with the world outside. Put another way, this includes observing conditions and circumstances of your life in each moment while holding a quiet space in your inner consciousness and entering the more aware space in your heart.

Surrendered alignment includes a deep space of neutral observing. It means looking carefully and honestly moment-to-moment at yourself, your life, your choices, your actions, your beliefs, and your desires and realigning them with your True Self. If your alignment is not fully with your soul, then you must take whatever steps are necessary to realign. Eventually you will stay in this state automatically, but until it becomes automatic, you must be observant and continually realign yourself. This is a discerning skill that everyone will ultimately evolve to learn.

To develop this skill you must take some moments through the day, turn your attention inward, and ask, "Where am I living from right now?" If I am not aligned with my soul, then what has caused me to loose my alignment?" Once you have determined the source of the distraction, take the necessary steps to realign by releasing it, and reestablish your soul connection.

To maintain alignment means attending to your heart, being in a surrendered state, and opening and refining your senses to attune to what is before you, as well as what is within you. Alignment is doing what is necessary to return to the source of love, peace, and completion. At first, this is the space you are in when you meditate, but eventually you can be in this space all the time without having to think about it because you will automatically be living from higher consciousness.

The Alignment Process

What you seek is already present and the alignment process leads you to discover it. Acknowledge there is part of you that seeks to awaken and evolve. As you deepen your connection with the presence behind all form, you awaken your consciousness and find more happiness, peace, clarity, insight, and love. The soul presence is love and the creative and sustaining force of the universe. It is the essence of what makes you feel alive. As you become aware of that presence within you, you connect with the source of love as it moves through your heart and mind and clears off past pain.

STEP 1: Everything you perceive is energy in motion, and everything is changing all the time. The way you sense it will likely change over time, but right now just notice the sense of presence that is with you and surrender to it. You don't have to try to do anything other than surrender yourself and be present with what you are noticing and feeling. Sensing and feelings are what give you access to soul alignment. In addition to being aware and present, put yourself into a receiving mode. Say silently to yourself, "I relax, surrender, and open to receive."

Your soul already knows all of this. You are just opening yourself to receive in order to be more consciously aware and established with it. Open your heart to the awareness of what it is that gives you life, awareness, and movement. It is often helpful to rest a hand over the upper center of your chest to help you make the connection. You'll notice that it feels comforting.

STEP 2: Tune into your inner space now and just observe the feelings. Do not analyze, but feel. Take a little time to go into the feelings. They should feel quite nice. If you experience anything else, take a deep breath and release, relax, and let go. The more you let go, the more you receive peace and happiness. Release all expectations of how you experience inner presence.

Be like a cloud effortlessly floating across the sky. Be completely accepting, empty, and open to receive in the deepest humility. Let your heart melt into deep receiving of peace and acceptance.

STEP 3: Open your heart very deeply and imagine your heart is a very beautiful chalice. Welcome and allow the source of love and light to pour that love and light into your heart. As it fills your heart, let it melt all the places of contraction, hardness, pain, suffering, and separation. Let yourself be cleansed with the light presence of transformation. Be attentive to any areas of resistance. Let them melt and let them go. Surrender it all. Relax and surrender.

STEP 4: Now say "Yes," and accept what you are being given. This is a very important part of the process, maybe the most important. When you say "yes," your heart aligns with the love and light of creation and opens to unity consciousness and clear light.

STEP 5: The last step is a deepening of acceptance and surrender even more. Allow the true self that you are to come in deeply and transform you into peace and purity.

Each time you sit in meditation, observe the feelings and sensations. Meditation may start with a mental process, but then you let go and feel, and sense the open awareness around you. You will start feeling mellow and relaxed, and, in time, the feelings deepen into peacefulness, contentment, and happiness. You spiritually evolve by surrendering and letting go of all you have been holding onto and merge into the awareness of your deepest inner truth. So take a deep breath and invite your heart-space to open and expand to receive. Allow yourself to be carried with the energy of your intentions. The more you do this type of practice, the clearer your connection becomes, the more you are guided, the more you evolve, and the happier you become.

Chapter 35

THE ENLIGHTENMENT PATH TO ASCENSION

Ascension refers to rising to enlightened levels of consciousness, which in turn leads to living in higher dimensional realities. As your consciousness ascends there are corresponding releases from lower level attachments, karma, people, emotions, and circumstances. Negative energy patterns stored in the physical body gradually dissolve and are replaced by higher frequency patterns supporting clearer perceptions and improved health and energy levels. In addition, the structure of the etheric energies in your DNA sequence becomes cleared and more strands activate, enabling a natural increase in capabilities of higher sense perceptions such as clairvoyance, telepathy, mind projection, remote viewing, healing, and channeling beings from higher planes.

When you are cleared of much of the ego's patterns and your consciousness inhabits higher frequency states you are automatically ready for the next quantum leap in your evolution. In early stages of seeking truth, you may be most interested in finding relief from the pain of your past and current suffering and limitations, but as you continue clearing you will realize you are evolving. As your consciousness ascends you reach dimensions where all the beings have evolved to higher realizations of love and service and consequently live beyond the pain and suffering of lower dimensions. Knowing this you no longer need to worry about your future lives and where you will find yourself. Regardless of your initial motivations to pursue a spiritual path, your rewards will be many ranging from greater happiness and fulfillment to higher levels of synchronicity and preparation for living in higher planes of love, light, beauty, and kindness.

Many are waiting for a planetary shift to carry them into a higher reality, but if your consciousness is still attached to negative and limiting beliefs and karmic programs, you will take the issues with you wherever you find yourself. The traits you carry determine your level of vibrational frequency. If you are driven by fear, anger, guilt, shame, blame and other low frequency traits, they will lock you into lower dimensions.

The vibrations of people and circumstances that trigger you are like links in a chain, and you will repeatedly be drawn to the level of your weakest link until you release that energy. At each level of clearing, your frequency rises until all the lower frequency components of your consciousness have been cleared and you enter and live in a higher dimensional frequency.

The dimension you occupy is a function of the vibration of the body you inhabit and your level of consciousness. So when planetary frequency shifts take place, you arrive with your current consciousness. Transitions like a planetary shift or the death of the physical body do not accomplish automatic releases of energy patterns you have carried for hundreds or thousands of lifetimes.

What guarantees moving to the most beautiful, loving, and peaceful planes is eliminating your attachments, lower vibration thoughts, and expanding your awareness to more purified states. This enables you to move into the more refined fourth or fifth dimension both which require a higher level of clearing and love.

Spirit guides, masters, and angels can help you as you ascend, but they do not do for you what you can do yourself. Time, commitment, and energy needs to be channeled into your self-transformation, as well as invoking help from those masters who have already accomplished the transformation. In the higher dimensions, what is held in consciousness manifests much more rapidly than in the more dense dimensions, such as what you are experiencing now in the third dimension. Therefore many will find they are not any better off than they were before a planetary or dimensional shift unless they have diligently cleared their lower frequency characteristics and negative karma.

Infinite Dimensions

As you rise through the dimensions, you find they are inhabited by beings with increasing levels of more refined consciousness. As you let go of ego defense mechanisms and characteristics, your level of attention naturally rises, and you move up to the next dimension. Many authors describe twelve dimensions, but since each dimension above the physical has an infinite number of sub-dimensions, these numbers only give general points of reference.

The evolution of your consciousness sequentially progresses from one sub-dimension to the next higher vibration. The physical dimension is somewhat unique because the dense vibration of the physical body carries a wide spectrum of consciousness levels in the beings incarnated here. So you find some very low vibration beings who are very negative living on the same planet with others who are more evolved and even enlightened. The physical dimension offers people the unique opportunity to address their beliefs and attachments and clear the lower frequency patterns if they so choose to do so. However, some are so intoxicated with fame, power, and wealth, that they have no interest in evolving spiritually.

As you clear negative and low frequency thoughts, beliefs, and feelings your consciousness ascends to higher levels with a corresponding positive change in your environment and quality of beings drawn to you. Your consciousness level determines your environment regardless of the lifetime and dimension you inhabit.

What Are the Densities We Ascend To?

Densities relate to the vibrational levels of each dimension. For instance, we speak of the Earth as being in the third density which vibrates at a level where everything has a solid form preventing two objects from passing through each other. Your body, plants, houses, and other structures have separate forms that do not interpenetrate each other. The components of the third dimension are dense compared to the nature of objects and materials in higher dimensions.

Beings who inhabit higher dimensions determine what is experienced through projections of their beliefs and consciousness level. In other words, intentions and desires manifest realities experienced there. In the higher levels everything is a projection of the consciousness of beings inhabiting that dimension, and the higher you ascend, the quicker your thoughts and intentions manifest. To some degree this is also true of the physical dimension, but the manifestations are far slower due to the greater densities here.

There are some differences that distinguish between the terms density and dimension, although some confuse the two and use them interchangeably. Dimension relates to consciousness level, while density refers to the vibrational frequency of what is manifest. In general, the higher density of a dimension, the higher the consciousness of the beings inhabiting it. How this relates to your experience will become more clear as we continue.

The term "Universe" relates to a narrow range of frequencies. For instance, everything in the physical universe is composed of tangible objects with solid densities. I'm also including gaseous matter and plasmas in the term "solid." As frequencies go up, other universes appear which are not visible to instruments or the senses in the third dimension. Within the fourth dimension are many sub-dimensions with beings who posess a similar range of consciousness levels. Sometimes these are referred to as planes of reality.

The Correlation between Consciousness Levels and Densities

Density Level 1. This density is composed of materials that are basic components of the environment such as soil, water, air, and simple life forms. Underlying their form are subtle energies that hold cohesive forces and consciousness. The consciousness level of these components keep them operating according to the laws governing their density level. Components of our physical universe are composed of first density materials. Entire planets, solar systems, and galaxies are composed of first density materials.

Density Level 2. Lifeforms at this level operate with second density characteristics which includes programming that motivates survival and everyday behaviors. These programs run mostly on automatic through instinctual behaviors. The lifeforms at this level react instinctively to their environment without analytical thought. The more simple lifeforms do not have self-awareness or complex thoughts, but run programs that govern their survival and procreation. Some also include elemental beings in this level which includes nature spirits, fairies, gnomes, leprechauns, and other entities who have finer characteristics than those in third density.

Density Level 3. The three lower density levels operate in duality and separation. Third density human beings are self-aware and capable of analysis and complex thoughts. Third density worlds have lifeforms with survival motivations characteristic of ego identities. This leads to conflicts, confusion, isolation, drives, and needs for more of what is thought to bring greater safety and security. This causes third density worlds to have drama, disagreements, and other ego characteristics on personal and collective levels.

Consciousness levels of beings living in third density range from very base emotions such as guilt, shame, pride, fear, anger, and hate to much more enlightened levels. Beings incarnate at this level to probe the nature of existence and motivations that sustain challenges. This gradually leads to awakening to higher levels of consciousness through avoiding struggles and suffering by free-will choices of surrendering and letting go of causes.

Many living in third density realities are unaware of their spiritual nature and operate primarily through the analytical mind and senses. Their heart center is often shielded and closed for protection, and as a result they live primarily through their intellect. This keeps them under the illusion of separation and they operate their lives through identities, roles, definitions, and archetypes such as victim, slave, ruler, warrior, savior, saboteur, teacher, scholar, and many others. The many fear-based identities create continuous streams of drama and struggle. Many if not most at this level are not motivated to look deeper into the nature of reality or spiritual realizations. Life is experienced mostly through physical pursuits and the ego's insatiable need for more.

Some wonderfully positive characteristics at this level include such attributes as being considerate, thoughtful, friendly, kind, charitable, polite, and appreciative. These traits become more frequent and freely expressed as the beings evolve to higher expressions of consciousness.

The upper levels many societies reach in third density include the positive characteristics of the lower levels plus the development of intellect, wisdom, knowledge, logic, and understanding. There is currently a consensus that our third density Earth is ascending to fourth or possibly fifth density. At these levels consciousness, and therefore life, is more refined. On the individual level, those evolving to higher awareness gradually open their heart center and begin feeling spiritually connected.

Density Level 4. We live in a multidimensional universe in which each dimension has a unique rate of vibration. Your body exists in the third dimension, but there are many frequencies above this that overlap with the third dimension. Entire realms of reality can overlap right where you are right now that you are unaware of. The most familiar example is of people who have passed on and are no longer in a physical body. Sometimes they are seen as ghosts and can walk right through a wall because they are now in a higher frequency than physical matter. Other examples are found in the stories of angels and ascended masters who live in refined dimensions that interpenetrate the physical but are not limited like the physical.

The consciousness of many is now rising automatically to the fourth density as they awaken to living a more polite, thoughtful, generous, and harmonious life. Negative ego is gradually being replaced by love, kindness, and service. The service to self so characteristic of third density Earth is giving way to service to others with an emphasis on cooperating, supporting, and helping others to have more fulfilling and happy lives.

The fourth dimension above the physical also contains the astral plane which has many sub-dimensions, some lower and some higher in vibration and characteristics. The lower vibration areas are hell-like and the higher vibration ones are more heavenly, beautiful, and peaceful. In the middle and higher levels of the fourth dimension are beings who are kind and helpful. They serve others rather than the self as is the case of many in the third dimension.

The mid and upper fourth density still have most of the characteristics of third density but the self-aware beings are generally more soul oriented and less ego driven. Many societies at this level are more technologically advanced than found in third density, and individuals often have much higher intellectual capacity than found in lower density worlds. As a result the societies have more cooperation, harmony, and happiness than are typically found on third density worlds. This doesn't mean that all is perfect or peaceful, as there are some societies with beings inhabiting the fourth density worlds who are still motivated by lower ego needs. Some fourth density worlds have cruel beings driven by greed, competition, power, and control who inflict their influences on victims. However, many fourth dimensional civilizations are operating at much more peaceful and harmonious levels than typically found in third density cultures.

The fourth density realm has a majority of beings with intellects more highly developed and capable than many of those in third density. As a result, they can be trapped with pride in their accomplishments and have strong commitments to their beliefs and skills. At this level the main hindrance to further evolution is being trapped by mental attachments and constructs. In order to evolve further, the mind's needs and fixations must be addressed, surrendered, and released.

One major obstacle stands in the way to becoming clear, free, awake, happy, fulfilled, and at peace: the ego-mind and how it operates. The mind can get you hooked with its stories, beliefs, conclusions, fears, regrets, guilt, blame, judgments, and justifications. The mind lives through the complete unabridged dictionary of perceptions. The mind goes over and over what it has collected from the five major senses and produces transitory perceptions and limiting conclusions. This is not to say that the mind is your enemy, for the mind can also enable you to experience virtuous qualities such as kindness, love, generosity, appreciation, beauty, and happiness. But, the way it usually operates can be in opposition to how you would like to live. The good news is that the blocks and limitations can be released and cleared, and at that point the mind functions as your greatest resource. What starts off as resistance in the form of fear, guilt, anger, pain, and struggle, melts and dissolves in the presence of the quietness and stillness of pure awareness

This was presented to me in a rather dramatic fashion through a vision some years ago. I was relaxing in a meditative state and requesting to be shown what I most needed to evolve to attain a higher realization and potential. I often make requests in meditations to be shown and guided to my next highest safe leap in consciousness. In this vision I was transported to something like an Egyptian museum with all sorts of statues and hieroglyphics, but this was a dimension where the beings seen on Earth in Egyptian paintings are alive. I have memories of several lives in ancient Egypt and I presume this is why I was drawn to this experience.

Several very tall beings who were spiritually evolved high priests led me to a stage where a high priest informed me I was going to be given an initiation. Needless to say I was thrilled at the prospect. Two of the beings on the stage appeared like pictures I've seen of Thoth and Annubis. Two guards carrying staffs with sharp curved blades joined them on the stage, one on each side of me. I was quite excited to have this experience, until one of the guards swung the blade and cut off my head. I was shocked and confused by this although somehow still completely conscious and aware of what had taken place. I had been expecting something wonderful to take place but instead found the opposite, or so I thought. I telepathically asked the high priest why this happened. The answer I received revealed an important lesson I had to learn that is difficult for many to realize: we must release the thinking analytical mind in order to have higher realizations.

This initiation emphasized the point as I was momentarily in shock until my head reappeared on my body, after which I was told to surrender all reliance on mental control. From that day on, I made it my mission to surrender all need for thinking and analyzing. I know this is a strange concept as the mind will question how a person can possibly function without thoughts. What I can tell you is that the soul takes over and you function quite well from higher awareness levels. Of course, you can utilize thinking if you want, but in most cases that need is transcended by the soul and direct awareness.

Many beings in fourth density are aware of their evolution and spiritual nature, and many engage in practices to address and clear ego motivations and take active roles to raise their consciousness. To transcend to the next higher density, it is necessary to further surrender the intellectual attachments and further integrate the fully enlightened soul awareness.

Density Level 5. The raising of consciousness eventually leads to ascension through enlightenment. In most cases, it takes place in consciousness first, but a special category of ascension includes raising the frequency of the physical body. It is commonly believed that we are living in a time when this is possible, whereas in the past, for many thousands of years this has been far more difficult.

The fifth density dimension is not only higher in frequency, but it is also characterized by higher states of consciousness and is the level to which those aspiring to ascend are most looking forward. It is oriented around service to others in love. Beings who live in this dimension have fine-frequency bodies and sometimes interact with those in the lower dimensions.

When you reach fifth dimensional consciousness and above, you will experience life in a permanent state of peace, love, and joy. You no longer need to work at having those experiences. The higher in frequency, the more effortless everything becomes, and at each unfolding level of consciousness, the experience of life changes for the better. For example, a person can feel love in many ways and to various depths. Each experience may be described as love, but the way it is experienced can be significantly different for each person. Another feature of attaining fifth density dimension of consciousness is that you will no longer need to struggle to be in present time awareness as you will always and automatically be in the now, the present moment. The mind no longer worries or fixates on the past, nor does it project to the future. Of course, you can recall any memory at any time, but you don't stay with the memories unless you deliberately choose to for referencing examples to help someone in the present. People reaching fifth density dimension of consciousness have a higher perception and intuition, enabling them to know things beyond what is obtained through the senses. There is an inner confirmation and knowing of truth.

In the fifth dimension not everyone experiences all the characteristics of the enlightened state to the same degree. Each person's consciousness level is unique, but as you go higher in consciousness after ascension, everything becomes easier and more beautiful. This is because the fifth density for the most part is composed of beings who are more heart-centered on love, kindness, and service. However, at the lower levels of this dimension some negative beings still seek control over others, but as the density level rises to the upper fifth, those beings are no longer able to inhabit those realms which are composed of unconditionally loving beings. These beings are benevolent and cooperative and have higher degrees of wisdom with much higher capabilities than most humans in third density.

The perception of separation characteristic of the lower densities no longer prevails. Struggling, suffering, and drama diminish as individuals raise their consciousness. Rising to fifth density also includes a natural emergence of mercy, forgiveness, love, sincerity, consideration, and kindness. This level of consciousness is not just about ideas of positive expressions but the full emergence of them through the individual's personality. To inhabit this level of density requires the integration of refined qualities and the exclusion of dualistic judgments such as good/bad, guilty/innocent, and deserving/undeserving.

Love at this level is not just a feeling or attraction, but a guiding principle apart from self-interest. It replaces self-interests such as neediness, selfishness, self-centeredness, and greed. The love at this level replaces the ego's mimicking of love which has elements of control and gain. The higher frequency levels of love reveal appreciation of beauty, peace, compassion, caring, service, and sharing. This love is all-inclusive without judgments and it spontaneously dissolves negativity and nurtures life, thereby deepening happiness, joyfulness, and fulfillment. At the lower levels of fifth density the love starts out as being conditional, but as the beings evolve, the love deepens and becomes unconditional and a natural expression of the personality in how it interacts with everyone and everything.

At the upper levels of fifth density the love is increasingly unconditional, and sustained joyfulness emerges more fully. This is not a joy in response to experiences, but rather a natural emanation that is constant and underlying all experiences. As a result of the emergence of these refined frequencies, life has more flow and ease and everything is seen as expressions of love. These beings discover that the more they experience love, the more capacity they have for love, caring, and compassion until their personality is completely overtaken with those qualities. Because of this, there is a desire to use one's talents and capabilities to benefit all creation. Previous commitments to express the deepest soul qualities and the willingness to surrender all obstacles and blocks facilitate the emergence of unconditional love.

Living in Fifth Density

Just knowing about fifth density life is not the same as integrating it and living it. As such, knowing what beings at this level are like creates an incentive for ego-clearing work to raise consciousness to join them. The beings inhabiting the refined frequencies of the fifth density live in higher vibratory bodies than humans experience in third density. These bodies do not require food to survive as the bodies are naturally energized. Eating can be enjoyed and transformed into energy when consumed and therefore there is nothing to be expelled.

Fifth density bodies can manifest in tangible forms such as angels and masters that some have witnessed throughout history. Many of their capabilities appear miraculous to lower vibratory beings as they are able to direct energy to create phenomena. The various psychic abilities are completely natural and common, including telepathy, levitation, and the full perception of subtle energies. Because their bodies are composed of higher energy vibrations, travel through dimensions and the universe is accomplished nearly instantaneously by thoughts and intentions. These abilities also enable the beings to share and integrate their souls with others in the most intimate and exhilarating exchanges imaginable.

The fifth density is a most wonderful and desirable dimension to experience the creation since most negative ego traits no longer exist there, nor do most of the limitations experienced in third and fourth density. The systems that enslave the masses at lower densities do not exist in fifth density. Fifth density beings have complete freedom to explore every aspect of creation. Consider any topic you find fun to explore and participate in now, and imagine having access to all resources you could ever want to take adventures to their highest levels of exploration. If you love science, music, art, creative expression, loving, and more, you'll have full and free access to it all without limitations or reservations.

Density Level 6. At this level of consciousness polarity no longer exists. There is a realization of unity consciousness and as such individuals are interconnected with groups of similar interests and frequencies. Unity consciousness includes a deep-level of loving acceptance of all, and an ease of flowing with life. From the sixth density and beyond, many beings are integrated into groups that function with single purposes and agreements. Although these beings have form, they exist in what we would consider light bodies. When these beings appear to humans, they resemble hologram projections. They look tangible, but your hand would pass through them.

Third density beings who have sufficiently evolved can experience this level of consciousness, but it is currently relatively rare to find such people. These are those who are fully enlightened, non-dual, and completely clear of all negative ego. Sixth density is the dimension where many ascended masters and angels exist.

Sixth density beings are fully aware of the underlying nature of reality and illusion, and participate in harmonious creation. They maintain a high level of harmony, peace, and love and enjoy a refined spiritual vibration. They are the embodiment of beauty, love, and joy and share their souls in ways that transcend what is possible at lower levels. They enjoy exploring, loving, and being entertained by the creation. They play through their individuality but without experiencing separation. Their experiences are all full of wonder and the fulfillment that comes from deep-level sharing with others.

At this level negative ego has vanished and therefore only positive and happy experiences are created. This is the level of complete mastery, happiness, and fulfillment. Prior to the sixth level, traces of struggle and suffering still occasionally intrude, but they manifest far less as consciousness rises.

These beings are completely soul integrated and as such inhabit high vibratory levels of love and service beyond individual actions in support of the creation. With their consciousness they sustain the harmony and balance of all universes. They are automatically drawn to support needs of the lower density realms. Instantly aware of thoughts and actions throughout the dimensions, their expressions of love manifest through waves of support they are able to transmit. Their objective is to sustain harmony and balance throughout creation.

Since long ago they have transcended negative thoughts, feelings, stories, and attachments, their existence and evolution is tied to furthering expressions of the highest frequencies of love. Their entire existence is joyful, fulfilling, and thrilling but not in the way we think of emotions. Words fail when trying to describe the depth of their blissful existence and satisfying vibrations.

They do not usually make appearances in third density because to do so requires lowering their vibrations, but occasionally they make themselves known through dreams or visions to convey important messages.

I can tell you of such an experience I had many years ago with the appearance of a being who presented himself as Saint Germaine. He certainly appeared as I would have expected Saint Germaine to look, and he said that is who he was. I had just finished facilitating a week-long meditation retreat in Santa Barbara and was meditating alone in the evening at my home. Whether it was literally whom people identify as Saint Germaine or an archetype, or other advanced being taking that form to present a teaching to me, I cannot say. It could have been any of those three.

I was reflecting on the week and exploring the sensations of higher frequencies that carried over from the previous week when I noticed a small violet light suspended in the center of the room. It was about the size of a softball and was undulating like a ball of plasma energy.

What I found curious was that I could see it with my eyes open or closed. Since it was in motion, it held my attention as it gradually grew larger and larger until the violet light filled the entire room. At that point I witnessed Saint Germaine walking toward me out of the violet light and he stood about six feet in front of me. I saw him vividly clothed in elegant, multi-colored garments, and he seemed tangible and solid. I was so in awe it never occurred to me to reach out to touch him. He communicated telepathically that he had an important teaching to help me and others transcend the many illusions and traps in place on Earth regarding karmic attachments. I had an audio recorder with me so I repeated what I was being told as he led me through a process of releasing a plethora of karmic attachments that have affected nearly everyone.

The process consists of acknowledging the effects from past lives but also the group karma trapping almost everyone. When you are part of any group you take on some of the beliefs and karma of the group. This includes the karma of the entire human race, nations, cities, families, and organizations. To effectively release yourself from these energies, they must be addressed. An important aspect of the releasing is to address all the places the karmic programs are held, including the causal body or the release will not be complete. This does not in any way diminish the manner in which you can participate in groups, but it does free you from negative consequences from the limiting beliefs or karmic obligations all groups have. This entire experience lasted about 45-minutes. He then told me to tell others of this experience which I have done, and then the vision faded away.

Sixth density beings are able to instantly project to any dimension and location simply by thinking of it and expressing the intention to be there. This is what I believe Saint Germaine did. The level of intelligence and wisdom of sixth density beings surpasses anything at the lower densities. They live in a continuous flow of harmony and love that is deeply peaceful and abundant in every sense of the word. Everything they experience is richly wonderful beyond what words can express.

Density Level 7. These beings exist in a unified field with group intentions that support creation and energy patterns underlying manifestation. These beings are overseers and sustainers of all creation. With their expanded awareness beyond illusions, universes exist within their consciousness and are maintained by their attention. This includes everything from subatomic levels through all manifestations and lifeforms. These beings can be considered the creators and sustainers of all lower dimensions. We call them beings only as a reference for they are not beings in the sense of separate individuality.

Some of these beings also fill roles of directly overseeing specific planes of reality such as watchers, guardians, creators, and intercessors. The watchers at this level are nothing like the lower density watchers sometimes referred to in texts. These beings observe the manifest creation and facilitate energy transmissions that foster evolution. They communicate to other beings where they recognize what is needed to support entire systems of planets, galaxies, and universes.

Everything in creation is held in their awareness and their intentions and directions support evolution. They know everything about everything and all is in their awareness. They do not take usually take form but exist as light beings of vastly expanded awareness. They remain at this level of service and involvement in the support of all creation. In some cases, some of them may choose to temporarily experience lower levels of existence to play a more direct role in the creation. In those cases, they have the ability to incarnate aspects of their consciousness into more individualized forms.

The 8th Density and Higher are composed of those who have made choices to merge more completely with the sea of consciousness. Some refer to twelve planes of reality and I'm including them in this discussion. It is impossible to adequately represent the beings and experiences at these levels in words, but I can give you some sense of their consciousness if not details of what their "day-to-day" life is like.

The eighth density is where full merging with unity consciousness is integrated. There is complete satisfaction and fulfillment without any needs. It is consciousness that is complete, aware, and satisfied in every way imaginable. It is a dimension without words. They exist in ethereal light bodies with virtually limitless lifespans in this dimension until they choose to merge further into Source.

An analogy would be that they are like a facet in a diamond. The facet is an individualized point of awareness but they are not separate from the whole. The way this applies to you is that what you think of as your soul is a container for your individuality that expresses consciousness through you with various qualities, but underlying your soul is the vast spaciousness of eternity and all manifestation. Individuality implies a sense of duality, but the individuality contains the consciousness of the whole. As you raise your awareness there is no sense of being separate from all existence.

Sometimes the word Self or Soul with a capital "S" refers to the large expanse of awareness, the totality of all existence and all consciousness which is the Source of all. So Self-Realization with a capital "S" is recognizing and realizing that this totality is who and what you really are beneath the veneer of appearances. This is also referred to as God realization. Meditation enables you to experience this level of realization and when some have experienced this, they said, "My God, I am God." In the past, some have been martyred for saying that because those hearing it misunderstood what they were saying. They were not exalting themselves in some delusion that they were a supreme or all-powerful being; they were having the realization of their continuity and oneness with all creation and existence. It is not a blasphemous statement, but an awakening of awareness that we are one with all there is and this is true of everyone.

The beings in eighth density and above view everything as a manifestation of love, and all is regarded as overwhelming beauty. Everything is seen as perfect with no judgments attached. In these higher dimensions the beings exist as mind groups without individual form but yet possessing individuality interconnected with others in the same density and group.

An example of the perspective beings at eight density and above perceive I'll relate what happened during a clearing session I was doing with a person who was having a strong reaction of fear and terror. I tried several approaches to clear the fear but it persisted, so I put out a call for any helper who would know how to relieve this person from the intense fear he was experiencing. A mind group from ninth density showed up, and I asked them who they were. They showed me what they called themselves but the word was so complicated I couldn't pronounce it, so I just called them, "They that have no name." They said that was as close an interpretation as I could comprehend at that time.

They telepathically transmitted to me they were willing to help and they asked me to explain the problem. I told them the person was in extreme fear and terror and asked what I should do. They answered with just two words that shifted what I was doing to a realization beyond the fear. They said, "What fear?"

I instantly realized, of course, the fear doesn't exist except as a belief this person had in his unconscious memories from long ago. From the high perspective of this mind group, fear is impossible to perceive. As soon as that realization occurred the fear and terror were instantly gone. Interestingly, this mind group consists of many thousands of souls in a unified field. Needless to say, they were far removed from our third dimensional reality.

The higher dimensions from eight density and above are the realms of the avatars who are perfected beings sometimes choosing to leave their groups and incarnate in lower densities to directly assist in the evolution of beings at the lower levels. It is difficult to describe in words what their experiences are because words are insufficient. They live in realms of light with levels of fulfillment and happiness that can only be experienced when the limitations of the lower frequencies have been completely transcended. The beings and groups in the ninth through twelfth density dimensions do not experience anything relatable to what we do in third density, as they have evolved far beyond ego-motivated needs. The higher realms can all be accessed through meditation. The discussion on the Stillpoint that follows will give further insights into their awareness level.

Accessing the Stillpoint

The beings in the higher realms have a consciousness of non-duality and stillness. This is also possible for beings incarnated at lower levels to experience and is directly related to enlightenment and ascension of consciousness. The non-dual awareness emerges in a Stillpoint of consciousness. Something magical happens when you experience the expanded awareness in the Stillpoint. The Stillpoint in consciousness is non-duality where there is expansive quietness, clarity, emptiness, awakening, and pure awareness.

When you put your attention on some reaction, stress, anxiety, fear, anger, or other upset, it vanishes because there is no resistance there. There is nothing for the reaction to get traction on. The Stillpoint is pure awareness well beyond the thinking mind. The mind of course wants an explanation of what is happening so that it can relax around the process. So when you meditate to reach non-duality, the mind will question, doubt, analyze, and project stories onto it, deducing conclusions about whatever draws its attention. Knowing this ahead of time prepares you to let go of the need for the mind to intrude.

By going to the non-dual Stillpoint in consciousness, you can release thoughtforms so that lifeforce will return to you in a completely neutral form without any emotional charge. This amazing process will facilitate you disassembling or unwinding the energy of even the most complex thoughtforms such as personality traits, negative emotions, identities, and ego structures. The non-dual Stillpoint contains no cohesive force holding anything together. By contrast all manifestation is held together with lifeforce energy and the focus of beliefs or intentions that caused it to form originally. When these forces are removed the thoughtform can no longer hold itself together so it uncreates and dissipates. I recognize that this is somewhat of a mechanical way of conceptualizing the process, but this helps give the mind a way of relating to this process.

The Stillpoint is a point of awareness in which you are fully conscious and aware, yet without any movement or involvement. There are no thoughts, no manifestations, no judgments, or reactions. It is perfectly clear and perfectly still. From that point of consciousness, impulses and desires of creation radiate like ripples in a pond. Each ripple is interpreted uniquely as creations in every frequency and dimension, but in the Stillpoint itself, there is total stillness and peace. The Stillpoint is not a New Age fad idea. It is what some call Nirvana and full enlightenment. It is also called non-duality and Buddha awareness, and thus the goal of serious meditators on a spiritual path.

Another way to think about the Stillpoint is emptiness, nothingness, and void, concepts that are difficult for the mind to grasp. It is like trying to picture infinity or catch the wind with your fingers. There seems to be nothing to anchor to, this causes problems because the mind is endlessly trying to connect and attach to something such as an idea, a concept, a conclusion, a story, a theory, a judgment, or control. In the Stillpoint none of these constructs can exist, so the mind will usually grasp at memories or worries. When this happens, you can acknowledge the thought, surrender all need for it, and let it go. It then disappears forever and uncovers the next layer of thought which can then be addressed. And so the process goes until only emptiness remains with no more thoughts.

The mind typically struggles with this because this process dismantles what it has long believed is its very purpose for existence. But this is not quite true, as it has only erroneously concluded what its purpose is. When emptied the mind is still very aware and clear in perceptions. When all the clouds of misperception dissolve, the clarity of consciousness is experienced. The mind then is able to embrace the emptiness, quietness, and peaceful expansion into all awareness. There has always been a presence and awareness but the mind was always distracted and hidden from it.

In the Stillpoint thoughts are like snow flakes falling into a lake. Snow flakes are, of course, frozen water and when they land on the lake, they merge with the lake. In the Stillpoint thoughts dissipate in the ocean of emptiness. They simply disappear. I used to say they dissolve, and in one way of looking at it, they do, but then I realized that they were not actually real in the first place and therefore there was nothing to dissolve other than the thought. When you turn on a light in a dark room, where did the dark go? It ceased to exist in the light. Thoughts also vanish in the clear light of empty reality. In one sense you are not making emptiness, you are discovering it. When you are there, non-conceptual wakefulness replaces all need for conceptual thinking. You will be operating from awareness rather than analytical thinking. In all-pervasive mindful awareness, no distractions or judgments exist. Awareness becomes all-encompassing.

On your way to the pure awareness you may find bliss, euphoria, and other sensations of lightness, love, and inspiration. They are all wonderful but they can also be traps that cause you to keep trying to experience them more and more, and you could mistake the sensations for evidence you have become enlightened. Be grateful for every experience, but do not grasp at them or try to sustain them or recapture them. The awakened state is not something that can actually be defined, for as soon as you attach a label or a sensation, you have missed the truth. As long as you are identifying yourself as a feeling, belief, condition, personality, sensation, you are still in the realm of concepts. Beings at the higher dimensions of eight and above inhabit non-dual awareness where having "negative" feelings about anything is not possible. These beings are the embodiment of all wisdom and knowledge.

As we release ego perceptions and reactions we evolve our consciousness progressively from one dimension to the next. Everyone will become enlightened and ascend to the higher realms when they have surrendered attachments to non-enlightened desires. This is certainly available to everyone in this lifetime and it can happen in the twinkling of an eye.

Chapter 36
EPILOGUE

The search for the meaning of life goes back to the earliest chronicles of recorded history. Ancient records are replete with accounts reflecting rich traditions of cultures looking beyond themselves for meaning. Today we are on the threshold of a New Age in which breakthroughs in science are finding parallels with the ageless teachings of mystics and philosophers. The exploration of inner space has become as important as outer space as meditation and visualization practices are increasingly being used for breaking new frontiers in the transformation of consciousness that leads to the realization of our greatest potentials.

We at this very moment are standing at the gateway of the greatest leap of the human spirit. We are unraveling the deep inward mysteries of life and coming to understand our nature and the place it plays in the complexities of the universe. Much of what was once esoteric and paranormal is now being understood and revealed as quite normal and perhaps even easy to understand in the light of a new matrix presented by theoretical physics. We have now arrived at an age of new discovery, self-discovery, and growth unparalleled in human history. We no longer accept the limitations imposed on us by past thinking. Your evolutionary journey is about learning to understand the flow of the universe and your rightful place in that flow. For it is true that the less you are in harmony with your environment and the more you try to resist your destiny, the harder you have to work to achieve what you want from life.

Since metaphysics, enlightenment, and ascension are concerned with the meaning and purpose of existence, they encompass the underlying teachings of Christianity, Buddhism, Gnosticism, Jewish Mysticism, Indian philosophy, and Sufism as well as many ancient cultures such as those of the Egyptians, Greeks, and Mayans. In more recent times Jungian psychology, transpersonal psychology, parapsychology, and the theories of quantum mechanics have all been associated with the vast aspects of spiritual evolution. The paths leading to spiritual truths offer freedom from superstitions and fear-ridden beliefs. They give understanding of the forces that influence our lives and of how we determine our own life circumstances.

In quantum physics, physicists have demonstrated what practiced meditators have long said: space and time are not absolute, matter isn't actually solid and "empty" space isn't empty at all. We are only now learning that mysticism and the new physics both reveal the oneness of all things and the nature of reality itself. The perception of oneness with the universe that is often spoken of by meditators is not only the central characteristic of mystical experiences, but also one of the most important revelations of modern physics.

We are on the frontier of knowledge that could eventually create a world free from physical and psychological pain and limitations. Nothing, however, will change until you decide to delve into the depths of who you are and explore beyond all boundaries. Your life can be different. It can be better and closer to an expression of who and what you really are.

To reach these goals you must remove layer upon layer of false premises and programming and all the self-created and self-defeating illusions by which you have lived life. The progress and rewards that await you are wonderful beyond what you might imagine. Only on the path of enlightenment can you find true success, health, abundance, abiding happiness, joy, contentment, fulfillment, pure love, and a love of life.

Are you ready to release your limitations and reach out to new levels of your evolution? Your destiny is in your hands and no one else's!

You hold the key to your own discoveries of a higher, happier, and more thrilling way to live.

Appendix

100 QUESTIONS AND ANSWERS ON YOUR SPIRITUAL JOURNEY

Over the years, I have been asked thousands of questions about our spiritual journey and in particular about enlightenment. This appendix consists of some of the questions I've answered about how the process of spiritual discovery and releasing takes place, thus furthering your evolution.

1. Question. How can I reach enlightenment when I am in so much pain?

Answer: You've probably heard of the term "Dark Night of the Soul." A 16th century Spanish monk, Saint John of the Cross, originally mentioned it in a poem. Some people use the term "dark night" when they are feeling troubled or depressed, but the actual meaning goes much deeper.

The good news is that while it can lead to a significant spiritual awakening it is preceded by deep feelings of abandonment, desolation, and despair. It is a state of feeling very disconnected from soul, spirit, and the Divine, and therefore a person thinks he or she is spiritually lost and hopeless.

Some indications that you might be going through a Dark Night of the Soul are:

Something happened that leads to hopelessness and despair.
You feel a deep sense of being worthless and lower than a worm.
You feel as though you have been rejected and a failure.
You feel like your misery and suffering have no solution.
Your ability to take action has been destroyed.
Your energy is very low and you are emotionally paralyzed.
You have no ability to look forward to anything.
You feel like you just want to die.
You feel helpless and deeply depressed.

The Dark Night is a special place of deep spiritual darkness. As horrible as all this sounds, what is unique about The Dark Night is that it can be a trigger for profound spiritual awakening and transformation. In fact, this is what distinguishes the Dark Night from depression. It can lead to an epiphany because when you feel as low as you can go, all that is left is to say, "I give up. I surrender." Since you are devastated, your surrender is very deep. You have little or no fight left, nor is there ego to defend. This is what opens the door to the light coming in.

A big difference between being discouraged or depressed and being in a Dark Night is that with depression, your outlook and beliefs don't change much. You may project blame on yourself or others for your conditions. You may even curse God and fume with anger. But the Dark Night can lead to feeling spiritually connected more deeply than ever before if it leads to deep surrender. A true Dark Night experience leads to permanent change of some of your previous beliefs and interpretations of life.

A Lesson from Nature

Have you ever seen how a butterfly struggles to emerge from its cocoon? The struggle is what strengthens it to be able to fly. Similarly, the wind blowing builds a tree's structural strength. The Dark Night of the Soul works like the cocoon for the butterfly and the wind for the tree. The struggle is the releasing of the ego in order for the soul to emerge. As you evolve, you will eventually have to address all ego components and surrender them. The Dark Night of the Soul is one way of triggering that process. Fortunately, you don't have to go through all of that.

Those who have experienced a Dark Night of the Soul or are currently experiencing a Dark Night will know that something very fundamental at a core level is out of focus or completely lacking in their lives. Those going through a Dark Night will sense that so much more is possible in their lives, even though they don't exactly know what that "so much more" is. Surrender is the key that eventually eliminates the ego and all of the causes of the Dark Nights.

2. Question: How can I accelerate my spiritual awakening?

Answer: The best way is to work with a wise and awakened spiritual teacher, but all the paths require letting go of old ways. Spiritual awakening requires many changes in beliefs and outlooks. You will evolve, but the rate at which you evolve is up to you.

Often people experience "Flash Realizations" when awakening. These are profound spiritual experiences that can put you in an elevated state for days or weeks, but they gradually fade and leave you wondering if you lost your spiritual connection. This can cause you to feel discouraged and/or impel you to search for answers to reclaim your spiritual realizations. This is actually a normal and natural part of the process because awakening happens in stages as deeper and deeper levels of the ego are revealed thus causing a "roller coaster" ride of experiences. At times, you might even feel like you are going backwards or losing the beauty of spiritual experiences. You actually haven't lost anything, but different aspects of the ego surface to be addressed and let go. Each aspect will continue to affect you until you address it and release it. It won't go away by itself even if it seems to submerge at times; it will resurface until you address it. That's why circumstances keep repeating in your life.

To accelerate your awakening, you must explore how to shed old beliefs and comfort zones and move into more refined ones. While you are going through this, you enter unknown territory that can be a bit scary, so it is really helpful and important to have a guide on your journey. Reading a few books or listening to lectures does not resolve the ego's complexity. Apects of it are hidden and difficult to clear on your own. Meditations are certainly an important part of the process, but having personal support helps the most.

3. Question: How do I stay positive all the time?

Answer: Affirmations and willpower will only sustain the positive feelings for a limited time. This is because ego programs run at subtle levels that will eventually break through to the surface and undermine your best intentions. The simple truth is that these ego programs will not go away by themselves even if they seem to disappear at times. If you avoid addressing them, they will find ways to reappear and trigger you again. In addition, they keep you locked into a limited level of consciousness that keeps repeating the same situations even if it takes years (or lifetimes) to recognize this pattern.

Dealing with this problem takes a certain courage and commitment because shying away from what is uncomfortable or painful is natural. Facing these things head on is the best way to resolve them, and the best way is to have someone guide you through the process or at the very least address the issues yourself in a meditative state.

4. Question: If I keep repeating love and light affirmations, will I grow spiritually?

Answer: Being on a spiritual path is not about anything external such as going to church, praying, repeating affirmations, or meditating. These, of course, can be helpful, but the spiritual path is more than those activities and more than being a nice person. Spiritual people often fall into the trap of using their spiritual practices to reassure themselves they are spiritual or even enlightened.

While spiritual practices are wonderful to implement, they are a means to an end and not the end in themselves. I've been with teachers who put tremendous emphasis on sitting a specific way when meditating, following specific prayer formulas, and applying certain rituals to become enlightened. Not that there is anything wrong with any of these, but an over-emphasis on formulas can easily be a distraction or even an impediment to your spiritual evolution. So avoid being attached to any outer form.

5. Question: I understand many spiritual truths, so how can I know when I am enlightened?

Answer: I see strongly opinionated posts on social media of people convinced their beliefs are right. They defend them and argue with anyone who disagrees. This is a normal ego defense pattern. Of course, you believe what you believe is correct or you wouldn't believe it, and changing beliefs is the most difficult thing there is because it undermines what you've based your life on and can be very scary. This is why people prefer their status quo even when it is painful. The ego will always defend its beliefs.

Eventually, you may realize that some beliefs are limited or even completely distorted or untrue, and a new set of beliefs must be adopted. All beliefs come from observations and conclusions. You can't function without beliefs and stories. The problem arises from the attachment to them and the belief they are real and absolute. Gradually, when more and deeper truths are revealed, you are forced to change your beliefs and thereby evolve.

Many understand the mechanics of spiritual growth. However, falling into an intellectual trap of spiritual explanations is easy. Here's a true example: A famous spiritual teacher a few years ago led retreats all over the world on enlightenment. He spent time in India studying with an enlightened teacher. He published many works over many years and was regarded by many respected people as enlightened. Then he had an epiphany and realized he was not really enlightened despite having all the vocabulary and credentials, so he ceased publications and retreats. His experience attests to the power of self-deception on spiritual matters.

After David Hawkin's came out with his scale of enlightenment which goes from 0 to 1000, I encountered many people calibrating themselves in the highly enlightened numbers while they calibrated most others significantly below them. This is because the ego wants to be enlightened and has many tricks to convince itself it is enlightened. Think of all the religious figures with their costumes and rituals. Some have very large followings who proclaim their enlightenment.

All I'm saying is that it is a tricky proposition to know about enlightenment and then convince yourself you are. Discovering and admitting this is the first step to breaking free and discovering the truly enlightened life. You'll be enlightened when you no longer wonder if you are.

6. Question: What do people do that prevents them from leading meaningful lives?

Answer: If people don't think they are having a meaningful life it is because they are disconnected from their spiritual nature and operating through ego perceptions and defenses. This often happens seamlessly as situations arise and a person meets them with their defensive nature rather than the soul. I have found that people experience satisfaction, completion, meaning, fulfillment, happiness, enjoyment, and lightness of being when they raise their consciousness and integrate their soul into their mind, body, and feelings.

7. Question: How can I deepen my spiritual journey in meaningful ways?

Answer: Deepening your participation in your spiritual awakening starts when you desire to connect with the truth and presence that lives within. Desire is what carries you along the pathways life puts before you. The more you engage in the discovery practice, the more deeply you will initiate the realizations. The beginning stages can seem as formidable as starting to climb a high mountain, but the journey gets progressively easier the higher in consciousness you rise.

To help with this I suggest the following technique. Put one hand over the center of your chest and acknowledge the comfort that naturally emerges. This helps connect you with the soul presence. Next, spend some time allowing yourself exploring your inner space while calling to your spiritual soul presence to emerge and integrate through all your thoughts and feelings. Through this process over time, the spiritual presence replaces all else and becomes the predominant experience causing you to experience life through an enlightened awareness.

8. Question: Is the ego a shell we must destroy to find the real us?

The ego is composed of many identities or personas. It is what holds a person's needs, wants, fears, and desires. The ego formulates interpretations that come through the senses which lead to false perceptions of reality.

Over lifetimes, the ego has created a complex system of beliefs and survival mechanisms attempting to perpetuate its existence. Beneath the costume the ego has woven is the true self composed of the essence of who you truly are. This is often referred to as the soul.

If you try to destroy the ego you will find it is a most worthy opponent. If there is one thing the ego knows how to do well, it is defend itself and survive. For this reason many people have battled it for decades and continue to be frustrated in their attempts to defeat it. The secret to success is to surrender all resistance and let it go. It is more effective to approach any ego pattern with a caring intention to heal it rather than destroy it.

9. Question: How do I deal with the ego and the problems it creates?

Attempts to treat ego-based issues with conventional approaches such as talk therapy utilizing coping strategies or medications which can somewhat subdue the ego by masking symptoms don't adequately address the underlying causes of the ego's characteristics, and as a result, the conditions resurface. Most people experience conditions repeating in their lives many times, but a person can eliminate the ego causes and reveal the inherent true nature of the soul. This entire process is what I call the "soul solution" which is a combination of processes to bring the soul to the surface and replace the ego, and this is why I titled my first book, *The Soul Solution*.

The soul has a completely different way of experiencing life. It is a different operating system from the Ego. It brings a peaceful, satisfying, comforting, loving, empowering quality to life. It embodies all the aspects of goodness that most people want. The Soul does not vie for power or control, but the ego does and as a result is usually what people end up experiencing and dealing with.

10. Question: Why is it so important to eradicate the ego? What are signs that the ego is controlling actions or beliefs?

Answer: The ego is a term that applies to a vast collection of disturbances to one's peace and harmony. Anytime you react negatively, you are operating from the control of the negative ego. This includes the mental and emotional components of all negative emotions as well as all judgments, fixed opinions, criticism, and blame. The ego tends to engage a person in fear-based outlooks that result in such conditions as futility, struggle, depression, hopelessness, guilt, doubt, victimization, anger, resentment, neediness, and the like.

As long as the ego is exerting itself in your life, your contentment, happiness, peace, fulfillment, love, and fun will be fleeting. When the ego is replaced by bringing the soul to the surface, all of the soul qualities become sustained.

As your consciousness rises, the effects of the ego diminish. I prefer to think of the process as helping to heal the pain and struggle of the ego rather than using language that includes eradicating or killing the ego. The ego is a survival mechanism driven by fear and when you use language such as destroying or killing it, the ego's natural reaction is to dig in and defend itself as it fights for survival. On the other hand, when the components of the ego are approached from a perspective of healing and bringing peace to it, the resistance relaxes, making it much easier to reduce the ego's defenses. This approach removes the perception you are taking anything of value from the ego, so it doesn't fight the process. Eventually, the soul replaces the ego.

11. Question: What impact does fear have on my ability to connect with my soul's inner voice? How can I overcome fear to create change in my life?

Answer: The core of nearly all blocks, including feelings of being stuck and mental and emotional disturbances is fear. Fear can manifest in many ways that you may not regard as fear-based but which are. For instance, it's easy to know fear is present when you have anxiety, panic feelings, and are terrified, but there are other forms of fear as well, such as worry, jealousy, insecurity, uncertainty, self-doubt, feeling the world is unsafe, and experiencing life as a struggle. Fear in all its forms functions like a filter that affects your outlook and decisions. When it is present it can distort inner guidance and generate negative self-talk.

The best solution is to replace fear by meeting it with the inner light of the soul. This process requires addressing each form of fear and then releasing and letting go of the way it engages your attention. The second step is to invite the soul to merge into every place the fear is found. With practice, this will diminish the lifeforce energy that fear engages and replace it with the peaceful and enlightened soul presence.

12. Question: Is quantum theory related to the discussion on enlightenment, and if so, how?

Answer: We exist in an intelligent quantum field that sustains all creation, and you and the soul are integral parts of the creation as well as participants in creation. All thoughts and impulses arise from the field of awareness and express through your individuality. The soul is your container of that expression. When you are integrated in the soul's awareness, you experience the reality that you are one with the creation as it plays out through your life in the quantum field. You write the scripts, bring in the props and people to populate your stage, and then interact in the play of life expressing through you.

13. Question: Can you elaborate on the concept that the Universe is our Mirror? How is life a mirror of our beliefs and a mirror of our consciousness?

Answer: The Mirror Universe is a fundamental insight into how the universe works. It is another way of saying, "You reap what you sow," which is a universally recognized principle. Your actions, thoughts, beliefs, and feelings reflect back on you.

In his classic book, *Think and Grow Rich*, Napoleon Hill wrote about a secret that many successful people have discovered which is that people attract what they think about. This is similar to something Buddha is reported to have said, "All we are is a result of what we have thought."

This is an acknowledgment that you are the creator of your own reality because you attract, create, and become what you hold in your mind both consciously and subconsciously. On the surface, this seems to offer a simple solution to all the challenges you experience since it would seem by these statements that all you have to do is start thinking about success and you will have success. However, two obstacles get in the way.

One problem is you probably are clear on what you don't want, but you may not be as clear on what you do want. I have often asked people what they want out of life, and I generally find that most people haven't thought much about that, but they are quick to say what they don't want. This causes your lifeforce to energize what isn't wanted.

The second problem is everyone has unconscious "blind spots" that undermine efforts to accomplish goals. While pondering the idea that you attract or create what you don't want may seem like a negative scenario, it is actually quite an empowering realization. Joseph Campbell put it this way on his video *A Hero's Journey*: "When you follow your bliss...doors will open where you would not have thought there would be doors...and the world moves in and helps." While Campbell is referring to positive aspects, the reverse is also true. When you dwell on negative outcomes, you block the very good things you would like. As for Campbell's comment, the question becomes what is the bliss he is referring to? He does not mean "blissed out" in some transcendent state of euphoria. The bliss he refers to is the happiness, contentment, and joyfulness that are the natural characteristics of the soul.

When you have integrated the bliss, happiness, and goodness of your soul, you more naturally attract and manifest the wonderful results you want in your life. This is the most profound of gifts from The Mirror Universe.

14. Question: What is the difference between soul and spirit?

Answer: What I call the spiritual soul some others call the higher self, authentic self, or true self. The soul is the intelligent non-physical core essence of who you truly are. It is the individualized expression of the intelligent spirit essence that pervades all existence.

The soul is characterized by all goodness in the form of unconditional love, acceptance, happiness, fulfillment, joyfulness, lightness of being, profound beauty, and spiritual awareness of oneness. Anytime you are not experiencing these qualities, you are operating from the ego and is a call to return to the soul.

15. Question: How does a person go about finding their soul?

Answer: First of all, it was never lost. It is just that most people haven't tried to connect with it and they have never had anyone guide them in how to do it, so it has remained a mystery to most. Because the soul is not physical it does require some time to refine a sensitivity to its presence. The soul is not yet discovered with the five senses or scientific instruments. The way you go about finding your soul is to start with the intention to discover it and connect with it. This can best be done with the eyes closed in a meditative state.

In the beginning, the biggest challenge is to get the mind to calm down so you can sense what is going on below its activities. The mind throws up questions and doubts and tries to analyze the situation. A person probably won't notice anything in the beginning stages of making the soul connection, but with practice over weeks or months, one learns to be more aware of its presence. But even if you don't see anything or feel anything, and many won't, that doesn't mean it isn't there or isn't working. For instance, we are generally not aware of the sensations of the clothing in contact with our body, but when we put our attention on it we become aware of it. Unless we are in an extreme temperature we usually don't think about what the temperature is either, but if you put your attention on it you can become aware of the temperature.

The way I started on my soul discovery journey with the simple statement, *"I feel my soul in my heart,"* with a hand over the center of my chest, and I repeated it many times with my eyes closed like a prayer while in a meditative state. I didn't feel anything at first but by repeating that statement many times over a number of weeks I started to notice a subtle presence. The awareness of the soul's presence is somewhat similar to what you may have sensed when a person is standing next to you even if your eyes were closed. You can sense their presence. That is similar to how I began experiencing the soul's presence and I then discovered that the more I put my attention on it the more aware of it I became. In the beginning it is subtle, but in time it becomes more tangible.

The soul has a quiet, peaceful presence. When people first make contact they may have a variety of sensations such as a mild vibration in their body, a ringing in their ears, a warm feeling, a tingling sensation, or simply a deeper sense of peace. Like any skill, it just takes practice.

16. Question: How can people break free from repeating patterns in life?

Answer: For the most part, unconscious or subconscious beliefs cause repeating patterns. It may seem strange to suggest that a belief can be unconscious, but most people are not aware of why they have the feelings, reactions, and judgments they do. This is because most of them formed many years ago, and the circumstances have been long forgotten that contributed to the conclusions people reached, but the beliefs continue to function like an autopilot that takes a person's life in certain directions. Merging the soul into the symptoms helps dissolve the subconscious beliefs causing them while simultaneously creating new, positive patterns.

17. Question: What is the difference between soul healing and energy healing?

Answer: Many forms of energy healing can bring physical and emotional relief by addressing the subtle-energy components of a disturbance. While these techniques can be palliative and sometimes curative, if the underlying beliefs are not addressed that caused the disturbance, they could find another way of coming to the surface and cause another disturbance. The soul, on the other hand, goes to the depths of the causes of difficulties and replaces them with a new level of consciousness that does not support the creation of future problems.

18. Question: What is the difference between meditation and prayer?

Answer: The type of prayers I recommend are what I call prayerful intentions. They are positive statements or declarations of the result you want. They engage the positive flow of creation through your verbalizing the intention. The power of the intention is augmented through the soul's presence that brings its qualities and resources. In fact, the key to what triggers engaging the soul is knowing about it, acknowledging it, and requesting its participation. Therefore, in a real sense, this is an active form of meditation utilizing intentions done in a relaxed state. Here are some examples:

I ask my soul to merge in my heart.
I merge deeply into the presence of my soul.
I feel embraced by my soul's presence and healing light.
I surrender to the soul's presence.

I feel my soul in my heart.

Meditation, on the other hand, is a passive process of being surrendered and allowing yourself to open to whatever awakening and revelation you are ready for.

19. Question: What are your thoughts on subjective vs objective reality?

Answer: For the most part, objective reality is an illusion. Objective reality is what the five major senses respond to; however, everything is subjective. Living inside of each person is a perceiver that creates points of view, opinions, and conclusions about everything and then warehouses them. The perceiver gives birth to identities that run like programs creating sub-personalities a person thinks are part of who they are. This perceiver believes its perceptions are real, yet they are all subjective interpretations of reality and work subtly, behind the scenes, out of day-to-day awareness. But often the perceiving mechanism draws conclusions with incomplete information and treats those conclusions as facts. This leads to fear, anger, depression, and other emotional responses that are essentially a construction of perceptions, stories, and myths that form the basis of everyone's life.

If you take the position that something is real, you imbue it with reality, and then act as if it were real. This is why people are passionate about their points of view which they are convinced are true and real, when in many (or most) cases, they are actually arbitrary opinions based on self-determined beliefs of what truth is or judgments on what is right or wrong.

You can readily see how life is composed of ideas and stories derived from perceptions. You can also see how this can lead to trouble. It wrecks relationships between husbands and wives, between governments and citizens, between employer and employees, between friends, and, of course, between enemies.

20. Question: Are experiences in life stored at the cellular level in the tissue of our bodies? If so, how does that affect our experience of life?

Answer: We are complex beings composed of many aspects. Largely humans are the accumulation of their beliefs, emotions, conclusions, and perceptions, and these components are stored at many levels. This can create challenges in eliminating the negative elements a person doesn't want. Here is a partial list of some of the places where the subtle energy of beliefs, emotions, conclusions, and perceptions can be found:

the brain
the nervous system
the subconscious mind
the aura and chakras
various subtle bodies such as the causal body
the organs and systems of the physical body
the cellular level including the DNA
the person's belief universe

Issues can arise from any of these areas and cause reactions and conditions. The clearing process must address all of these areas because they may contain issues you are unaware of.

21. Question: What is the one life lesson that has had the greatest impact on your life?

Answer: I'm not inclined to think of my life as a series of lessons as much as a series of awakenings, and I would put the realization that we are more than our physical bodies as paramount. My first experience of this happened more than 40 years ago in my early explorations through meditation. When it happened I felt as though I were recalling an ancient memory of what felt like home, but it was not of the earth. I felt like I was pulled into a vast ocean of love at the beginning of time, witnessing the creation of my soul and the universe out of the deepest and purest love imaginable. I realize we all have an ancient past and a dynamic destiny and our life journey is the discovery of that.

22. Question: If we talked in a few months, what would be something that might have changed? Perhaps you can speculate on an internal shift, freedom, or new frontier you are trying to reach.

Answer: I view our spiritual journey as an ever unfolding and expanding experience. Part of the fun of the journey is not knowing what revelation or discovery is next. Every shift in consciousness I've experienced was never what I thought it would be like. For this reason, I do not project or anticipate what is next.

23. Question: What is the difference between Christ consciousness, cosmic consciousness, and enlightenment? In addition, what steps are required to attain these?

Answer: The terms are somewhat related yet include some differences. Cosmic Consciousness refers to the perception of oneness with all awareness. It is a state usually attained through meditation in which individuality and separation vanishes and the underlying interconnectedness of all existence is realized. It is similar to Self-Realization.

Christ Consciousness includes Cosmic Consciousness but incorporates the elevated level of awareness one attains with refined qualities. It is sometimes also referred to as the ascension of consciousness which means dissolving ego characteristics of separation and raising one's consciousness to the level of pure love and light.

The term "Christ Consciousness" as used today is a close equivalent to awakening or enlightenment. Some also apply it to a more specific level of spiritual attainment in which a person's consciousness has ascended beyond the ego and his or her heart-center is fully open. The term is most often applied to certain saints or "ascended masters."

The use of the word "Christ" is not specific to Jesus, but rather the word Christ refers to one who is "anointed," which implies "set apart for a holy purpose." Some groups use the term "Christed" to refer to a person who has become one with Christ or ascended to the level of the consciousness of a Christ.

Christians are opposed to using the term in this way because they regard Jesus as a unique being, whereas those using the term are referring to elevated states of consciousness available to all. Sometimes these terms are used interchangeably although enlightenment more broadly includes higher realizations and non-duality.

24. Question: Why do people seek Enlightenment?

Answer: Asking this question is like asking why a moth seeks a light. The moth doesn't know why it is drawn to a light, it just is. In our case, it is our nature to know who and what we are. Here's why—at our core is a soul essence that naturally desires to rise to the surface and express itself. However, what most people identify with are many constructs of personality traits overlaying the soul. These traits are so compelling that people are convinced these created identities are who they are, but they are mostly driven by various forms of fear. The fear can include motivations for safety and security and drives to avoid anything perceived to be dangerous or threatening. Hence, many people have paranoia, anxiety, fear of making a mistake, fear of rejection, and many other variations of fear.

Over time as a person addresses the illusory nature of the identities, more and more of the soul rises to the surface to reveal its nature, and the person's consciousness rises. The more people are in touch with this spiritual nature, the more they are motivated to understand it.

25. Question: What can trigger spiritual awakening?

Answer: Spiritual awakening can happen in an instant and often unexpectedly. In some cases, it can seem to happen for no obvious reason. However, much like plants in springtime that seem to burst forth in bloom spontaneously, much preparation laid the foundation for the blossoming. Spiritual awakening also requires preparations. In past lives and dedication in this life, people only awaken when they have let go of sufficient illusions that mask their deepest truth. For some it is through difficulty and struggles that motivate them to seek, for others it is through devotion to spiritual quests and practices.

The most common activating cause derives from sincerely following a spiritual path that usually includes having a teacher or guide who has already awakened. By being in the presence of one who is already awake, some have found it much easier to access higher states of consciousness. Even in those cases, a person usually must genuinely be living in integrity with a desire to deepen into spiritual awareness for full awakening to occur.

All this said, it should be noted that sometimes people have epiphanies with little outward seeking or dedication. These cases are rarer, but do occasionally happen when a person has given thought to a topic, read accounts about awakening, or posed questions exploring the nature of life. Surrendering and dissolving the many ego-beliefs that mask the already enlightened soul that lives within you is the most reliable trigger for awakening. The more you clear the illusions and distortions of the ego, the higher your consciousness naturally attains.

26. Question: How long does a spiritual awakening take?

Answer: This is one of the most commonly asked questions by people on a spiritual path. Awakening usually feels like a never-ending journey filled with pitfalls and plateaus. For most, the process is a lifelong one and usually spans many lifetimes. Of course, the process is accelerated when a person becomes more committed to the spiritual path and engages in spiritual practices.

In the early stages, there is a lot of searching to find answers to many questions on the subject. Usually, people read many books and attend numerous workshops seeking to discover the truths they need to support their journey. This phase alone can last a decade or more.

In the next phase the search is narrowed to teachers and sources who are best able to guide people in their struggles with ego and illusions. This phase can span another decade or more.

In later phases, a person arrives at the threshold of ego dissolution through extensive inner work and meditation. When they have surrendered and released illusions sufficiently either with the support of an enlightened teacher, or more rarely on their own, an inner enlightening shift occurs. Sometimes it is a single monumental shift, and in other cases it initiates a series of incremental shifts, expanding awareness each time. Evolving from one phase to another takes unwavering commitment and dedication to move through the frustrations and struggles encountered along the way.

Marianne Williamson gives one of the best answers to this question, in her book the *Age of Miracles*. "It takes a decade to understand the basic nature of spiritual principles, another decade while the ego tries to eat you alive, another decade while you try to wrestle it to the ground, and finally you begin to walk more or less in the light. Anyone who thinks a spiritual path is easy, probably hasn't been walking one."

27. Question: Do enlightened people see and relate to others in a significantly different way than un-enlightened people?

Answer: The enlightenment experience is a continuum of higher awakenings. As the enlightenment deepens, ego-based motivations diminish and finally disappear. This results in progressively less anger, judgment, criticism, and blame, as well as other negative reactions and emotions. If those issues do come up, they typically dissipate fairly rapidly and do not result in moods or brooding. Negative characteristics fade away, and a natural opening of the heart center causes more compassion, kindness, caring, happiness, and unconditional love to occur.

In addition, because the higher chakras open in enlightenment, there is a higher awareness that results in higher perception, patience, and understanding. The more enlightened people are, the more they see and relate to others on a soul level rather than a personality level.

28. Question: Since many spiritual teachers say to enjoy life and live in the moment, why do people run around seeking enlightenment? Shouldn't they just enjoy the present moment?

Answer: Being mindfully present is always helpful on a spiritual path, for that is all we actually ever have. The past no longer exists other than as memories, and the future has not yet arrived. Most people fluctuate from processing the past repeatedly to worrying or planning their future.

Seeking enlightenment is an ego-mind driven condition in which the mind is seeking what it thinks it doesn't have. The ego-driven mind thinks something is missing, so it pursues enlightenment, usually through many diverse pathways in its never-ending search for more control, more safety, more security, and more answers.

The mind doesn't really know what enlightenment is, but it has heard about it and thinks this is what is missing from its experience. Therefore, it drives a person to read books, go to retreats, and travel to remote places to find enlightened beings with answers.

The many ideas the mind has about enlightenment are never what the experience turns out to be because enlightenment is not a cognitive analytical process. Enlightenment is being in the present moment with no thoughts going to the past or future. It is where you find peace. Most people can sustain present moment awareness for specified times, but when full enlightenment awakens, it becomes a permanent and natural awareness; you no longer have to pursue it, work at it, or try to hold onto the present; it is there in quiet awareness all the time.

29. Question: Why are some people naturally more enlightened than others are?

Answer: We are all on a long journey to our spiritual home. Our experiences both in this and previous lives determines our understanding and realization of spiritual principles. When some seem to awaken more easily and quickly to spiritual realizations, they have probably had numerous lifetimes in pursuit of them. They undoubtedly went through their struggles a long time ago and perhaps even attained enlightened levels in previous lives.

Sometimes when people hear how simple it was for some to awaken, it is easy to think they are flawed because enlightenment seems so difficult. But an apparent delay only means more remains to surrender. There is no judgment about the realization level a person has experienced, for all will eventually arrive back to the Source.

30. Question: Is the path of enlightenment for everyone?

Answer: In one sense, everyone is on a path to enlightenment, but most don't know it. An evolutionary current carriers everyone, but some become more actively involved in accelerating their awakening. Everyone could benefit from awakening, but most are too distracted to be devoted to what is required. It takes commitment, persistence, patience, and sustained desire to stay on a path.

In addition, the many teachers and teachings today make sifting through the confusion to find the gems of truth that resonate with where you are on your path a difficult and timely process. No one path exists for everyone. You have to find the best one for you now, and it will lead you to the next one when the time is right.

31. Question: Why is spiritual awakening so painful?

Answer: Often the process of spiritual awakening highlights the suffering a person has experienced. The causes of the suffering are often elusive and yet keep presenting themselves until they are acknowledged and surrendered. Until fully awakened, the pain accumulated through karma, beliefs, and emotional reactions perpetuates. The very desire for awakening puts people on a path of shedding the struggles and suffering caused by their attachments. The more strongly people identifiy with opinions, needs, desires, fears, etc., the more painful the process will be as they surface.

The path of spiritual awakening is a process of elimination. Each and every attachment and illusion must be released. In the early stages, it can at times seem overwhelming, but as more is released, the journey becomes easier.

32. Question: What does it mean when people say "everyone is already enlightened"?

Answer: Beneath the identities people think they are is an awareness of enlightenment. Most people are so strongly hypnotized by the projections they assume are reality that they have little or no experience with the awareness below the illusions. The claim that everyone is already enlightened refers to the underlying truth beneath all appearances. As people gradually wake up from the stories and dreams running their lives, they become increasingly aware of an enlightened consciousness that does not identify with anything the mind projects.

33. Question: Is the enlightened mind freer or less free than the normal mind?

Answer: This question possibly answers itself, as by definition, enlightenment is an awareness of being freed from the mind. The "enlightened mind" is in a state of freedom and acceptance. It no longer fights with what is. It is acceptant and peaceful. This said, using the term "enlightened mind" is self-contradictory because the sense of mind disappears with enlightenment. Some refer to this as "no mind" or the unconditioned mind as opposed to the "normal mind," which is conditioned through judgments and beliefs.

This question is a form of definition of enlightenment if the normal mind is defined as the ego mind. The ego-driven mind is what most people experience as their normal mind; however, enlightened teachers usually define the enlightened mind as the natural mind. Therefore, for purposes of answering this question, I'll define the "normal" mind as a mind driven by ego defenses that are primarily various forms of fear. The very definition of enlightenment hinges on attaining a consciousness free of ego.

Full enlightenment means being free from all forms of psychological fear, control, anger, judgment, pride, guilt, depression, and all other aspects of the ego. This being the case, the closer one approaches full enlightenment, the less ego exists, or to use the terminology posed in the question, the more free of the normal mind the person becomes.

34. Question: Is spiritual awakening just a myth applied to a psychological condition, perhaps a mental aberration?

Answer: Attempts to define or describe spiritual awakening often project ideas, definitions, and judgments. However, enlightenment is non-conceptual awareness and therefore any attempt to label it falls far short of what it is. All we have to communicate with is words that are symbols of ideas. Properly chosen words do help point to underlying truths but when applied to enlightenment, they create concepts that are inaccurate. For instance, explanations are conceptualizations with stories attached to images and qualities; however, spiritual awakening or enlightenment is waking up from such illusions. Spiritual awakening detaches from the mind that continually formulates and projects and opens one to an awareness that transcends all definitions to a consciousness of non-conceptual awareness.

35. Question: What are signs of spiritual awakening?

Answer: One of the most common experiences upon awakening is the sense of being one with everything. The separation experienced through the senses in everyday life melts away. This is also accompanied with a realization all is simultaneous with no past or future. There is a feeling of being complete and content with underlying equanimity. In addition, this is usually followed with a sense of being in an automatic flow of effortless effort. In some cases, heightened intuition and clarity also occur. In cases where the awakening is more complete, mood shifts are rare and outer circumstances do not affect internal peace. When experiencing this shift, people sometimes feel they are losing it after days or weeks. This can be due to acclimating to the new level of consciousness or being pulled back into the distractions of everyday life.

36. Question: How common is spiritual awakening?

Answer: I'll assume the question relates to what is commonly referred to as enlightenment. If it were to include any spiritual epiphany, the number would be many millions since there are many "born again" Christians who feel they have had a spiritual awakening, not to mention comparable occurrences in all religions.

"Spiritual awakening," however, is a term usually used in reference to a shift in consciousness that includes awareness of the oneness of all, freedom from illusions, a quiet mind, and sustained present moment awareness. While this has historically been thought to only happen to a small population of dedicated spiritual aspirants, in our modern age it has become more common. With the wide availability of information through books, the internet, and access to awakened teachers, the knowledge that was once hidden and difficult to discover has now become readily accessible. This combined with the ability to travel distances to interact with those who are already enlightened has opened more opportunities for spiritual awakening than was available to our ancestors.

37. Question: What kind of meditation is effective for enlightenment?

Answer: Numerous approaches to reaching enlightenment are available, but one way or the other they all reduce to eliminating what prevents it. An important key to any method is exploring and deepening one's understanding of self through surrender.

The major obstacle is the mind projecting illusions it clings to as truth. Everything the mind believes is really just a collection of perceptions and conclusions. In other words, they are mythologies, stories, or delusions, but they are so strong that once you are caught in them, you believe they are truth and reality. Because of this, most people are living stories projected by their deepest beliefs, loves, and fears.

To arrive at an enlightened consciousness, you have to deconstruct the mind's projections and shift into the awareness that underlies all thoughts and manifestations. Any meditative practice that you are drawn to can help facilitate this process, and what is effective for you at one time will likely be exchanged for other approaches as time goes on. This is where a skilled and enlightened teacher can be invaluable in helping you recognize the traps of the mind and offer direction on how to free yourself from them.

38. Question: What are the pros and cons of spiritual awakening?

Answer: I've already answered many of the benefits in this book, so now I'll list some "cons" which are usually centered on being disappointed.

One "con" to spiritual awakening is being disappointed it was not what was expected. This can be a major challenge as the mind always tries to project what it thinks will happen, and what does happen is rarely what the mind expects.

Many people expect that when spiritually awakened, all their pain and problems will instantly disappear. Sometimes this does happen, but often it does not.

Some expect they will automatically receive treasures and gifts.

Some think that everything in their life will magically change to everything they ever dreamed they wanted.

Some think life will be easy forevermore.

Some think they will find the love of their life.

Some find they lose what they formerly cherished.

Many find they lose their passion.

Some expect to have "super powers."

I once heard an "enlightened" teacher say that if you are offered spiritual awakening or one million dollars, take the money. I think that teacher missed something important. I hope this list isn't discouraging. It shouldn't be because an endless list of wonderful reasons to awaken exists. All the "cons" are mind-projected expectations and not the reality.

39. Question: Are there any shortcuts to enlightenment?

Answer: The most effective technique I have found is first to go into a good meditative state and ask to be taken to the next level of evolution. Second, be in a surrendered state and pay attention to what is important for you because life will always reveal what your next step is. Regardless of what comes up, the path of surrender will take you deeper. A natural tendency is to hold on to what is familiar, but letting go reveals your deep inner truth.

Once something is being revealed to you, give permission for the transformative work to take place. "Permission" opens a doorway to your transformation, and sometimes it helps to say to yourself, "I give myself permission to let go of this." Alternatively state, "I give myself permission to receive that blessing."

The path of enlightenment is essentially a process of letting go of attachments and negative patterns such as fear, doubt, anger, judgment, criticism, blame, and others. Any techniques you find that enable you to do this will move you along your path. If you do not deal directly with these issues through releasing techniques, you will play out a series of scenarios that dramatize them in ways that force you to eventually deal with them. This is what sometimes leads people to experience "The Dark Night of the Soul."

Another way of approaching the pathway to enlightenment is to become the most complete and loving being you can. The love energy will naturally dissolve the parts of you that are keeping you from an enlightened state. If you combine both the path of love and the path of releasing, you will have the fastest way possible to enlightenment.

40. Question: What is self-realization and why can't I get a straight answer?

Answer: I'll answer the second part of the question first with the well-known tale of four blind men each touching only one part of an elephant. There are several variations of this tale, but you'll get the point with this one: One touches the tail, one touches a tusk, one touches a leg, and one touches the trunk. Then they get together to discuss what they thought they were touching. Each had a very different and inaccurate interpretation of what an elephant is. How this applies to self-realization is that each person describes his/her own experience and often thinks he or she has the "right" answer or "best" answer. This is the point to the story. Each person had a different subjective experience, none of which accurately described the elephant. Self-realization also is subjective; hence, it has some latitude in definitions. If you flip the two words to "realization of the self," you'll come closer to the spiritual definition; however, there are varieties of levels to the experience.

One prominent aspect of self-realization is the awareness of being one and connected with all there is. The analogy of the ocean is often cited to depict this impression, namely that we are all like waves with individual expressions, yet an aspect of the one ocean. When one has the awareness of being one with all creation, all sense of separation vanishes.

41. Question: What motivates the search for enlightenment, if not desire?

Answer: Nothing would exist without desire if you think of desire as the urge behind all creation. Desire provides motivation, and therefore is useful for everything you experience. Desire is necessary for any movement, including the search for truth and enlightenment. Therefore, it is important. Once enlightenment has become a permanent awareness, desire is no longer the driving force. Awareness becomes the field in which all appears.

42. Question: Does spiritual awakening lead a person to ignore the problems of life instead of dealing with them?

Answer: Some have had that experience. There are stories of the enlightened teacher Ramana Maharshi who lost interest in school, friends, and relations. He became so absorbed in Samadhi that he was unaware of his body and surroundings and food had to be placed in his mouth or he would have starved. Over time, he did become more active in life with establishing an Ashram. A phase of passivity sometimes occurs as the realizations of the impermanence of everything arises. Many feel they lose their passion for life for a time, but this usually passes in a few months or years, as a person re-engages in more meaningful ways with people and life. Not everyone who awakens has this type of experience, however. Many find themselves becoming more loving, kind, and caring and engage in ways to express these ideals.

Along the awakening path, confrontations with ego needs challenge a person's equanimity, but as the awakening deepens and the ego melts, the painful issues are replaced with contentment, happiness, and fulfillment.

43. Question: Do you think we go through hardships to become enlightened?

Answer: One way or the other you will evolve, either by wisdom or woe. In most cases, it is a combination of the two. Those who have not experienced the shift to liberation can be entangled in the consequences of negative karma and negative ego. Often the most meaningful course-correction lessons are learned by trial and error. Pain avoidance and fear are stronger motivations than the pursuit of happiness. Because this is so, hardships can be the stepping-stones to seeking relief, healing, and ultimately enlightenment, but it certainly doesn't have to be this way.

44. Question: In order to become enlightened, do I have to abandon my conscious self?

Answer: You don't abandon the conscious self, but your perception of what it is will change. The obstacle the conscious self presents to enlightenment is its many fixations and attachments. By becoming enlightened, what the conscious self has believed and held is released. In the evolution of your consciousness and the awakening process, you will become more aware of your conscious self, and the many illusions the conscious self clings to will fall away and a neutral observer or witness will emerge.

45. Question: How would an enlightened person mourn the loss of a dear one? Will he just go about his day, completely unnerved by his or her loss?

Answer: The shortest verse in the Bible is John 11:35 which says, "Jesus wept." An enlightened person is not a zombie or without feelings. Although an enlightened person is not attached, when someone close passes he or she naturally feels loss and sadness. Feelings are part of being human, but enlightened individuals do not sink into the depths of negative emotions. If negative emotions do arise, they are less intense and more short lived than they would have been prior to enlightenment. The level of many feelings an enlightened person experiences is heightened, such as encompassing unconditional love, deep caring, and heartfelt compassion.

46. Question: When has one achieved enlightenment?

Answer: My usual answer to this question is when you no longer need to ask the question. However, I know what you mean by the question, and there are indications of enlightened awareness. It depends on where people's consciousness is on their spiritual journey whether they would consider themselves enlightened or if anyone else would.

Here's what I mean: One of the common experiences usually associated with enlightenment is the opening of a sense of being one with everything. This is often called Unity Consciousness. It is quite common for people to have this experience in meditations, but it can also expand into everyday awareness. When people have this awareness, they may consider themselves enlightened, but not everyone would agree. Some would say that even if Unity Consciousness becomes permanent and isn't lost after the meditation, this still is insufficient to indicate enlightenment.

Some people also think of themselves as enlightened when they experience bliss and/or deep love. While these are also common experiences with certain meditations and are very beautiful experiences, they too are not indications of enlightenment. There are also those who wouldn't consider either of these examples of enlightenment because they are still identifying with certain conceptualizations, and they would regard true enlightenment as beyond all conceptualization.

The examples above are good indications a person is on the way to enlightenment, but no one agrees on a single indicator. In general, when your mind is perpetually quiet all the time and you inhabit emptiness and non-duality as your sustained inner experience, you are probably enlightened. In the meantime, look for emerging happiness, completion, peacefulness, effortlessness, and freedom from the tyranny of the mind.

47. Question: Can one be partially enlightened?

Answer: According to David Hawkins, M.D., PhD, who created a scale of consciousness, the answer is yes. On his scale which goes from 0 to 1,000, enlightenment begins at 600. He says the ego completely disappears at 850 on his scale. I know a lot of people have strong positions against having such a scale, but these are only attempts to describe the differences observed in people's consciousness, so I suggest just appreciate it for what it is, or take it with "a grain of salt" if you prefer.

At 600 Hawkins describes transcendence, illumination, self-realization, enlightenment, and deep peace. At this point, wants, needs, desires, and aversions start to dissolve. At 600 the mind is no longer judging and being present is automatic. Experiences arise from awareness rather than planning or linear thinking. A state of effortless effort is attained in which life has a natural ease and flow.

48. Question: Are enlightened people happy?

Answer: Consider the answer to the previous question which encompasses levels of enlightenment. Most of the time a person at 600 on Hawkin's scale is at the beginning levels of enlightened and is mostly happy, content, satisfied, and peaceful. In addition, an enlightened person is mostly beyond staying in negative moods, but as long as a person is still in a human body, when facing a loved one's death or a tragedy sadness is always possible, but usually passes in a short time. The major differences between how an enlightened person reacts to situations that most people get negatively emotional over is by experiencing the emotion for a very short time and by feeling negative emotions infrequently and with less intensity than most people.

49. Question: Do truly enlightened people share the same point of view?

Answer: Existing without opinions is impossible, and regardless of one's consciousness level, differences in opinion will occur in some matters. An enlightened person can still have preferences different from others and often express them. For example, there can be a wide variety of opinions in matters of everyday life, but usually most agree on spiritual matters although how subjects are explained can vary.

50. Question: How do you achieve enlightenment in one lifetime?

Answer: Although attaining enlightenment does not depend on just an approach, all true paths include letting go of attachments, causes of negative karma, releasing judgments, and other ego reactions and needs. How a person goes about this and how fast he or she succeeds is a matter of personal commitment.

The word enlightenment is used very loosely today to apply to many different spiritual practices and mental states. Two major aspects pertain to what is called enlightenment. First, there is enlightenment that comes from the mind. This includes receiving realizations, and understanding of the nature of transcendence, oneness, and non-duality. The second aspect to enlightenment is of the heart. Enlightenment of the heart is a different focus from that of the mind, and enlightenment of the mind is incomplete without the enlightenment of the heart.

In order to bring the soul into the physical dimension, one takes on a body that functions in physical density. This body also operates with personality. What happens in the process of life is that your soul submerges as the activities of the analytical mind, emotions, and personality dominate. This in turn, causes sub-personalities to form around the pain and other illusions that are characteristic of the physical dimension.

The experiences in this third density could be love, beauty, kindness, and generosity, but due to the ego, life distorts these ideals. People become immersed in pain, suffering, limitations, and disease. Additionally, every time someone projects emotions at you, maintaining love and peace is challenging. If hooked by the other person's emotions, you loose your center and become entangled with like emotions. This further encases you in the illusions of the lower emotions.

To progress on the enlightened path, you must become neutral and unaffected by any pairs of opposites. When you are equal-minded, you will experience joy and feelings of love and satisfaction regardless of outer circumstances. When you reach this state, others can no longer hook you with their emotions or illusions. This is a very high way to live and brings great freedom with it. Let go and be free. Yes, you can certainly become enlightened in one lifetime provided you are relentless and dedicated to the pursuit of becoming clear and free of the ego.

51. Question: Does achieving enlightenment require emotional detachment?

Answer: Emotional neutrality is a by-product of enlightenment not a cause of it. As consciousness rises, equanimity emerges. Before enlightenment, there is often emotional fixating or attaching through positive or negative emotions. For instance, a person could be filled with anger and hate and thereby be attached to the object of that anger. An enlightened person would not experience this but would be acceptant without judgment and therefore non-attached. In the case of being attached to a person with the emotion of love, an enlightened person's love is unconditional, non-possessive, and non-controlling.

52. Question: Why don't all humans become enlightened?

Answer: Enlightenment is not a goal or of interest to most who are busy raising their families, following their career path, or involved with recreational activities. For many the struggles of everyday life are all they can deal with, and they are too overwhelmed to put the attention needed on such a high goal.

A large percentage of people are also trapped by their strong beliefs. In many cases, those beliefs include aversions to enlightenment, believing it is a path away from their concept of God. Some religions instill fear in exploring outside their doctrines. The path to enlightenment takes commitment, dedication, and perseverance over years, and most people are not that motivated.

53. Question: Does enlightenment change the brain?

Answer: I can only tell you about my experiences concerning this, and I recognize this may not apply to everyone. When I went through one consciousness shift years ago, all my thinking stopped and has never returned. For a while, it was a strange experience not to have any uninvited thoughts, just dead silence all the time. I can deliberately think something at times, but most of the time the words I say seem to arise spontaneously from awareness with no pre-thought or analysis afterwards. I remember thinking, "How am I going to do anything without thoughts? How do I drive a car, balance a check book, or even make decisions?" These all resolved themselves over time as I began operating from awareness rather than planning.

I had yet another strange sensation with my brain when I went through another consciousness shift; I felt my brain moving around in my head. It felt somewhat like there were fingers in my head moving my brain around. This lasted for maybe a minute, and I've had a few others tell me they had similar sensations. This happened to me twice, and I do not know the significance of it. I am not saying any of these things are related to enlightenment, just that they both happened when I was experiencing some rather dramatic shifts in consciousness.

54. Question: Can you be spiritually enlightened, then lose it?

Answer: The perception of losing enlightenment sometimes happens, but nothing is ever lost. I know that sounds like a contradiction, but here's what I mean. When you are in early stages of enlightened awareness, especially during meditation, you may no longer project judgments nor fixate on beliefs, but as you return to everyday life you may experience some positions, beliefs, and interpretations re-engage and re-create some attachments. It isn't that you lost something; it is just that the mind re-engaged and distracted you.

In rare instances, some who awakened to enlightenment levels became reabsorbed in ego desires that lowered their consciousness level. The deeper you go into enlightened emptiness and non-duality, the longer it will stay with you until eventually this becomes permanent.

55. Question: Did you ever mistakenly believe you were enlightened?

Answer: I did early on my spiritual path. Because I had some remarkably transcendent and beautiful realizations in meditation, I assumed I was enlightened. It took going through a health crisis and other stresses for me to reexamine my beliefs and conclusions. I realized that having a few amazing meditations was not the same as actually being enlightened. I've met many people over the years who similarly think they are enlightened and sometimes fool themselves into thinking they are highly enlightened. It is not for me or anyone else to judge the degree of enlightenment of anyone who claims to be or thinks he or she is.

Deceiving oneself on the matters of enlightenment is easy, but self-judgment in this regard has no value. People who are truly enlightened have no need or desire to refer to themselves as enlightened or attempt to determine how enlightened they are. We are all evolving beings, and enlightenment itself is a progression of realizations with many characteristics.

56. Question: Are there enlightened people who don't believe in reincarnation?

Answer: Some non-dualists and enlightened ones would say there is nothing to reincarnate since everything is an illusion. From a non-dualist perspective, we are all projected illusions. These projections are apparently persistent enough that we experience existence. You arrived here somehow, and the prevailing projection is that you arrived here through a reincarnation process even though it is all an illusion.

57. Question: Why is it that feeling spiritually enlightened is sometimes interpreted as being depressed and indifferent?

Answer: Here is what I have observed with quite a few people on the way to enlightenment. Many go through a phase prior to enlightenment in which they feel like they have lost some of their passion and purpose. This can cause some to become discouraged and loose touch with others. When some realize that life is an illusion, they find this causes them to feel everything is futile. If it happens, just continue with spiritual practices and those feelings will pass. Enlightenment brings peacefulness, contentment, caring, and happiness. If people are not experiencing these qualities, they are more likely in a pre-enlightenment phase that will pass as they continue on the path.

58. Question: How can a spiritual teacher who sounds so wise and enlightened do so many bad things?

Answer: This question answers itself. If the teacher sounds enlightened, what makes the teacher sound that way? Some teachers have spiritual sounding language, tone of voice, costumes, and gestures that some associate with being enlightened. Such a teacher may even think he or she is an enlightened being as self-deception is a defense mechanism of the ego. An enlightened person does not violate the boundaries of another, nor engage in activities that take advantage of anyone.

Some spiritual teachers have had enlightening experiences that they use as credentials to validate their claim that they are enlightened. However, this does not indicate they are fully enlightened, and they may even engage in some lower consciousness activities or struggle with karmic patterns from past lives. This is not to conclude these teachers have nothing to offer spiritual seekers as they may help many a great deal.

59. Question: Does being more enlightened than others necessarily mean that one will be more successful than less enlightened ones? By success, I mean possession of material wealth, fame, and other al things.

Answer: Enlightenment is about consciousness and awareness and not about anything material or physical. This being the case, some may be materially well off, while others are not. Nothing outward in the form of success or possessions that indicates a person's spiritual consciousness.

60. Question: Do enlightened people easily recognize other enlightened people?

Answer: Once people have gone through the awakening, they are familiar with what the experience is and the effects it has on perceptions. If a person has not awakened, whatever he or she thinks enlightenment is arises from the ego's analysis and therefore is not accurate. Enlightenment is rarely what the mind thinks it is. With enlightenment comes clarity. An enlightened person is able to recognize the characteristics reflected by the consciousness level of others and therefore usually able to recognize others who are enlightened.

61. Question: What does it feel like to be spiritually enlightened?

Answer: Enlightenment is about becoming free of fixated opinions, judgments, concepts, and ideas of the mind that act as filters between you and your experiences of life. The mind rarely allows a person to experience life without judgments. Input is constantly being interpreted, evaluated, colored, and filtered by your conditioning, past pain, past ideas, judgments, and choices.

In enlightened consciousness, the senses experience reality without the mind interfering. Because of this, if you are enlightened, you can use the mind rather than being used by it. You become free of the mind's need for drama, for being right, for judging and valuing, and for being in control. The uninvited thoughts stop, and you become free of the emotions and decisions based on past realities. You experience life in the moment automatically.

In the early experiences of awakening, feelings can fluctuate as the entirety of the ego has not completely dissolved. As the ego finally disappears, a sense of being complete emerges, yet with non-dual awareness. The seeming of opposites is gone. Reality is all and nothing. There is full timelessness, you live in the ever present now, and it is all automatic.

62. Question: How can I stay in the enlightenment state?

Answer: Sometimes when people experience something beyond physical sensations, they take it as an indication of enlightenment. These experiences, however while beautiful and sometimes spontaneous, are not evidence of enlightenment itself. They can be enhanced and extended with practice, but if you are truly wanting a sustained awakening shift in consciousness, you must let go of every ego perception, reaction, and judgment. As more of the ego is surrendered and released, enlightened awareness is maintained for longer durations.

Some non-dualists object to the use of words such as "state," "phase," "level," "qualities," or even the words "ego" and "enlightenment" itself. However, to answer the questions asked, I am relying on certain words to point to underlying truths. The challenge is determining what the ego elements are. Some are very subtle and fade into the background of awareness and are barely noticed. The obvious ones may be more easily identified, but they can also be more challenging to unravel and release. Full enlightenment can take years if not decades, so do not be discouraged. Be persistent in surrendering until you live in a "state" of complete surrender and the ego dissolves. As you near the threshold of complete ego release, you might experience a surge of fear that you will cease to exist. This, of course, is the ego projecting its fear of what it thinks will happen. The paradox is that even though the ego is gone, consciousness and awareness are ever present.

The answer to reaching and maintaining enlightened states always comes down to surrender. Everything must be surrendered: every thought, judgment, emotion, need, want, and attachment. The paradox is that even though all is surrendered and released, nothing is ever lost, for there was nothing to lose. Through surrender arises the awareness that everything is a mind projection onto the screen of consciousness. Once complete surrender is achieved, you will experience deep peace, satisfaction, happiness, completion, and contentment.

63. Question: When enlightened people experience desire, how do they perceive it? How do they react to desire?

Answer: Enlightened people move through life as an expression of awareness and are not attached to desires, nor do they experience the suffering some desires can create in those not enlightened. An enlightened person does not experience desire the same way an unenlightened person does. The enlightened person is very neutral and moves with the flow of creation. Desire is not wrong, bad, or anti-enlightenment. Existence itself requires desires since nothing would exist without it. An enlightened person, however, is not controlled by desires nor attached to desires or outcomes. The enlightened person is a neutral observer of what is and is not driven by desires, so there is no suffering derived from desire.

64. Question: Are there any truly spiritually enlightened people living today?

Answer: One of the problems with discussions on enlightenment is the fact it is somewhat elusive to define. Myths describe what an enlightened person is like, and some of these ideas elevate these people to super-human beings. While some have achieved remarkable extra sensory abilities, enlightenment is about consciousness and awareness far more than attainment of skills or powers.

If the qualities of enlightenment hinge on such characteristics as transcendence, self-realization, radiant light, deep peace, non-duality, and the dissolution of wants, needs, desires, and aversions, many will qualify as being enlightened. But only those who have attained these qualities are sufficiently aware enough to know if others have. Nothing the mind defines is the answer to this question, and therefore no amount of analysis or comparison can arrive at accuracy in this matter. Knowing whether someone is enlightened or not depends on realization and awareness and though the number of enlightened ones may be small, it is far larger than those who have become spiritual legends.

65. Question: How does a spiritually enlightened person deal with pain?

Answer: Through extensive discipline and practice, some have been able to compartmentalize conditions of the physical body and emotions and thus mediate pain. This, however, is not necessarily an indication of enlightenment, but such people are able to shut off reactions to what would otherwise be painful. Enlightenment is a matter of awareness level, and whether the pain is physical or emotional, enlightened people are more acceptant of circumstances. They do not judge the cause of such conditions nor anyone who contributed to them. One notable characteristic of enlightenment is being at peace with what is. The peace is deep, transcendent, and not dependent on anything external. The enlightened person is not in resistance to any circumstance, while continually moving into balance and applying resources available to alleviate suffering.

Enlightenment is an internal shift in consciousness that does not necessarily create physical changes, but there are some accounts of extraordinary endurance. Some highly spiritually advanced people have apparently been able to handle extremes in their environment. For instance, Sai Baba is reported to have been immune to extreme hot and cold weather, as he would appear to be comfortable walking barefoot in snow with only a very thin garment when the people with him were quite cold. He was also comfortable in very hot weather. Another extraordinary example was Shiva bala yogi who was bitten by cobras more than once and survived.

Whether extraordinary abilities are a byproduct of enlightenment or the practice of mental disciplines is difficult to determine. Some regarded as enlightened seem as subject to the same levels of pain and suffering as everyone else. Therefore, it does not appear that enlightenment itself is the factor.

66. Question: Would a spiritually enlightened person think of himself or herself as being enlightened?

Answer: A spiritually enlightened person is somewhat of a pragmatist, which is a logical way of approaching topics and situations, rather than approaching them based on mythologies, emotions, or opinions. An enlightened person is non-self-judgmental in recognizing consciousness levels; however, for the most part, enlightened people are not concerned with defining whether or not they are enlightened, but they are usually open to discussing their spiritual experiences and realizations. Enlightened people wouldn't normally even think about whether they are enlightened or not because they experience a very naturalness about consciousness. Most of the time when such a person is asked if he or she is enlightened or not, the reply sounds evasive.

67. Question: Would an enlightened person act illegally or unethically?

Answer: Legality is a matter of human created rules. Enlightened people operate outside of rules. That is not to say they are looking for ways to be in violation, but they operate beyond rules. In some cases, they may face the consequences imposed by their society for breaking rules, such as was the case with Jesus, Socrates, Galileo, and many others.

An enlightened person is aligned with love, kindness, and grace, and therefore would not normally do anything offensive unless in a very rare instance to teach a principle. Enlightened people live in integrity and therefore all they say and do is coming from a place of consideration, honesty, and respect. They would not violate another person's boundaries or do anything unkind.

68. Question: Is life easy for an enlightened person?

Answer: An enlightened person has to deal with most of the same circumstances everyone else does, but his or her reactions are quite different. "Easy" in this case relates to how a person contextualizes or judges situations. For some maintaining a household is perceived to be burdensome, but an enlightened person flows without resistance through the tasks necessary. Therefore, in this sense, their life has ease.

Once enlightened, people experience sustained inner peace that also creates a feeling of ease. Since they have transcended most, if not all ego, they are no longer generating negative karma, and hence not creating the types of circumstances around themselves that cause others to struggle or suffer. They live with a sense of automatic flow and effortless effort, but that does not mean they are automatically healthy, wealthy, or accomplished by external measurements of success. Some, of course, are, but that type of success is not an indication of being enlightened. The ease of life of one who is enlightened is more a matter of the manner in which he or she is acceptant and at ease with circumstances.

69. Question: Is a spiritually enlightened person interested in every moment?

Answer: Not only are enlightened people very present in each moment, but they are also mindful and attentive to it as well. They are neutral observers of themselves and others every moment. Some may or may not have thoughts or desires, but most have feelings such as happiness, joyfulness, peace, and contentment. In many cases, whatever they find themselves doing, they are having fun.

70. Question: Does a spiritually enlightened person make mistakes? If so, does he/she feel regret?

Answer: Mistakes are a matter of definition, but enlightened people do not always perform perfectly. For instance, if an enlightened person were playing golf, tennis, or basketball without any mistakes, he or she would always perform perfectly, but we know this isn't the case. Enlightenment is about consciousness and awareness, not outward performances. However, since an enlightened person is not generating negative reactions or negative karma, he or she often experience greater synchronicity than others do. The enlightened person wouldn't define any circumstance as a mistake, but rather simply an action leading to certain consequences. The enlightened person would be surrendered to those situations while flowing toward healing, harmony, and peace.

If through a mis-step or choice that creates a negative reaction in others, the person would feel apologetic and forgiving. Regret implies a judgment which enlightened people do not experience, but they would seek to make amends where appropriate.

71. Question: How do the enlightened masters suppress all desire, aversion, and delusion when these are part of human experience?

Answer: In the process of becoming enlightened, the ego dissolves, and many of the so called aspects of what are usually considered parts of being human are replaced with a different prevailing consciousness and presence. This new consciousness and presence does not require the suppression of negative emotions, resistance, judgments, or desires, as enlightened consciousness operates without these needs. In other words, what formerly drove a person with needs, wants, and reactions is no longer there. At this point, the person lives with deep peacefulness, clarity, and awareness. The degree to which this is so is the degree the ego has been let go.

72. Question: What would a country be like if it were governed by only enlightened people?

Answer: In general, enlightened ones are not interested in running for political office with the systems currently in place. On a world where those forming policies are enlightened, love would be the motivation, and cooperation and kindness the manner. This would be taught from birth.

Yes, an enlightened person is engaged in life and makes positive differences. Retiring to a cave is not necessary, and, in fact, when the Golden Age arrives, there will be many enlightened beings participating in creating a flourishing life for all.

73. Question: Is it possible to be enlightened and not know it?

Answer: It is not very likely. If a child lived around all enlightened people so he or she never knew otherwise, the child could be enlightened and not ever think anything unusual about it. After all, the enlightened state is often called the natural mind. No such environment now exists. We all come out of ego-driven societies with ego-driven personalities. As one awakens, he or she becomes quite aware that transformation of consciousness is underway. This cannot be missed.

74. Question: Is meditation the only way to get enlightened?

Answer: In some rare cases, people have awakened spontaneously without a meditation practice. Sometimes this is referred to as having an epiphany. The vast majority of the rest of us can best reach higher awareness through meditation, but it depends on what is considered enlightened. If having epiphanies were the benchmark, then meditation would not be required, but to refine consciousness and integrate high awareness, some form of meditation is most likely necessary.

Meditation, however, is just a tool, a means to an end. Many regard meditation as an essential practice and often regard it as a most important one. Some meditate for hours each day, and at times this may be a good choice, but normally it is not required. The quality of meditation is more important then the quantity.

75. Question: Other than following a life of meditation, what are some other ways a person can reach enlightenment?

Answer: Reaching and maintaining enlightenment comes down to letting go of every judgment, negative emotion, and attachment. Meditation is the best way since it enables you go do deeply into the underlying unconscious patterns that sustain the responsible ego identities. However, another approach that is effective is self-inquiry, which also is best done in a relaxed state. The way self-inquiry works is to ask yourself questions designed to release the hold the mind has on one topic after another.

All types of inquiry can be valuable because while in the searching phase of a spiritual quest, as you refine the questions, you refine the realizations, but perhaps the most valuable form of inquiry of all is self-inquiry which is a powerful approach to transcending analytical mental processes and delving into consciousness itself. It is a way of diverting attention away from the mental analysis of the mind to observe consciousness itself.

It's not the situations themselves that hold you in non-enlightened consciousness; it is the conclusions, points of view, fixed-opinions, beliefs, perspectives, and perceptions, that determine your state of consciousness. A judgment is a position, and positions are arbitrarily created myths. They are only ideas, so they are essentially illusions life is based on. The inquiry process can help deconstruct what the mind fixates on. Here are a few suggestions for the type of questions to apply to self-inquiry to get you started:

What do I really want?
Who is thinking this?
Who is wanting?
Who am I without a body?

Who am I when there are no thoughts?
Who is observing me ask the questions?
Who is suffering?
What am I?
What do I believe about spirituality?

As you keep asking these types of questions repeatedly, answers will change. Self-inquiry eventually leads to a state of consciousness that is beyond mental activity or analysis and even beyond beliefs or perspectives.

Actually, self-inquiry leads to a suspension of any sense of self. You, the meditator, disappear in a stream of consciousness. This awareness leads to a profound understanding of life and a total sense of being one with all existence. No amount of thinking or analyzing can prepare you for this experience or lead you to it. As you engage self-inquiry, regardless of answers to the questions, always say to yourself, "Thank you. I am not that. I surrender and release the need for that."

The more you do this process, the more questions you will ask yourself, and by continuing to surrender, you will eventually arrive at a quiet mind. This opens the way for enlightenment.

76. Question: Will an enlightened person take action to prevent someone from doing harm?

Answer: If an enlightened person believes he or she can help keep a person from making a mistake the person might step in if possessing the skill-set to do so. But not everyone who is enlightened is equipped to handle outrageous situations. It depends on the degree of violence or harm the person is engaged in or contemplating. If a person were under the influence of a drug or alcohol, the better wisdom would be to let the proper authorities attend to it.

77. Question: Would an enlightened person care more about certain people than others?

Answer: Enlightened people's perspective is that all are one and the same beyond any illusions. They have great compassion for all suffering, and they often play a role in the alleviation of suffering for those they encounter, but enlightened people are still people. They have family and close friends and only have twenty-four hours a day like everyone else, so much of their influence is with those closest to them or those who seek them out for help, but this does not mean they care less for others. Because they believe all are equal and on a spiritual journey, their caring is for all.

78. Question: Are spiritually advanced people also full of flaws and faults just like the rest of us?

Answer: The answer to this question lies in how you define "spiritually advanced" and how you define "faults." I'll assume a spiritually advanced person is somewhat enlightened and therefore would not judge anyone.

It may be that in asking this question you are wondering if a spiritually advanced person has become a super-human who never makes a misstep. Leaving aside any judgments about what this means, a spiritually advanced person has not necessarily mastered every aspect of life. This means they can make mistakes. They can stub their toes. They can have illnesses. They can make business decisions that don't work. They may not have a great singing voice and they may fail a math test.

79. Question: In what ways is an enlightened person different from a non-enlightened one?

Answer: Most of the differences are internal so many people may not have any idea an enlightened person is that much different from others. Externally the person looks the same as everyone else, but the internal landscape is quite different from those non-enlightened. For instance, they have a sustained deep peacefulness, do not judge anyone for anything, and are perpetually happy, fulfilled, and content. They are perceptive, insightful, and wise, and always loving and kind. A clairvoyant would perceive an enlightened person having a pure and radiant aura with open and clear chakras.

80. Question: Why is it that someone who claims he or she is enlightened is considered unenlightened by some others?

Answer: Typically, those who have attained non-duality (which is enlightened awareness) would say there is no one to be enlightened, so how could an "enlightened person" be said to be enlightened, when, in truth, no one is there? Therefore, a person who has attained full enlightenment wouldn't claim to be enlightened. Those approaching enlightenment or having some of the experiences associated with enlightenment often think they are enlightened and sometimes claim to be enlightened. The ego wants to think it is enlightened and often makes such claims.

Some have greater realizations and freedom from ego-issues than others. In that sense, we could say some are more enlightened than others are, but the perspective of one who is fully enlightened realizes no one is there to be enlightened. This said, there is a practical side to our Earthly experience, and it is clear that some operate with more enlightened awareness than others. I don't think we need to be so paranoid about using the word "enlightenment" in a sentence describing what such a consciousness level is. Maybe the word "illumined" would be a better choice because it wouldn't have the same connotation. Some people have strong feelings about not claiming to be enlightened.

81. Question: In short, how can one can describe Enlightenment?

Answer: Enlightenment is difficult to define, but its characteristics can be identified. I usually describe enlightenment with two other words, "acceptance" and "freedom," and of course, more explanation is usually needed.

Enlightenment is usually equated with "awakening" which comes in stages. In rare cases, it can be complete in one shift, but usually a series of consciousness shifts happen over years or decades. These consciousness shifts typically happen spontaneously in a few seconds, but the full realization and integration can take days, weeks, or months.

Some, or most, of the qualities associated with enlightenment are not deeply experienced with the first enlightening experience. Sometimes when consciousness shifts or expands into unity consciousness, people consider themselves awake, and may settle into a very satisfied condition and plateau at that level. Others may continue evolving.

82. Question: How can I become more awakened?

Answer: Awakening occurs as the mind releases what it holds. Two effective methods to help with this are self-inquiry and surrender. Ultimately, it always comes down to surrender. This means releasing all holding and resistance around every belief, feeling, and reaction. This leads you to greater equanimity, peace, and expansion of awareness. Self-inquiry is a powerful approach to transcending analytical mental processes and delving into consciousness itself. It is a way of diverting attention away from the mental analysis of the mind.

83. Question: Do enlightened people feel emotions? Things I read say enlightened people only feel blissful and calm. Does this mean they do not have other emotions? If so, this sounds weird and sad - like they are cyborgs.

Answer: The answer to this question reflects what each person has experienced and it couldn't be otherwise. The mind (or the person) does not know what it has not experienced. Intellectually comprehending characteristics of the enlightened state is not the same as the full realization in which there is a total release of conceptualizations and emotional reactions. People often think their experience is the answer to what an enlightened person experiences because they have had enlightened moments, but a significant difference lies between having some awakening realizations and a full-sustained enlightened awareness.

In early awakening experiences, certain realizations of truth and illusion occur, but the mind still attempts definitions and explanations. Over time, the mind becomes increasingly quiet until no uninvited thoughts appear day and night. At that point, being in the now and sustaining a thought-free state is effortless. What were formerly negative emotions also vanish into the nothingness out of which the mind created them.

Enlightened people are not disengaged robots. I make a distinction between feelings and emotions. An enlightened person has positive feelings of happiness, caring, love, fulfillment, joyfulness, contentment, and a lightness of being, while being free of such negative emotions as fear, anger, depression, guilt, resentment, and other ego reactions.

84. Question: How is it possible, or even good not to experience fear? For instance, if they were about to be murdered, would enlightened people be fearful? Would they be more likely to be harmed because they do not feel healthy fear to protect themselves.

Answer: Certain survival fears are "hardwired" into our body and nervous system. Also a part of the human brain called the reptilian brain triggers some negative emotions. Because of these facts, in most cases, even the enlightened can experience a fear response when facing imminent threat, but it wouldn't normally be a frantic or panic reaction. It would be more of a heightened attention and focus on what needs to be done. There would be more composure, calm, and ability to be present with what needs to be done than what most would expect.

The majority of fears experienced by most people are projections of what might happen in the future, and since enlightened people live in the now automatically all the time, they, therefore, do not experience these type of fears.

85. Question: Is Non-Duality the key to losing the fear of rejection or another's judgment?

Answer: Non-duality is one way, but other methods to address fears or the judgments of others are also effective. What anyone says or thinks about you is only an opinion. Claim your power by not conceding that anyone else's opinion is more important than your opinion of yourself.

The title of Terry Cole-Whittaker's book *What You Think of Me is None of My Business* can be a very helpful mantra. This is not to make you insensitive to others, but to put you in your own power by not letting anyone demean you. Addressing these sensitivities with non-duality will take some dedication to a practice that can lead you there.

86. Question: Is spiritual awakening an instantaneous process or is it gradual?

Answer: Spiritual awakening is an ongoing process that takes place over time with many shifts in consciousness. Oftentimes, those shifts happen in a matter of a few seconds, but they can take weeks or months to integrate. Each person seems to experience much of the process in a unique way, so no blanket statement can fully explain the occurrences for everyone. However, generally, each shift is based on releasing something the mind has been holding. This can include beliefs, emotional reactions, or patterns a person has been mired in. The awakening shifts usually happen over many years in which each realization forms the foundation for the next awakening. In most cases, this is a lifelong process.

87. Question: What is your conception of God?

Answer: An enlightened perspective of God is beyond all definitions. God is not comprehended by the mind trying to formulate a definition. God is the most incredible being you can imagine and God is also the formlessness underlying all creations. This is the great paradox beyond the mind's capability, for God is both form and formlessness. In other words, God is not contained by any conceptualization, because all conceptualizations are limitations. Every time you open your eyes, everything you see is God, and every time you close your eyes, every thing you imagine is God. Moreover, when you are in deep sleep God is there in the perfect stillness.

88. Question: Can chronic pain be a path to spiritual awakening?

Answer: It may not be the path of choice, but for some it has worked. When people go through deep and severe pain and suffering, they can, in some cases, come to a deep place where they say, "I've done everything I can and I have no more I can do. I give up the fight and I let go." This can be an indication of the ego giving up. At this point of deep surrender, a beautiful opening can occur as a higher presence takes over. The person may feel surrounded by and filled with light, which leads to transcending to higher realizations. I've known people who have experienced this, but I've also known those who have suffered a great deal who did not reach that same level of surrender and therefore did not awaken.

Some have mistaken suffering as a way of accelerating the payment of negative karma and therefore as a way to attain "salvation" or awakening. But this is a misinterpretation of why suffering can, in some cases, lead to awakening.

89. Question: Would meditating in a "cave" help me reach enlightenment?

Answer: The enlightened state is not dependent on location or anything external. Some find it easier to reach and maintain elevated states of consciousness by withdrawing from people and activities; however, it is not a requirement. The "cave," of course, is a metaphor for isolation and retreat into the deeper self. A cave experience can be a means to an end of achieving elevated consciousness. The cave provides minimal distractions, which makes it easier to sustain a peaceful and expanded state of consciousness than is often possible by living in a society with its requirements. Once the ego fades and enlightened states become sustained, a person will find comfort in any situation.

90. Question: What is the best way to reach enlightenment?

Answer: Trying to find enlightenment on your own can be a long and discouraging process as it can lead to a lot of trial and error. Books, audios, and videos are a way to gather background information but they will not usually lead you to the enlightened state. Participating in group meetings can also help, but to really move forward more quickly it is very helpful to spend time with a person who can offer not only guidance, but also help you clear what is blocking you, and who is able to transmit clear consciousness to you.

Eliminating what prevents it can cause enlightenment. The major obstacle is the mind clinging to projections it believes are true but are really just what it clings to as truth that are just perceptions and conclusions. Most people are walking around living a dream or nightmare projected by their deepest beliefs, loves, and fears. To arrive at an enlightened state requires that you deconstruct the mental projections and shift into the awareness that underlies all manifestation. This is where a skilled and enlightened teacher can be invaluable pointing out the traps of the mind and offer direction on how to free yourself from them.

91. Question: Is it really possible for people to be without ego for prolonged periods?

Answer: What is helpful to know is that ego contains two aspects. One is negative and includes painful emotions, judgments, and projections, but another aspect of ego is composed of the core essence of who you are. In ancient Eastern philosophy individuality is referred to as your unique expression in all creation. This uniqueness is sometimes referred to as your soul or higher self, which encompasses peacefulness and other qualities everyone seeks. When the full realization of this truth is reached you are aware of individuality without a sense of separation. Yes, it is possible to function without negative ego.

92. Question: Does our concept of enlightenment affect our path toward it?

Answer: The mind is constantly working to define things and work things out, so it projects what it thinks the enlightened state is. No matter what the mind thinks enlightenment is, distortions will occur, for the mind can't really know what it has not experienced.

How you define enlightenment impacts what you think is necessary to attain it. For instance, the mind might well think that certain spiritual practices, prayers, or ceremonies are necessary, but these can become traps or ends in themselves. Religions were formed to systematize the spiritual process, but they contain many doctrines and codes of conduct to formulate the path as it was understood to be.

Attaining enlightenment is a process of eliminating everything that gets in the way of what enlightenment is. The best way to do this is to become a master of surrender.

93. Question: How do some people attain accidental enlightenment?

Answer: This is a particular phenomenon that rarely happens and when you hear about it you may think something is wrong with you if you haven't experienced it. Alternatively, a person may conclude that those it happens to are especially chosen by some higher power to have the experience. Neither conclusion is true.

Each lifetime picks up where a pervious one left off, but it usually takes two, three, or more decades before the awakening in this life takes place. People who have spent several lifetimes in the pursuit of spiritual goals are the ones most likely to experience enlightenment in this lifetime.

Because we have advanced technologically in our society, we have access to knowledge and teachers that most people in past ages didn't. This has enabled a larger number of people to initiate awakening experiences more rapidly than was commonly available in the past. Enlightenment is now within reach for any dedicated spiritual aspirant.

When there is an awakening, it usually seems to be spontaneous and can actually happen in a matter of seconds, but what is not usually known by others is the detailed preparation that preceded the spontaneous experience. When you observe a rose bush in the springtime, you see the buds forming over days and weeks, but then suddenly one day they burst open spontaneously into a beautiful flower. At that point, you don't think much about all the preparation that went into the "birth" of that rose.

94. Question: What do I do after spiritual awakening?

Answer: Having an awakening experience is really just the beginning of a new perspective on everything. It does not mean that your outer life needs to change a lot or that all challenges magically vanish, but you'll have a more peaceful way to handle them. Don't mistakenly think you've somehow reached the end of your evolution. It just means many of the distortions the mind previously projected are seen with more clarity.

Some people having spiritual awakenings become more inward and passive or withdraw from society. On the other hand, awakening can also present an opportunity to participate in life more fully. You actually have that choice. So you are at a cross roads having to decide which way to go.

Some who have experienced a spiritual awakening call it a natural awakening because, at last, they understand what they are, which feels totally normal and natural. They realize that experiences before were hazy dreams. In other words, life goes on, and will be what one makes of it. =

95. Question: How do I stay in a state of enlightenment longer? My mind can stay inactive for a short time but not a full day.

Answer: The analytical mind is the only obstacle to sustained enlightenment. Applying mindful practices and methods will help you to have a quieter mind and over time you will sustain enlightened awareness for longer periods. In the beginning a quiet mind is often fleeting, but over time you will achieve full awareness and sustain it.

A method I find useful is to observe your mind and its activities and then release whatever it is engaged with. This is most effective when done in a relaxed, meditative state. Set an intention to check in with yourself every hour and notice what the mind has been doing for the previous hour. Then deepen your surrender and release whatever it was doing until you feel at peace. You won't need to do this forever because you'll soon become more and more mindful and less engaged. Then you can stretch out the intervals between checking in with yourself and eventually you'll find it is no longer necessary for because the awareness will be sustained.

Be patient because your mind has been conditioned for many years by education and career to be analytical and attached, so some time will be necessary for the mind to release.

96. Question: Where can I go to learn enlightenment?

Answer: All approaches and practices that can aid you in reaching enlightenment come down to various forms of meditation and surrender. You'll want to experiment to find an approach that is the most efficacious for you.

All techniques are a means to an end and not the end in and of themselves. I mention this because I know people who have been meditating with a particular form for decades, and they still haven't reached the enlightenment they have been seeking, yet they persist with their practice for hours every day. To avoid this find an approach that you like and stay with it for several weeks or months and then determine if you are moving toward what you want. If you aren't progressing, experiment with other forms. In other words, don't stubbornly stay with something that doesn't produce the results you seek.

Sometimes reaching higher awareness is quicker and easier when you meditate with others. A multiplied effectiveness happens when several are together meditating. Even meditating with one other person can be helpful, but for even stronger support, meditate with teachers who demonstrate they have reached higher states themselves. When you do this, a resonance effect makes reaching higher consciousness easier for you.

You do not need to join an ashram to accomplish this, although if you feel strongly drawn to this life, it can be helpful for the short term. An attraction in this direction could be due to past lives. One caveat is that such an environment by its nature imposes beliefs, practices, and rules that themselves can become traps. Once in their system, members talk themselves into complete compliance assuming the teachers know the answers. Following the group's requirements is typically necessary to maintain membership.

The enlightened state in contrast, is one of freedom on all levels, including the illusions and mythologies imposed by systems created to perpetuate themselves. I recommend that you explore several teachers you are drawn to and find the one with whom you resonate closely.

97. Question: I have felt enlightened several times, but I always fall back to my everyday state. What should I do?

Answer: One of the most commonly reported "enlightenment" experiences people describe is feeling like they've lost their enlightenment after the "event" happened. Most people who experience enlightening awakenings do not immediately jump to full ego release, non-duality, and sustained enlightenment. While it can sometimes seem that enlightenment comes to some effortlessly and spontaneously, for most it happens progressively. If the awakening shift was not complete, the ego components that remain will gradually reassert themselves causing a sense of loss. In reality, the experience is not lost, but other memories, emotions, and ego reactions emerge, all of which cloud the awakening. As the evolution of consciousness continues, the elevated state will sustain for longer periods until it is permanent. The process can be accelerated somewhat by continuing with meditative and clearing practices that address and release the remnants of the ego.

After each shift in consciousness you acclimate to the new state which becomes your new baseline. Therefore, it feels normal or what is referred to in the question as the "everyday state." Consciousness shifts are most noted when they first occur because they create a different internal experience. As the days pass, you get more used to the new sensations and adjust to them and feel like yourself again. The new level of consciousness now becomes your new baseline for your next enlightenment shift.

98. Question: Does becoming enlightened affect family members?

Answer: Becoming enlightened is a process. Along the way some rather eccentric topics might be pursued that "normal" people would be aversive to or frightened by. If you feel the need to let them know what you are exploring, refer them to books on the subject. If that piques their interest, then let them ask you questions. Otherwise, the less said, the better.

As people move along a spiritual path, the energy they carry will change. This creates a resonance effect on the mental and emotional state of those around the person. The closer to enlightenment one becomes, the more he or she becomes unconditionally loving, patient, kind, compassionate, and peaceful. This produces an energy field that radiates those qualities that positively affects others. However, the effect may not be noticed immediately. As a person pursues enlightenment or spiritual awakening, considering the beliefs and value systems of others is important. One must use wisdom in what is discussed. Gently introducing new ideas and toning down any excessive enthusiasm goes far in placating negative reactions in others.

99. Question: Has anyone actually reached a point of eliminating suffering and maintaining peace within?

Answer: If by eliminating suffering you mean physical pain, that would be less likely, but if you mean being acceptant and at peace with what is, that is not only more likely, but also a state achieved by many.

Early on the path of enlightenment much rises to the surface to be addressed. Difficult and painful memories from the past replay, and disappointments and frustrations with the present can be obstacles. As long as you address what is presenting itself and you deeply surrender and release reactions and attachments, you will move continually closer to not only eliminating the suffering that circumstances can trigger, but also to attaining sustained peacefulness. This is not an impossible dream, although until you arrive it can sometimes seem that way.

100. How do you maintain a focus on God all the time?

Answer: What you can experience much of the time is a dual awareness where the transcendent aspects of reality [God] are present as a backdrop in your consciousness. Usually this carries no particular sensation apart from an awareness of its presence, regardless of what else has your attention. The nature of having a body requires dualism. The underlying question is how to reach higher levels of consciousness and sustain them.

The best way to arrive and become stabilized at a higher level of consciousness is to let go of what interferes with attaining it. This is obvious, but to become stabilized you must be a detective to determine in very great detail every belief you hold at the deepest levels that blocks it. All assumptions, opinions, and perceptions must be surrendered, let go, and dissolved. Surrender everything until you attain a surrendered state of consciousness in which you no longer project any resistance, reaction, or judgments. In addition, ask to remove and dissolve all obstacles keeping you from being one with the Soul.

Subtle-energy clearing is certainly an important part of this process. Limiting patterns persist because they are warehoused as subtle-energy thoughtforms in many different areas, most of which are unconscious, such as ancestral energy patterns impressed in the physical body, old beliefs, and karma in the causal body, and the programming carried over from past lives.

Once you no longer have any attachment or investment fixated in beliefs, you can immerse yourself in whatever activity or adventure that you enjoy. You'll then recognize that all life is play, fun, and an expression of love. The purpose of existence is to take part in a continual unfolding of adventures and experiences that are ever evolving. The entire creation is continually transitioning into something other than its current state. Since forces have brought each of us to where we are, to seek escape from the journey would go against the whole reason for existence. When I am asked how long it takes to become enlightened, I tell people to forget about any duration and instead focus on due diligence to become as clear as possible without attachment to any beliefs, conclusions, or judgments. Once this happens, you are enlightened and free.